W9-CHP-873

Crystal Reports:
A Beginner's Guide

About the Author

David McAmis is an IT consultant, journalist, and author living and working in Sydney, Australia. His work has appeared in computer magazines and trade journals, and he is a regular contributor to *Access-Office-VB Advisor, Advisor Expert: Exchange & Outlook, Component Advisor, Developer's Review, E-Business Advisor, Enterprise Development, Exchange/ Outlook Magazine, Internet.au, Intranet Design Magazine,* and *Visual Basic Programmer's Journal.*

In addition to writing product reviews, general interest, and how-to articles, David has been a guest columnist for *Enterprise Development* magazine and writes a monthly "Expert Advice" column for *Internet.au*, Australia's best-selling Internet magazine.

When not writing, David works as an IT consultant and is a partner in a consulting firm in Sydney that develops and supports Windows, Web, and mobile applications. In his varied career, he has been a consultant, technical trainer, university lecturer, and consulting services manager, and has served as vice president of a software and services company in the United States. David holds a B.S. degree in management information systems and is a Microsoft Certified Professional.

David has been working with Crystal Reports since Version 4.0 of the product and is a Crystal Certified Consultant and Trainer, having taught over 700 students in his career.

He is considered to be an expert in the field of business intelligence and is a frequent conference speaker. You can reach him at dmcamis@hotmail.com.

Crystal Reports:
A Beginner's Guide

David McAmis

McGraw-Hill/Osborne

New York   Chicago   San Francisco
Lisbon   London   Madrid   Mexico City   Milan
New Delhi   San Juan   Seoul   Singapore   Sydney   Toronto

McGraw-Hill/Osborne
2600 Tenth Street
Berkeley, California 94710
U.S.A.

To arrange bulk purchase discounts for sales promotions, premiums, or fund-raisers, please contact McGraw-Hill/Osborne at the above address. For information on translations or book distributors outside the U.S.A., please see the International Contact Information page immediately following the index of this book.

Crystal Reports: A Beginner's Guide

Copyright © 2002 by The McGraw-Hill Companies. All rights reserved. Printed in the United States of America. Except as permitted under the Copyright Act of 1976, no part of this publication may be reproduced or distributed in any form or by any means, or stored in a database or retrieval system, without the prior written permission of the publisher, with the exception that the program listings may be entered, stored, and executed in a computer system, but they may not be reproduced for publication.

567890 FGR FGR 019876543

ISBN 0-07-219326-3

Publisher   Brandon A. Nordin
Vice President & Associate Publisher   Scott Rogers
Acquisitions Editor   Franny Kelly
Project Editor   Laura Stone
Acquisitions Coordinator   Alexander Corona
Technical Editor   Leah Steele
Copy Editor   Judy Ziajka
Proofreader   Pat Mannion
Indexer   Jack Lewis
Computer Designers   Carie Abrew, Tara A. Davis, Lauren McCarthy
Illustrator   Michael Mueller, Lyssa Sieben-Wald,
Series Design   Gary Corrigan
Cover Series Design   Greg Scott
Cover Illustration   Kevin Curry

This book was composed with Corel VENTURA™ Publisher.

Information has been obtained by Osborne/McGraw-Hill from sources believed to be reliable. However, because of the possibility of human or mechanical error by our sources, Osborne/McGraw-Hill, or others, Osborne/McGraw-Hill does not guarantee the accuracy, adequacy, or completeness of any information and is not responsible for any errors or omissions or the results obtained from use of such information.

To my mother, Evelyn Rose, who proved she would do just about anything to have the family home for Christmas. You will always be "The Most Beautiful Girl in the World."

Contents at a Glance

Contents

Acknowledgments

A very big thank-you to the team of people behind the scenes who have worked on this project and made this book possible, including Fran, Alex, Laura, Julie, Marie, Lyssa, Michael, and the entire Osborne team. Fran, I appreciate your patience and perseverance, and I am indebted to you for the opportunity to work with such an incredible team of people.

Thanks to Leah Steele, who has been with me every step of the way and made sure I didn't lose the plot.

Thanks to Neil Salkind and the entire Studio B family for taking care of business and letting me do what I do best.

Thanks to Chris, Kelly, Rhody, Steve, Tracy, Fred, and the entire Crystal Decisions Australia team for their support.

And finally, thank you to the worldwide support network of peers, family, and friends who have provided support and encouragement throughout this project and many others. I could not have done it without you. *Nunc scio quit sit amor.*

Introduction

Before every introductory Crystal Reports training class I teach, I like to point out that there is just a shred of knowledge that separates the beginner from the report expert. Regardless of how many years someone has been using Crystal Reports, everyone had to start at the exact same place. I decided to take on this project because I believe that new Crystal Reports users are neither "dummies" nor "idiots"—chances are, you have an in-depth knowledge of your business or organization and are using Crystal Reports to extract the information you need to make better business decisions.

Crystal Reports: A Beginner's Guide has been written with you in mind. What you can find in this book is solid, practical advice for creating Crystal Reports, focusing on the most commonly used features and functionality.

Who Should Read This Book

This book is perfect for anyone who has little or no prior experience using Crystal Reports. For business users, it provides the knowledge you need to start creating reports relevant to your business—the only limit is your imagination! For application developers who are just getting started with Crystal Reports, it also provides an excellent primer before you move on to more advanced reading.

What This Book Covers

This book is separated into a number of modules, which range in content from creating a simple report to complex formulas and analysis features of Crystal Reports.

Module 1, "Getting Started," covers the basics of report design, focusing on the process you go through to design a report (before you even open Crystal Reports!).

Module 2, "Creating a Simple Report," starts you on your journey by focusing on creating a simple report using one of the Crystal Reports Experts.

Module 3, "Working with the Report Design Environment," helps you learn about the report designer itself, how to work with objects, and more.

Module 4, "Organizing Your Report," takes your report design a step further by showing you how to use Crystal Reports features such as grouping and sorting to make your report more meaningful.

Module 5, "Analyzing Report Data," gives you an introduction to the features within Crystal Reports that allow you to present an analysis of your information.

Module 6, "Using Parameter Fields," discusses how parameter fields can be used in your report, as fields on their own or with record selection, to create interactive reports.

Module 7, "Distributing the Results," explains how your reports can be exported and distributed to users who may not have a copy of Crystal Reports themselves.

Module 8, "Formulas and Functions," introduces you to the Crystal Reports formula language, which can be used to add complex calculations and manipulate fields that appear in your report.

Module 9, "Advanced Record Selection," teaches you to use record selection to narrow your report's focus to just the data you want to show.

Module 10, "Working with Sections," will prove invaluable, as this module shows you how to use sections to create statements and form letters, and apply formatting to sections of your report.

Module 11, "Using Subreports," gives you an insight into how to use subreports to display disparate data sources within the same report, and how to use subreports to overcome common data-linking problems.

Module 12, "Cross-Tab Analysis," provides a look at cross-tabs and how they can be used to create well-organized, information-rich reports.

Module 13, "Charting and Graphing," proves the point that a picture is worth a thousand words. In this module, you learn how to create charts and graphs from the data within your report.

Module 14, "Geographic Mapping," illustrates another way to display report data, using maps.

Module 15, "Working with Data Sources," provides one of the missing links when working with Crystal Reports—how to access the data your organization collects.

Appendix A, "Mastery Check Answers" contains the answers to the Mastery Check questions found at the end of every chapter.

Appendix B, "Crystal Reports Dictionaries," provides an overview of Crystal Reports dictionaries, how they are created, and how they can be used to simplify reporting for end users.

Appendix C, "Crystal SQL Designer," demonstrates the advanced SQL querying functions of Crystal Reports and shows how a query can serve as the data source for a Crystal Report.

Appendix D, "Troubleshooting (FAQ)," provides answers to some of the most frequently asked questions that arise when working with Crystal Reports.

How to Read This Book

How you read this book depends on your personality—if you are the type of person who likes to sit down and read a book from cover to cover, you'll find that the modules contained within this book logically follow each other, so you should be able to start at the very beginning and go right through to the end. If you are like me and prefer to find the information you need quickly, you can use the table of contents or index to quickly find a topic and jump straight to that module. All of the modules can be read as stand-alone topics, and the projects can be completed without having completed previous chapters. (If a project does call for a report file from a previous chapter, you can download it from the Osborne Web site at www.osborne.com.)

Special Features

If you flip through the book, you may notice some of the special features included in this series. Within each module, there are a number of **Hints**, **Tips**, and **Notes** that have been inserted—they provide extra information that may be of use or explain a concept not fully covered in the text. You'll also notice there are some sections titled "**Ask the Expert**"—these sidebars contain commonly asked questions and their answers.

Each module also includes a number of step-by-step **Projects** that help you learn and understand the concepts presented within the module. All of these projects are based on a sample database that is included with every copy of Crystal Reports, created for a fictional company called Xtreme Mountain Bikes.

And finally, **Mastery Checks** are included at the end of every module. When you have finished reading each module, try to answer the Mastery Check questions—if you get stumped, you can look back through the module for any concepts you may have missed or check out Appendix A, where the answers to the Mastery Check questions are located.

If that wasn't enough, you can also download sample report files, completed exercises, and resources from Osborne's Web site (www.osborne.com) or the companion site to this book (www.crystalbeginnersguide.com). On the site, you can also find additional links to other Crystal Reports resources on the Web and information about users, groups, and more.

This book is the product of a long journey—countless years of teaching Crystal Reports classes, working with report designers, and designing reports myself. If there is one hope that I have for everyone who reads this book, it is that you can take some bit of knowledge from this book and apply it to your work. Students are amazed in training courses when I admit that after seven years of working with the product, I still learn something new every day about Crystal Reports—a different way it can be used, another way to utilize a feature or formatting technique, or just through seeing its application to a different use or industry.

It is my hope that this is the start of your own journey. Don't get stuck in a cubicle creating the same old listing reports for the rest of your life; get out there and talk to other Crystal Reports users, expand your horizons, learn new ways of doing things, and share what you have learned. Like the title says, this is only the beginning.

Module 1

Getting Started

Goals

- Understand the report design process
- Learn how to create report prototypes
- Identify the tools available within Crystal Reports
- Understand the different types of reports that can be created with Crystal Reports

Crystal Reports has grown to become the de facto standard for report writing, with over seven million licenses distributed. Traditionally considered a tool for application developers, Crystal Reports has come into its own as a powerful ad hoc reporting tool for business users as well.

This module walks you through the basics of report design and introduces you to the tools within Crystal Reports that will help you get started. Whether you are a software developer looking to integrate reporting into your application or an end user looking to create reports, it all starts here.

Report Design Overview

Report design actually begins before you sit down at the computer and start using Crystal Reports. Report design has five basic phases:

- Defining the concept
- Sourcing the data
- Creating the design
- Developing and testing the design
- Deploying and operating the report

Defining the Concept

One of the seven habits in Stephen Covey's *The 7 Habits of Highly Effective People* is "Begin with the end in mind." This same principle applies to report design. Before you can actually sit down in front of a computer and create a report, you must first have some idea or concept of what you want the final report to look like.

A good starting point is a look at the sample reports that ship with every copy of Crystal Reports. These sample reports can be found in the C:\Program Files\Seagate Software\Crystal Reports\Samples\En\Reports folder (where C: is the drive where you installed Crystal Reports).

These samples are broken into two categories: Feature Examples, showing the various features and functionality available, and General Business examples, showing commonly used business reports. These reports were created using a sample database from Xtreme Cycles, a fictional company, and can get you thinking about how you would like to present the information in your report.

Other good sources of inspiration are any existing reports or spreadsheets you are currently using. It is always good to have a starting point for your report concept.

The easiest way to develop and communicate your report concept is to create a prototype, or mock-up, of the report you want to create. A sample prototype is shown in Figure 1-1. You can use a word processor, a spreadsheet, or the low-tech option of pen and paper, but you should try to make the prototype of your report as complete as possible. This will help you later when you are trying to determine the feasibility of creating the report that you want.

Report Title: Monthly Sales by State	Requested by: John Smith, National Sales Manager	Date: 05/15/02	Def No: 0036

Monthly Sales by State			NOTES
SALES REP COMPANY ORDER TOTAL COMMISION			FIELD DEFINITIONS
ALABAMA			SALES_HEADER.SALESREP
xxxxxxxx xxxxxxxx	$999999.99	$999999.99	CUSTOMER.CUSTOMERNAME
xxxxxxxx xxxxxxxx	$999999.99	$999999.99	SALES_HEADER.ORDERTOTAL
xxxxxxxx xxxxxxxx	$999999.99	$999999.99	COMMISION: CALCULATED FEILD
xxxxxxxx xxxxxxxx	$999999.99	$999999.99	ORDER TOTAL*.025,
xxxxxxxx xxxxxxxx	$999999.99	$999999.99	ROUNDED UP TO NEAREST
TOTAL FOR ALABAMA	$999999.99	$999999.99	DOLLAR
	(AVG)	$999999.99	
ALASKA			GROUPED BY STATE, RECORD
xxxxxxxx xxxxxxxx	$999999.99	$999999.99	LEVEL SORTING BY SALES REP
xxxxxxxx xxxxxxxx	$999999.99	$999999.99	
xxxxxxxx xxxxxxxx	$999999.99	$999999.99	SHOWING A SUM FOR ORDER TL
xxxxxxxx xxxxxxxx	$999999.99	$999999.99	AND COMMISION AS WELL AS
xxxxxxxx xxxxxxxx	$999999.99	$999999.99	AVG COMMISIONS @ EA. BREAK
TOTAL FOR ALASKA	$999999.99	$999999.99	

Created By:
David McAmis

Figure 1-1   A sample report prototype

Sourcing the Data

With a prototype in hand, the next step is to determine where the data for your report actually resides. Is it stored in a database, a log file, or a mainframe file? After you have determined the general location, you need to find the database or system administrator responsible for that particular database or system. Armed with the database or file schema (showing the big picture of where all of your data is stored), the database or system administrator should be able to tell you exactly where the data is located.

Hint

If it seems like your database or system administrator is speaking a different language, don't worry. While you may be describing the information you need in terms you are familiar with (invoices, purchase orders, and so on), he or she may be looking at it from a different angle, related to where the information is stored. To help with a meeting of the minds, check out Encyclopædia Britannica at www.britannica.com and search for the keyword *database*. The site provides a good overview of database terms and will give you the working knowledge of databases you need to get everyone speaking the same language.

A common problem is that the data you want to include in your report may not exist. Your accounting system, for example, may not have the capability to track budgets. Therefore, producing a report comparing actual sales to budgeted sales may be difficult.

You should also keep an eye out for any fields that need to be calculated and determine whether those calculations should occur on the database level or within Crystal Reports. Crystal Reports features a powerful formula language and function set, but you may want to consider pushing heavy processing back to the database where it belongs.

Creating the Design

After creating a prototype and determining your data source, the next step is to design the report. You're probably wondering if this is when you get to use Crystal Reports. The answer is no. The best report design is one that is completed first on paper and is then re-created using Crystal Reports. During the design phase, you want to revisit your prototype report and, given what you know about the database at that point, indicate which of the fields in your report are going to come from the database, which fields are going to be calculated, and what formulas are to be used in those calculations.

You should also have a good idea about how the data is organized, what grouping and sorting are required, and what records need to be selected to get the results you need.

Developing and Testing the Design

Finally, with the design completed on paper, it is time to open Crystal Reports and get down to business. After you have laid the groundwork, the actual report design process should be quick and simple after learning the skills in this book. After the initial report development is complete, you should test your report on a number of different platforms in a number of different situations. If you are distributing your report as part of a Web application, try to preview the report on a number of different computers or operating systems. Note any performance issues and revisit your report design to see if you can make any performance enhancements.

If you have created a report that prompts the user for start and end dates, try entering bad dates, the same date, or even some text in those prompts. You need to be prepared to handle any situation that a user may encounter.

1-Minute Drill

- What are the five phases of report design?
- Where can you find the sample reports that ship with Crystal Reports?

Deploying and Operating the Report

As a final step in the report design process, you need to consider how your report is going to be used. Will users want to export the report? How does the report design translate when you export to Microsoft Excel or Word? Try to export the report yourself. You may need to revisit your report design based on the results of your exporting attempts.

- Defining the concept, sourcing the data, creating the design, developing and testing the design, deploying and operating the report
- C:\Program Files\Seagate Software\Crystal Reports\Samples\En\Reports (where C: is the drive where you installed Crystal Reports)

Will users be able to modify the report? Are your formulas, naming, and coding conventions easy to follow? Again, you may need to modify the report design based on your answers.

Finally, when the report is in production, you need to monitor the operation of the report to ensure that the report performs as expected and that it is still relevant. Many organizations think that report creation stops when the report is handed to its users. On the contrary, the report design process should be ongoing throughout the life cycle of the report, with continual analysis to find ways to enhance the information presented and add value to the data.

Project 1-1: Developing a Report Prototype

An easy way to learn how to develop a report prototype is to jump right in and tackle an existing report request. If you are creating the report on behalf of someone else, you should start by spending a little time interviewing the user and making sure the report prototype meets the user's needs. If you ensure that the user is happy with the report's design before you begin, there will be no surprises when you deliver the final product.

The goals for this project are to complete the first three phases of good report design:

- Defining the concept
- Sourcing the data
- Creating the design

When this project is finished, you should have a well-documented report prototype that you can later use to create a report, using the skills you will learn in future modules.

Step-by-Step

1. *Defining the concept.* Find the user who submitted the report request and spend some time interviewing this person to determine what information the person would like to see in the report. A good way to get users thinking about what their own reports could look like is to bring along printed copies of sample or existing reports you have available.

Hint

Another way to help users communicate the information they want to include is to bring along screen shots of existing systems- or data-based applications. Frequently, users will refer to a piece of information according to where they see it in the course of their workday. They may not know where the data is stored in the database but can tell you where it is entered, updated, and so on. This information will prove invaluable later when you are ready to source the data, as your database or system administrator should be able to locate it in the database structures from the screen shots provided.

While there is not a hard and fast set of questions you should ask users during this phase, the following list should help you get started:

- Who will use this report?
- How often should it be run?
- What subset of data should it include (year to date, current month, one state, all states, and so on)?
- What information would you like to see in the report?
- What is the title of the report?
- What type of report should be generated (column-based report, mailing labels, form letters, statements, and so on)?
- Will the user be prompted for any information?
- What grouping or sorting is required?
- Do any fields need to be calculated?
- Are there any business rules that apply to these calculations?
- How will the report be distributed (hard copy, exported to Excel, and so on)?
- Is the running of the report likely to interfere with the performance of the database (in other words, should the report be scheduled to run after hours)?

2. *Sourcing the data.* With the notes from your meeting in hand, go to your database or system administrator and find out where the data resides for your report. During this discovery, the administrator should be able to provide you with a data dictionary and/or entity-relationship diagram for your database or application. A data dictionary, such as the one in Table 1-1, will show the names of all of the tables in the database, the fields they contain, and a description of each of the fields.

Field Name	Data Type	Length	Description
Product ID	Number	10	Product ID number
Product Name	Text	50	Product name
Color	Text	15	Primary color of product
Size	Text	5	Product size (S, M, L, XL, 14, 16, 18, 19, 20)
M/F	Text	10	Male/female flag (M/F)
Price (SRP)	Currency	N/A	Suggested retail price
Product Type ID	Text	10	Product type (references Product Type Table)
Product Class	Text	50	Product class (bicycles or accessories)
Supplier ID	Number	10	Supplier ID (references Supplier Table)
Re-Order Level	Number	10	Re-order level
UOM	Text	20	Unit of measure (kg, lbs, and so on)
SKU	Text	20	Sales key unit

Table 1-1 Product table, a typical data dictionary

An entity-relationship diagram is simply a graphic representation of how all of the tables fit together, as shown in Figure 1-2. If possible, get a copy of both the data dictionary and entity-relationship diagram, as they will prove invaluable in the report development process.

It is also at this point that your database or system administrator can advise you on the feasibility of the report you want to create. For instance, the user may want a report that shows ten years worth of historical sales data, but it may not be feasible to run a report to add up each and every sale over a ten-year period. Your database administrator may need to create a summary table, stored procedure, or other specialized data structure to make reporting on this information possible.

The goal of this phase of report design is to learn where the data for the report is held, so you may want to note the table and field names required, as well as how the tables are joined together.

1

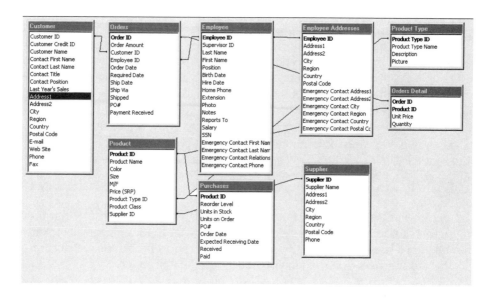

Customer		**Orders**		**Employee**		**Employee Addresses**		**Product Type**

Figure 1-2 | An entity-relationship diagram

3. *Creating the design.* With both your notes from your meeting with the user and the information gleaned from your database or system administrator, you are now ready to sit down and create the design of your report.

Ask the Expert

Question: What is a stored procedure?

Answer: A stored procedure is a compiled SQL program that exists and runs on your SQL server. Stored procedures are useful when creating reports from large sets of data, or when running reports that require long, complex calculations. In these cases, the stored procedure performs the work for you on the database server.

During this phase, try to create a prototype that is as specific as possible. Where you can, show all of the elements of the report accurately. If you want the column headings centered and the columns themselves left-aligned, mark this on your prototype. As reporting needs grow, there may be a number of people creating reports for users. Giving them a clear road map to follow makes things easier all the way around.

Hint

You can find a number of templates for different types of report prototypes in the Module 1 folder of this book's .zip file (available for download from the Osborne Web site at http://www.osborne.com).

During this time, you also should consult the user again to ensure that the report design and content are on track with what the user originally asked for. Again, gaining the user's approval of the report prototype will ensure that no surprises occur when you deliver the final product.

Project Summary

Before you can create a report, you need a plan, and developing a report prototype is a key part of that plan. With the report prototype created, most of the hard work has been done. All that remains is to create the report to specifications using Crystal Reports.

Report Design Experts Overview

To help you get started with the report design process, Crystal Reports includes a number of report design experts that will guide you in creating a report. These experts consist of a series of dialog boxes that take you step by step through a particular procedure. Whether you have dabbled in working with Crystal Reports or are a complete novice, the experts will help you quickly get underway.

Remember that anything you do using a report design expert can also be accomplished using the menus, commands, and icons within Crystal Reports itself. If you prefer, you can start from a blank page and add all of the elements of the report yourself, but the experts make the initial report design process easy.

─┼─ *Tip* ───────────────────────────────────

You can reuse the report expert after the initial design process to add elements to your report. Keep in mind, however, that any formatting you may have added after finishing with the expert will be lost. This is because the expert uses a template to create your report. When you use the expert to make additional changes, it reapplies the original template.

Standard Report Expert

The Standard Report Expert is used the majority of the time and allows you to create list reports and to add grouping, sorting, summaries, formulas, and so forth. You also can create reports for analysis using the Standard Report Expert (such as a report that responds to the request "Show me my top ten customers"), add graphs, and apply predefined styles to your report. An example of a report created with the Standard Report Expert is shown in Figure 1-3.

Product Listing

Product Class	Product Name	Color	Size	Price (SRP)
Bicycle				
Bicycle	Mozzie	jewel green	18.5	1,739.85
Bicycle	Wheeler	deep burgundy	18	539.85
Bicycle	Wheeler	deep burgundy	16	539.85
Bicycle	Romeo	radiant steel	22	832.35
Bicycle	Romeo	radiant steel	20	832.35
Bicycle	Romeo	radiant steel	18	832.35
Bicycle	Romeo	radiant steel	16	832.35
Bicycle	Endorphin	deep burgundy	22	899.85
Bicycle	Endorphin	deep burgundy	20	899.85
Bicycle	Endorphin	deep burgundy	18.5	899.85
Bicycle	Endorphin	deep burgundy	17	899.85
Bicycle	Endorphin	deep burgundy	15	899.85
Bicycle	Descent	steel satin	15	2,939.85
Bicycle	Mozzie	jewel green	20	1,739.85
Bicycle	SlickRock	champagne	15	764.85
Bicycle	Mozzie	jewel green	17	1,739.85
Bicycle	Mozzie	jewel green	15	1,739.85
Bicycle	Descent	steel yellow	22	2,939.85
Bicycle	Descent	steel satin	22	2,939.85
Bicycle	Descent	steel yellow	20	2,939.85
Bicycle	Descent	steel satin	20	2,939.85
Bicycle	Descent	steel yellow	18.5	2,939.85
Bicycle	Descent	steel satin	18.5	2,939.85
Bicycle	Descent	steel yellow	17	2,939.85

Figure 1-3   A report created with the Standard Report Expert

Form Letter Expert

The Form Letter Expert is used to create reports that combine database information with text you enter or import. Using the Form Letter Expert, you can create form letters (like the one shown in Figure 1-4), statements, invoices, and so forth that seamlessly merge information from your database (similar to the mail-merge feature found in Microsoft Word and other word processors).

Form Expert

Crystal Reports can be used to print information on existing forms used by your organization. Using the Form Expert, you can underlay a scanned image of the form that will be used when printing, allowing you to design the report directly on top of the form. With this method, you can align the fields in your report to match the form that you use for printing. After you finish creating the report, you can remove the underlying image, and your report will print correctly on the forms every time.

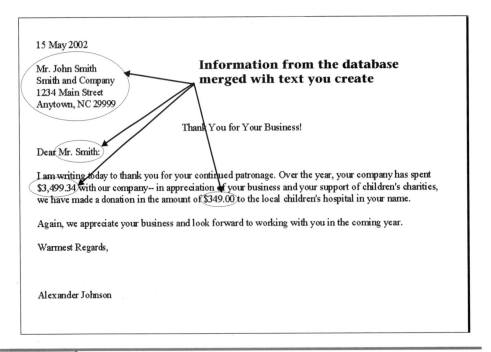

Figure 1-4   A form letter created using the Form Letter Expert

Cross-Tab Expert

A cross-tab report is a data presentation format that closely resembles a spreadsheet. The Cross-Tab Expert can help you create a cross-tab report that has rows and columns that can be stacked on top of each other to provide a summarized, hierarchical view of your data. In addition to rows and columns, a cross-tab report also has summarized fields that allow you to quickly read the report for the information you require, as shown in the report in Figure 1-5.

Subreport Expert

A subreport is a report inserted within a report and can be used to display two or more disparate sets of information or to join two or more data sets that do not share a common key. For example, you might use a subreport to show sales information for your organization next to sales information from a particular segment, such as retail. The data for the two sections comes from different data sources and is totally different, but you can use the Subreport Expert to create a subreport that displays the information next to the information on the main report, as shown in Figure 1-6.

Products by Class and Type

| | Accessory | | | | | Bic | |
	Gloves	Helmets	Locks	Saddles	Total	Competition	Hy
Total	576,544.60	1,091,435.90	338,416.89	409,437.40	2,415,834.79	3,553,136.14	6
Active Outdoors Crochet Glove	186,984.21	0.00	0.00	0.00	186,984.21	0.00	
Active Outdoors Lycra Glove	243,980.11	0.00	0.00	0.00	243,980.11	0.00	
Descent	0.00	0.00	0.00	0.00	0.00	Sum of Orders.Order Amount (N 2,291,712.50	
Endorphin	0.00	0.00	0.00	0.00	0.00	450,250.38	
Guardian "U" Lock	0.00	0.00	26,499.89	0.00	26,499.89	0.00	
Guardian ATB Lock	0.00	0.00	55,722.42	0.00	55,722.42	0.00	
Guardian Chain Lock	0.00	0.00	23,946.59	0.00	23,946.59	0.00	
Guardian Mini Lock	0.00	0.00	28,620.33	0.00	28,620.33	0.00	
Guardian XL "U" Lock	0.00	0.00	38,064.42	0.00	38,064.42	0.00	
InFlux Crochet Glove	71,043.71	0.00	0.00	0.00	71,043.71	0.00	
InFlux Lycra Glove	74,536.57	0.00	0.00	0.00	74,536.57	0.00	

Figure 1-5   A sample cross-tab report

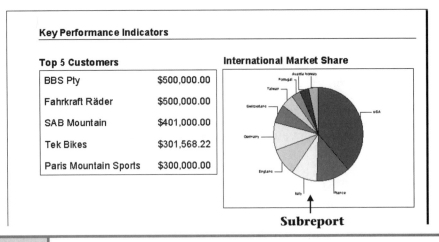

Subreport

Figure 1-6 An example of a subreport

Another common use of subreports is to join unrelated data sets. For example, you may want to create a report listing all of your organization's salespeople and then match them to a prospect database that you have purchased. Because the two databases are from different companies, they probably will not have much in common. Using a subreport, you can pick a field in the two databases that is similar (such as a region or a state field) and use that to match the data sets.

Mail Label Expert

Crystal Reports makes creating labels from your data source quick and easy by predefining a number of standard labels. Using the Mail Label Expert, you can quickly create labels in a variety of sizes and formats without having to work out the size, spacing, and so forth. If you are working with a label size or format that is not listed as a standard label, you can enter the dimensions, spacing, and so forth to create a custom label.

Tip

Most of the standard labels are for letter-sized paper only and correspond to an Avery label number.

Drill Down Expert

The Drill Down Expert enables you to create reports displaying a summary of information from your data source that hides all of the details that comprise the summary. When users want to see the details, they drill down into the data by double-clicking, and the details then appear. An example is a report created to show sales by state. A drill-down report might simply display the state and a sales total. To see all of individual sales that comprise that total, a user could double-click the name, state, or summary field to display the associated details, as shown in Figure 1-7.

Online Analytical Processing (OLAP) Expert

The Online Analytical Processing (OLAP) Expert can be used to create reports from OLAP data sources. Unlike relational databases, which store data in a number of tables in a two-dimensional view, OLAP data structures can be multidimensional. Instead of rows and columns (two dimensions), OLAP structures have multiple

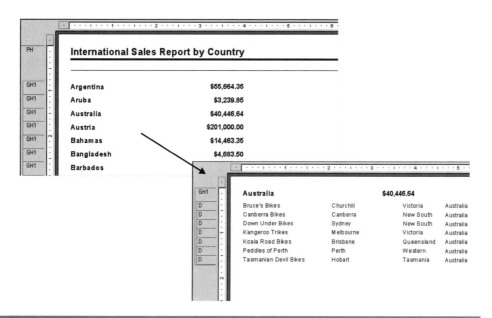

Figure 1-7 A drill-down report showing the details that make up a summary field

dimensions to help business users and managers analyze data extracted from their transactional systems.

Crystal Reports supports most of the major OLAP vendors, including Hyperion Cubes, IBM's DB2 OLAP Server, Informix MetaCube, Holos HDC Cubes, and many others using Object Linking and Embedding (OLE) Database (DB) for OLAP, including Microsoft SQL Server and Applix TM/1.

Tip

For more information on OLAP data structures and related terminology, check out http://www.moulton.com/olap/olap.glossary.html.

☑ *Mastery Check*

1. What are the five phases of report design?

_____

_____

2. Why is it important to create a report prototype before actually creating the report itself?

_____

_____

3. Where are the sample report files that ship with Crystal Reports located?

_____

_____

4. Subreports can be used to:

   A. Display related information from two or more different sources in one single report.

   B. Display unrelated information from two or more different sources in one single report.

   C. Both A and B above.

   D. None of the above.

5. What is a drill-down report?

_____

_____

Module 2

Creating a
Simple Report

Goals

- Identify the steps in creating a report using an expert
- Understand the options available when working with an expert
- Create a simple report using the Standard Report Expert

At this point, you are ready to get down to business. You should have a prototype of the report you want to create and should be well acquainted with the different types of experts that are available to help you get started. In this module, we take a look at the steps required to create your report using the report experts; then, at the end of the module, you will create your first report, using the Standard Report Expert.

Using the Report Design Experts

To create a new report using an expert to guide you, click the New icon on the standard toolbar or choose File | New. This action opens the Crystal Report Gallery, shown in Figure 2-1.

Each of these experts (described in Module 1) will guide you through the steps for creating a new report with the specified features. While this abundance of experts may seem a little daunting at first, all of the experts share some common steps, such as selection of the data source, fields, and so on. Once you are

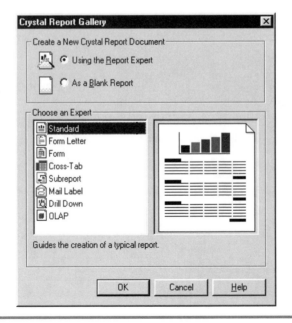

Figure 2-1 The Crystal Report Gallery

2

comfortable with the Standard Report Expert, you can apply your knowledge of how it works to other experts.

Selecting a Data Source

The first step in creating a report using the Standard Report Expert is choosing the data source on which the report will be based. You can select among three general types of data sources:

● **Database**   Virtually any relational or nonrelational database or data source accessed through a native driver or Open Database Connectivity (ODBC) connection

● **Crystal Query**   A SQL query (QRY) created using Crystal Reports' own query tool

● **Crystal Dictionary**   A Crystal Reports dictionary (DC5 or DCT) file created using Crystal Reports' own dictionary tool to present a simplified view of a database or other data source

Tip

For more information on working with Crystal Queries or Dictionaries, check out the appendixes at the back of the book.

To select your data source, use the Data Explorer, shown in Figure 2-2. The Data Explorer itself is really just a number of different views of the data sources that you have available to use in your report:

● **Current Connections**   This section of the Data Explorer shows any databases or sources that you are currently logged onto.

● **Favorites**   If you are familiar with Favorites in Internet Explorer, this option will be familiar; it works the same way, except that instead of saving frequently viewed Web pages, the Favorites option in the Data Explorer allows you to save frequently used data connections.

● **History**   The History section of the Data Explorer automatically saves connections you have recently used.

- **OBDC**   Most databases can be accessed through ODBC. Crystal Reports ships with a number of ODBC drivers for the most popular database formats, including Informix, SQL Server, and so forth. You need to install and configure the appropriate ODBC driver for your database.

- **Database Files**   You can also access some personal computer (PC) databases through a native connection, which eliminates the need for an ODBC driver. These databases include XBase, DBase, Paradox, Microsoft Access, and Btrieve.

- **More Data Sources**   In addition to using standard relational databases, Crystal Reports can report from the local file system, message tracking logs, Internet Information Server (IIS)/Proxy logs, Windows NT event logs, Microsoft Exchange, Microsoft Outlook, and more. You will find all of these data types under More Data Sources, as well as OLE DB, which is used to access relational databases, OLAP data sources, and nonstandard data sources. A number of native drivers for relational databases also appear under this heading if you have the appropriate database client installed.

- **Metadata/Query**   This is another option for creating reports using a Crystal Reports dictionary or query.

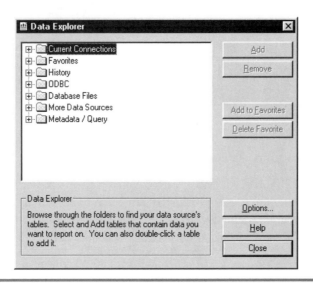

Figure 2-2   The Crystal Reports Data Explorer

The most common types of data sources are ODBC or native relational databases. If you select either of these two types of data sources, a second dialog box appears asking you to choose the individual tables where the data resides.

⟨?⟩ Ask the Expert

Question: What is ODBC?

Answer: ODBC stands for Open Database Connectivity and represents a common platform for accessing databases and database files. Instead of each database or application vendor coming up with its own database drivers and standards, almost all use the ODBC standard. This means that there is one standard interface for accessing data. If you open the Windows Control Panel, you should see an icon for ODBC Data Sources, which will open the ODBC Data Source Administrator. Using this tool, you can set up an ODBC driver that points to your data source and allows Crystal Reports to access the tables, fields, and so on that it contains. For more information on ODBC, check out http://www. microsoft.com/data/odbc/, and for information on setting up an ODBC driver, search the Crystal Reports help file for the topic "Setting up an ODBC data source."

1-Minute Drill

- What are the three options for data sources when using a report expert?
- Where could you find connections you have recently used?

─│Tip

You can move between the Report Expert tabs by clicking on the name of the tab or by using the Back and Next buttons located at the bottom of the Report Expert dialog box.

- Databases, Crystal Query files, and Crystal Dictionary files
- In the Data Explorer, under the History section

Linking Database Tables or Files

If you select one or more tables for your report, the Standard Report Expert adds a tab titled Links, as shown in Figure 2-3. Your database administrator should be able to provide you with an entity-relationship diagram that will show the relationships among the tables in your database. You need to re-create these relationships in Crystal Reports by drawing visual links between the tables.

If you are linking tables of a native PC-type database (Microsoft Access, dBase, Btrieve, or FoxPro), you have three linking options:

- Look up both at the same time.

- Look up all of one first and then all of the others.

- Look up all the combinations of the two files.

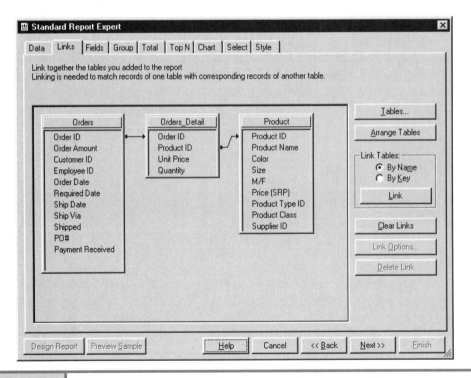

Figure 2-3 The Visual Linking tab helps you join two or more tables

For SQL databases accessed through native drivers or ODBC, you have a full range of join types available to you, including:

- Equal
- Left outer
- Right outer
- Greater than
- Less than
- Greater or equal
- Less or equal
- Not equal

Tip
If you are unsure about the type of join you should have between two tables, check with your database administrator or someone who is familiar with your database or application.

Choosing Fields

The Fields tab of the Standard Report Expert, shown in Figure 2-4, is split into two sections. The left pane of the dialog box lists all of the fields that are available to be inserted into your report, grouped underneath their table name. To add a field to your report, you need to move the field from the left pane to the right pane. You can accomplish this by double-clicking the field name or by highlighting the field and clicking the Add button. Additional buttons are also available to add or remove one or all fields.

Tip
To select multiple fields, hold down the CTRL key while clicking.

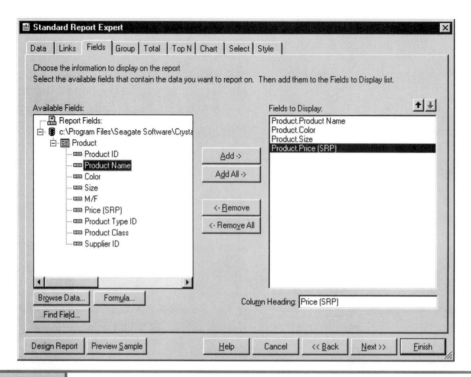

Figure 2-4 Using the Fields tab to select the fields for your report

If you are unsure of a field's definition or contents, you can use the Browse Data button to display a sample of the field's contents. Keep in mind that the sample returned is not based on the complete contents of the table; it is just a representative sample of up to (approximately) 200 records.

Another key feature of the Fields tab is the Find Field button, at the bottom left. This button allows you to search the selected tables for a field that matches your criteria.

Because we are creating a simple report to start with, we are not going to discuss the use of the Formula button to insert calculations and summaries at this time. If you can't wait to get started using formulas, you can go straight to Module 8, where formulas are covered in depth.

To change the order of the fields you are inserting in your report, you can use the up and down arrows that appear in the upper-right corner of the dialog box to move fields up and down. At this point, you can also change the column heading associated with a field.

2

Grouping and Sorting

The next step in creating a report using the Standard Report Expert is selecting the sorting and grouping to use in your report using the Group tab, shown in Figure 2-5. This tab is similar to the Fields tab. To select a field, you move it from the list on the left to the list on the right. By specifying a field on the Group tab, you can add sorting control breaks, or groups to your report. For example, if you were to group on the State field, your report would be printed with all the records for each state together, with a break between each state. Another example is shown in Figure 2-5, where the report is being grouped by a Product Class field; all of the products that fall into a particular class will be grouped and shown together.

After you select a field, notice that you have a choice of sort orders:

- **In Ascending Order** This option groups the records by the field you have specified and orders those groups from A through Z, zero through nine, and so forth.

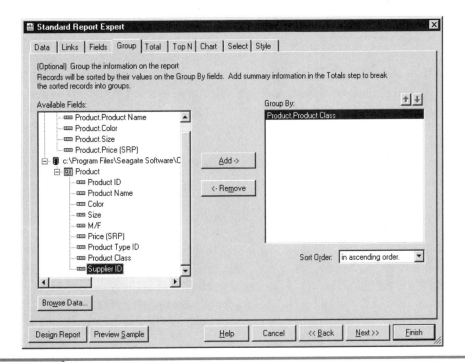

Figure 2-5 Choosing the grouping and sorting for your report

- **In Descending Order**   This option groups the records by the field you have specified and orders those groups from Z through A, nine through zero, and so forth.

- **In Specified Order**   Using this option, you can name and define your own grouping criteria. You might want to use this option, for example, if you want to group states into sales territories. You could create a group called Bob's Territory and set the criteria to North Carolina and South Carolina. When the report is printed, all of the records from North Carolina and South Carolina will be grouped together under the group name, Bob's Territory.

- **In Original Order**   If your database has already performed some sorting on the data, this option leaves the records in their original order.

Tip

The Group tab also features a Browse Data button that allows you to browse a field's contents and determine its type.

Inserting Summaries

The Total tab, shown in Figure 2-6, is used to insert Crystal Reports summary fields into your report. Crystal Reports provides these summary fields so that you do not have to create a formula every time you want to insert a sum, average, and so forth.

You can insert a number of summary fields into your report; the types of summaries vary based on the type of field, as shown in Table 2-1.

For some of the statistical functions, you are asked to provide additional information, such as the value for N. For other functions, you specify that a summary is a certain percentage of a particular field.

When you add a summary to your report using the Standard Report Expert, the summary appears immediately following each group, showing the summary for only that particular group. The option in the lower-right corner of the dialog box, Add Grand Totals, adds the same type of summary field at the end of the report and shows the value for the entire report.

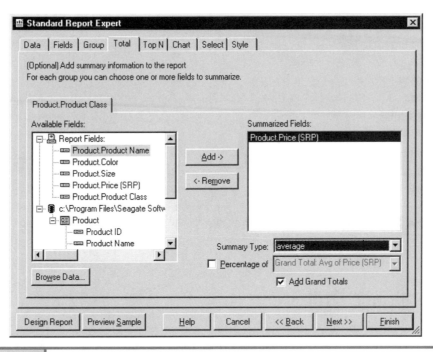

Figure 2-6   Inserting summary fields into your report

Summary Type	With Numeric Fields	With Other Field Types
Sum	X	
Average	X	
Maximum	X	X
Minimum	X	X
Count	X	X
Distinct Count	X	X
Sample Variance	X	
Sample Standard Deviation	X	
Population Variance	X	
Population Standard Deviation	X	

Table 2-1   Crystal Reports Summaries and Usage

Summary Type	With Numeric Fields	With Other Field Types
Correlation	X	
Covariance	X	
Weighted Average	X	
Median	X	
Pth Percentile	X	
Nth Largest	X	X
Nth Smallest	X	X
Mode	X	X
Nth Most Frequent	X	X

Table 2-1   Crystal Reports Summaries and Usage (*continued*)

1-Minute Drill

● What are the four different sort orders available for groups?

● How can you select multiple fields within Crystal Reports?

Using Top N Analysis

Top N analysis, shown in Figure 2-7, is a powerful analytical feature that allows you to order data based on subtotals or summaries, and is an optional step when using most report experts. For example, if you have a report totaling each customer's sales for the past year, you can use Top N analysis to determine your top 10 or top 20 customers by ranking their sales totals. (Likewise, you can also find your bottom 10 customers.)

In addition to doing Top N and Bottom N analysis, this feature can be used to sort all of your customers, placing them in order from highest revenue to lowest (or vice-versa).

When working with Top N Analysis and the report experts, you need to keep two things in mind. The first is that to use Top N analysis, you need to have a group inserted into your report and a summary field summarizing some

---

● Ascending, Descending, Specified, and Original Order
● Hold down the CTRL key while selecting

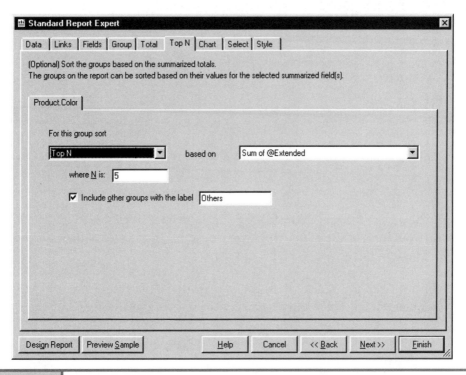

Figure 2-7   Top N analysis can be used to analyze report data to identify trends

information within that group. The second is that Top N analysis can be applied to multiple groups. You may want to show your top 10 customers, for instance, and, for each customer, the top 5 products purchased.

Crystal Reports uses a powerful third-party graphics engine to provide a wide range of graphs and charts, as shown in Figure 2-8. A number of standard chart types are available:

- Bar

- Line

- Area

- Pie

- Doughnut
- 3D riser
- 3D surface
- XY scatter
- Radar
- Bubble
- Stock

You also have the option of creating a custom chart type, based on your needs. In addition to the graph type, you can select the source of data for your graph. The four data types available are these:

- **Group Graphs** These are based on a group you have inserted and some summary field. These graphs can appear in the report header and/or

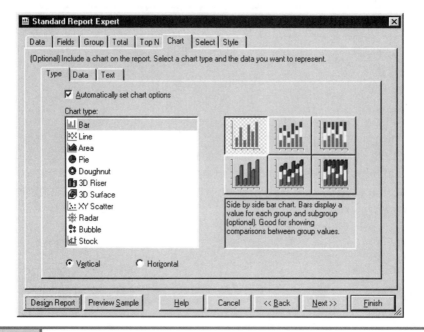

Figure 2-8 Charts and graphs available in Crystal Reports

footer, or, if your report has multilevel grouping, these graphs can reside in a group header and/or footer.

- **Advanced Graphs**   These are plotted on the change of a field to show values (corresponding to the X and Y axes). Using an advanced graph type, you do not need to have a group or summary inserted into your report. In addition, you can use special analysis functions such as Top N analysis and summary operators without having to insert the operators into your report. This type of graph can appear in the report header and/or footer or in a group header and/or footer.

- **Cross-Tab Graphs**   These are based on the contents of a cross tab that appears in your report and can be placed in the report header and/or footer or group header and/or footer, depending on where your cross tab appears.

- **OLAP Grid Graphs**   These are similar to cross-tab graphs except that they are based on OLAP data structures instead of the relational databases that you are probably familiar with. Like cross-tab graphs, they can appear in the report header and/or footer or a group header and/or footer, depending on where the OLAP grid is inserted.

Using Record Selection

One of the last steps in creating a report using the Standard Report Expert is setting the record selection for your report using the Select tab, shown in Figure 2-9. Record selection is important because you probably do not want to return every single record in the table for your report. You use record selection to narrow the data to get exactly the nugget (or subset) of information that you need. If you were creating a daily sales report, for example, you would probably want to return the sales records for only a single day.

Another key point about record selection is that you want to return only the records that you need for the report. It makes no sense running a report for 2 million customers when you are interested in only one particular customer. Using record selection, you can narrow in on that one customer and save on report processing time.

Using this tab, you can specify a field to use and then set your record selection criteria based on that field. If you are creating your report from a relatively small database, you can skip the Select tab and move to previewing your report.

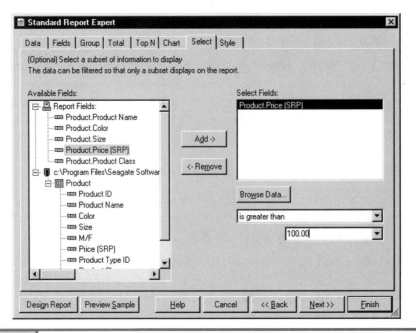

Figure 2-9 Choosing the record selection for your report

Previewing Your Report

The final tab in the Standard Report Expert, shown in Figure 2-10, is for setting the report style. At this point, you can give your report a title and can apply a predefined style, including coordinating colors, fonts, and so on. If you select any of the predefined styles shown, you see a preview of what that particular style looks like on the right. Unfortunately, Crystal Reports does not allow us to add custom styles to the list presented, but the predefined styles can be a great starting point for giving reports your own look and feel.

You can also add a picture or your company logo using the Add a Picture button at the bottom of the tab to select a graphic.

Tip

You will need to make sure the graphic you wish to insert is in one of the following formats: BMP, TIFF, JPG, or PNG.

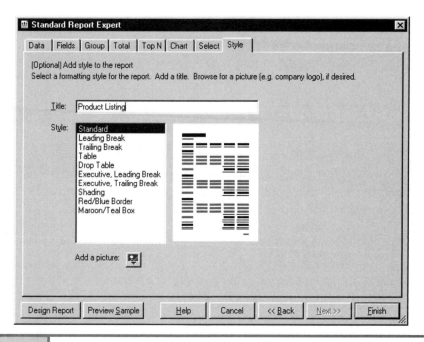

Figure 2-10 | You can apply a preformatted report style to your report

With the report expert settings complete, it is time to take a look at what you have. As shown at the bottom of Figure 2-10, you have three options:

●   **Design Report**   The Design Report button in the lower-left corner of the Style tab completes the report expert and opens your new report in the Design tab, allowing you to make changes to the design without actually connecting to the database and reading any records.

●   **Preview Sample**   To cut down on the processing time for your report while you are still working on the report design, you can choose to preview only a sample of the records. Using the Preview Sample button, you can preview the report with all of the records or select just a sample of the records (the default number is 100).

●   **Finish**   The Finish button opens your new report in full preview mode, reading all of the records you have requested from the database.

Tip

If you are a bit confused by the Design tab and Preview tab that appear, note that these subjects are covered in Module 3.

Ask the Expert

Question: Can I go back into the Report Expert to change my report design?

Answer: Yes, you can go back into the Report Expert at any time by selecting Report | Report Expert. The only problem is that when you edit your report using a Report Expert, all of the custom formatting and changes you have made will be discarded. Most report designers find it is easier to use the Report Expert just to get started, and then make any changes or additions to their report using the tools, menus, and icons within the report designer itself.

Saving Your Report

After you have finished with the report expert, you are returned to either the Design or Preview tab of your report. You can save your report from either view. Choose File | Save or click the Save icon on the toolbar.

Save Options

On the File menu, the Save Data with Report option is checked by default. The only reason to leave this option checked would be if you were going to send the report to another Crystal Reports user who did not have access to your database. This user could open the report with saved data and view or print the results without having to go back to the original data source. Otherwise, this option will increase the report file size unnecessarily.

In addition, under File | Summary Info, shown in Figure 2-11, you can enter an author's name, keywords, and so forth. Although most people do not ever complete the summary information for any file that they save, you should complete this information. Crystal Reports treats these fields as special fields that can be inserted into your report. You can also use the check box at the bottom of the dialog box to

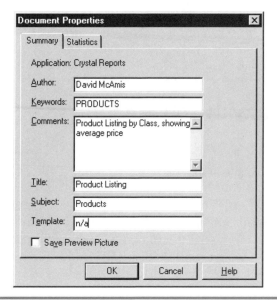

Figure 2-11   Summary information can be inserted into your report as a
special field

generate a preview of the report. With this feature, when you are looking at a long
list of reports, you can browse through a thumbnail picture of each report.

Previewing and Saving Your Report

The last step in creating a report is previewing it and saving your design in a
report (.rpt) file. You can preview your report at any time by selecting Report |
Refresh Report Data or by pressing the F5 function key. If you are working off
a database that has live data entry during the day, you may notice that your
report results change as new data is entered or deleted. There are a couple of
considerations when choosing the file format and save options.

File Format

Using Crystal Reports 8.5, you can save your report to an .rpt file in either
the current format or, using the Save As option, in a format compatible with
version 7.0 of Crystal Reports.

Hint

If you are planning to distribute your report to other users in Excel or some other format and don't see that option, don't worry. Crystal Reports can export to Excel and many other formats, as you learn in Module 7.

Saving Data with Your Report

Another issue to consider when saving your report is whether to save the data with the report. When a Crystal Reports report is run, a saved record set is written to a temporary file on the hard drive. (You may notice this feature when you make a change to your report or record selection and you are prompted with Use Saved Data? or Refresh?) When you save your report with the Save Data with Report option enabled, this saved record set becomes a part of the report (.rpt) file and increases the size of the file dramatically. To turn off this option, select File | Save Data with Report and remove the check mark.

Project 2-1: Creating a Report Using the Standard Report Expert

In this project, we are going to create a Product Listing report for the fictional Xtreme Mountain Bike Company. In our report, we want to show the product name, color, size, and price. We also want to group by product class and show the average price for each of the classes in our report (that is, the average price of bicycles, accessories, and so on).

Hint

If you have downloaded the information for Module 2 from the Osborne Web site, a finished version of this report is included.

Step-by-Step

1. From the Start | Programs menu, launch Crystal Reports.

2. From the Welcome dialog box, select Create a New Crystal Report Document and click OK. From the Crystal Report Gallery, select the Standard report expert and click OK.

3. Click the Database button to open the Data Explorer and navigate to the Xtreme Sample Database under the ODBC node of the tree, as shown in Figure 2-12.

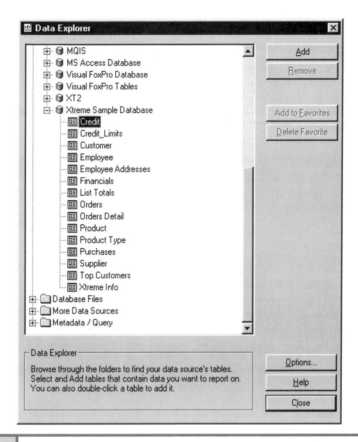

Figure 2-12   The Data Explorer is used to select tables and fields from your database

4. Under the Xtreme Sample Database node, select the Product table and click the Add button. A green check mark should appear next to the table name, and the Data tab in the background in the Report Expert should reflect your selection. Click Close to close the Data Explorer and return to the report expert.

5. On the Fields tab, select the fields that you want to see in your report. For this project, select the following fields:

● Product Name
● Color

- Size
- Price (SRP)

To select a field, highlight it in the list on the left and click the button marked Add -> to move it to the list on the right.

6. On the Group tab, select the grouping and sorting you want for your report. In this example, group on the Product Class field.

Hint

To group, use the same technique as for selecting a field to include: highlight the field you want to group by and click the button marked Add -> to move the field to the list on the right.

7. On the Total tab, select the summaries you want to insert in your report. Because you have a list of products, you will probably want to know the average price of the products in each category. At this point, Crystal Reports has identified that the Price field is numeric and has moved it to the list of fields to be totaled automatically. If it hadn't, you could have located the Price (SRP) field and moved it from the list on the left to the list on the right. Verify that this field has been added and change the summary type to Average.

8. Do not use the Top N, Chart, and Select tabs at this time. Don't worry— you'll work with these features later.

9. On the Style tab, give your report a name of "Product Listing" and apply a

Hint

You can preview the preformatted report styles by clicking the name of the style.

predefined style.

10. Click Finish to view the results. If you chose the Standard report style, your finished report should look something like Figure 2-13.

11. Save your report as **Product Listing Ch2-1.rpt**.

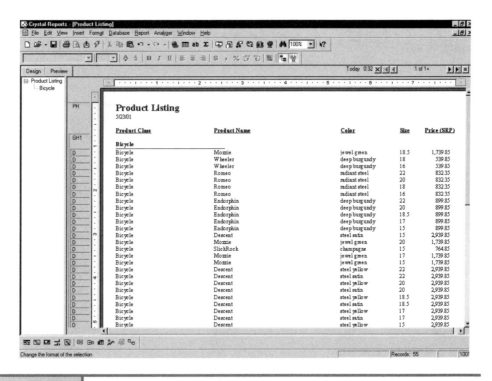

Figure 2-13   The finished report, using the Standard report style

Project Summary

The Standard Report Expert is the easiest means of quickly creating a report and is frequently used a starting point for more complex reports.

☑ *Mastery Check*

1. How many report experts are available?

    A. 8

    B. 10

    C. 12

    D. 6

2. What does ODBC stand for?

_____

_____

3. What types of summary operators are available within Crystal Reports?

_____

_____

4. Why do you need to use record selection in your report?

_____

_____

Module 3

Working with the Report Design Environment

Goals

- Understand the report design environment
- Learn how to customize the report design interface
- Identify the various sections of a report
- Work with report objects and text fields

With your first simple report created, it is time to take a look at the place you will spend the most time as a report designer: the report design environment. In this chapter, you learn the basic skills that you will need throughout the report design process. You will learn how to navigate through reports; to insert, move, and format different types of objects; and to use general report formatting techniques.

Report Design Environment

The report design environment is divided into several areas, each with its own purpose and unique properties. Some areas of the environment are standard with every report that you create, such as the Design and Preview tabs and the navigation toolbar and other toolbars. Other areas, such as report sections, depend on your report's design and may appear multiple times depending on your needs. Understanding what is happening in the report design environment is the key to understanding report design, and this section gives you an overview of the various areas of the design environment and their use.

Design and Preview Tabs

You can view your report in two modes: Design and Preview. Design mode, shown in Figure 3-1, offers a behind-the-scenes look at your report, and each section of the report is displayed once. Any changes you make to a section or objects in a section while in Design mode are reflected throughout the report. For example, if you change the title that appears in the Page Header section, that change is reflected in every page header regardless of whether your report is 1 page or 100 pages.

The Preview mode is a print preview that is prepared according to your default printer driver. It provides an accurate, multiple-page "what you see is what you get" (WYSIWYG) representation of your report. What you see in Preview mode is exactly what you see when you print your report.

For most operations, you can use either the Design or Preview mode, but it is sometimes easier to work exclusively in the Design mode because you can see precisely where you are placing objects. Also, when you are in the Design view of your report, you can view any objects that are suppressed or hidden in your report. (And believe me, this comes in handy sometimes!)

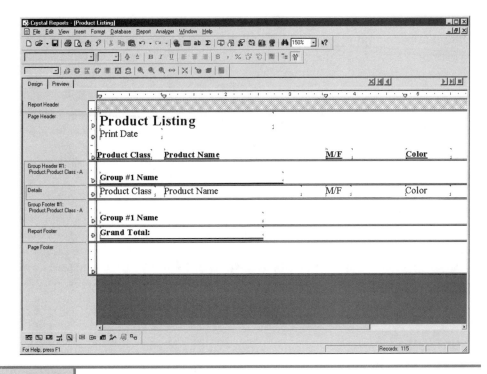

Figure 3-1   The Crystal Reports Design view

Navigation Methods

The navigation toolbar, shown on the Preview tab in Figure 3-2, is used to navigate between pages in Preview mode. The arrows move you a page at a time through the report, and the arrows with the vertical lines move you to the first or last page of your report. In addition, you can close preview windows and stop report processing using the same set of buttons.

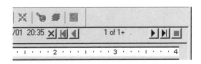

Figure 3-2   The navigation toolbar can be used to move backward and forward through your report.

To navigate to a specific place in your report, you can also use the group tree that appears on the left side of the Preview window, shown in Figure 3-3, or you can search for a value using Crystal Report's Find function (CTRL-F).

Note

This tree appears only if you have one or more groups inserted into your report.

Another navigation method, new to Crystal Reports 8.5, is the ability to jump to a specific page directly from the Report menu (CTRL-G).

Tip

Sometimes you may see the page numbers shown as "1 of 1+." This means that Crystal Reports knows that there is enough data to fill additional pages, but it doesn't know exactly how many. If you click the right arrow, Crystal Reports will advance to the next page. If you click the right arrow with the line (indicating to jump to the last page), Crystal Reports will show you the total page count.

Toolbars

A number of toolbars contain buttons or shortcuts to commonly used menu items. These graphics are also shown on the menus, to help you quickly locate the corresponding button on the toolbar.

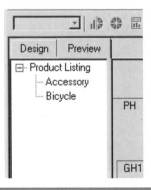

Figure 3-3   The group navigation tree

You can display four different toolbars (shown in Figure 3-4) and the status bar by right-clicking in the toolbar area and selecting a toolbar from the list. The toolbars and their associated functions are as follows:

- **Standard** Provides the standard Windows buttons for opening, saving, printing, and refreshing reports, as well as buttons for cut, copy, paste, undo, redo, and basic Crystal Reports operations. This toolbar appears by default when you start Crystal Reports.

- **Formatting** Supplies shortcuts to common formatting options, including font, size, and alignment. This toolbar appears by default when you start Crystal Reports.

- **Supplementary Tools** Includes tools for drawing lines and boxes, adding graphics to your report, inserting groups and cross tabs, and so on.

- **Analyzer Tools** Analyzes geographic maps or charts and contains buttons and functions relating to this type of analysis.

- **Status Bar** Appears at the bottom of the report design page and shows object names, measurements, number of records, processing status, and so on. The status bar is shown by default when you start Crystal Reports.

Report Sections

Another important concept to understand in the creation of reports is that the report is broken into separate sections. On the Design tab, the different sections that make up a report are shown on the left side of the screen, as shown in

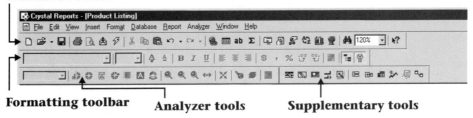

Figure 3-4 Crystal Reports toolbars

Figure 3-5. The following sections may appear in your report and are commonly used as described here:

- **Report Header/Footer** These appear at the top of the first page of the report and at the bottom of the last page. The report title appears most often in the report header, and a record count or end-of-report marker may appear in the report footer (that is, 10,000 records processed—end of report), in addition to any grand totals for your report.

- **Page Header/Footer** These appear at the top and bottom of every page. The page headers and footers are used to display information that is critical to understanding the data represented and may include field headings, page numbers, and the print date of the report.

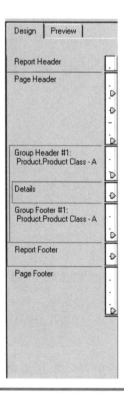

Figure 3-5 A number of sections comprise a Crystal report

3

- **Group Header/Footer**   These appear immediately before and immediately after any groups you have inserted. The group header or footer usually contains the group name field, which provides a label for the group, and the group header or footer may also contain formulas, subtotals, and summaries based on the data in the group.

- **Details**   This appears once for each record in your report and (unless you are creating a summary report) contains most of the report's data.

On the Design tab, each of these sections is represented once, but when the report is previewed or printed, these sections are repeated as many times as needed, as shown in Figure 3-6.

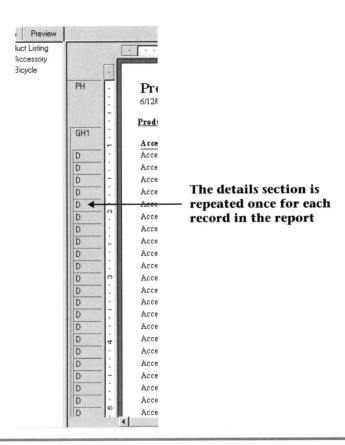

The details section is repeated once for each record in the report

Figure 3-6   An example of a report preview

Tip

It is easy to become confused when switching between the Design and Preview modes, especially when you are looking at a preview of a report and wondering where that field came from. One trick to help you understand where different objects are placed is to click the object to select it. When you switch back to the Design mode, the object will still be selected, and you can see what section it appears in.

Note, too, that you can split report sections into multiples, so you may see Page Header A and Page Header B (as shown in Figure 3-7) to indicate that the page header section has been split into two segments. You can use this technique to create complex reports that may be impossible to create with just a single section. For example, if you were creating a report for distribution in two different languages, you could have one report header set up with the English title, comments, and so on, and a separate report header with the same information in Spanish. By looking at a database field (like a Country field), you could determine which header to display.

Tip

If you are interested in working with multiple sections, turn to Module 10.

1-Minute Drill

● Which toolbars are shown by default when you start Crystal Reports?

● What is indicated by the page count of "1 of 1+"

Customizing the Design Environment

The report design environment can be customized to suit the way that you work and the reports that you need to design. Environment settings are established using two main option sets: global options and report options.

● Standard, Formatting, and Status Bar
● That there are additional pages of data available, but they have not yet been formatted to be displayed

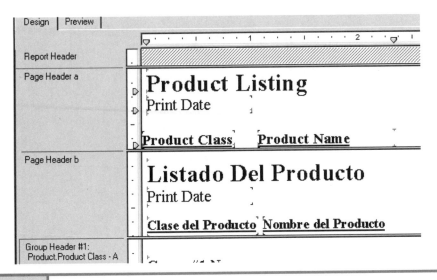

Figure 3-7 An example of a report with multiple sections

Global Options

File | Options contains global options that affect all reports that you create using Crystal Reports. Using the options shown in Figure 3-8, you can customize the layout of the report design and preview windows, define where reports are stored, and set other options that apply to the report design environment.

Report Options

File | Report Options, shown in Figure 3-9, includes settings that apply to a specific report, and these settings take effect immediately. Report options specify how null fields are handled and whether data and/or summaries are saved with the report, and they define preview page options and other properties.

Layout Options

Everybody has his or her own work style and preferences when working with a software package, and Crystal Reports caters to your individuality. You can configure the design environment according to your preferences by selecting File | Options | Layout. You can control rulers that appear, guidelines (which

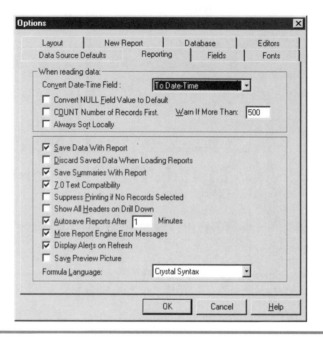

Figure 3-8 Options accessed using File | Options can be set globally and take effect with the next report you create

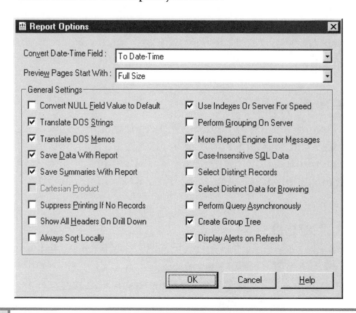

Figure 3-9 Options accessed using File | Report Options apply to a specific report only

Ask the Expert

Question: What is a null field?

Answer: A null field is a field within your database where no information has been entered. You may have a contact database that has four fields for different phone numbers. In some database records, the contact may have only one or two phone numbers; the other fields would be null (meaning that no information had been entered there).

we will talk about later), the display of section names, and more. Common layout options, shown in Figure 3-10, include the following:

- Show Rulers in Design
- Show Rulers in Preview
- Show Guidelines in Design
- Show Guidelines in Preview
- Show Hidden Sections in Design
- Show Short Section Names in Design
- Show Section Names in Preview
- Show Page Breaks in Wide Pages
- Show Tool Tips in Design
- Show Tool Tips in Preview

Which of these options you set is up to you. Some report designers prefer to view just the basics, without the rulers, guidelines, and so on to clutter up the design window, whereas others find that the rulers and guidelines help them get a feel for the report's dimensions and layout.

There are also options that apply to the objects shown on your report. Some of the options available include these:

- **Show Field Names**   This option displays the full field name instead of a placeholder such as XXXXXXX.

- **Insert Detail Field Titles**   When a field is inserted into the Details section, a text object is automatically inserted into the page header with the field heading.

- **Insert Group Name with Group**   A group tree can be inserted to aid in report navigation and organization.

You can also choose options for the preview page, starting with the initial image set to Full Size (100 percent), Fit Width, or Fit Page. You can use the Create Group Tree check box to control whether a group tree is generated from the contents of your report.

Tip

In the report you created in Module 2, a group tree was generated and appeared on the left side of the report preview window. Choosing not to generate the group tree aids in report performance, as there is one less item for Crystal Reports to display.

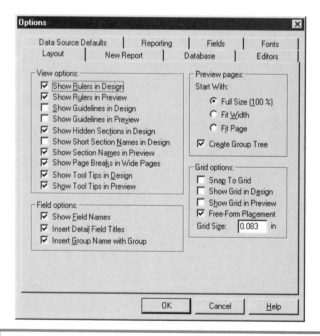

Figure 3-10   Options for the design environment

And finally, to help you keep your report design evenly spaced, Crystal Reports has an underlying grid that can be used to align objects. Options for this grid include the following:

- **Snap to Grid**   Aligns all inserted or moved objects to the underlying grid
- **Show Grid in Design**   Displays the underlying grid in the design view
- **Show Grid in Preview**   Displays the underlying grid in the preview
- **Free-Form Placement**   Disregards the grid's placement of an object and places the object where you indicate
- **Grid Size**   Provides the size of the underlying grid in inches or centimeters, depending on your regional settings

Tip

Alternatively, you could use a shortcut to access some of these options, following these steps: Switch your report to the Design mode by clicking the Design tab in the upper-left corner of the report design environment. In any white space (where no objects are placed), right-click, and a menu headed by Snap to Grid should appear, showing most of the options. Use the check boxes that appear on this menu to configure the underlying grid.

Project 3-1: Customizing the Report Design Environment

To help us understand how global options can be used, we are going to customize some settings of the report design environment. To start, we are going to set the autosave feature, which will periodically save your report (just in case anything should happen), and then we are going to set the default directory where your reports will be stored.

Step-by-Step

1. From the Start | Programs menu, launch Crystal Reports.

2. Choose File | Options and click the Reporting tab.

3. Select the Autosave Reports after xx Minutes option.

4. Enter a time interval to be used (5 minutes is the default, but you can select any interval you like).

5. Click OK to accept your changes.

Crystal Reports will now save a copy of your report, and you won't need to worry about losing your work if anything should happen. Next, set the default directory for any reports you create.

6. Choose File | Options and click the New Report tab.

7. Click the Browse button, shown in the dialog box in Figure 3-11, to browse to the subdirectory where you want to keep your reports.

8. Once you have selected a directory, click OK. The path and name of this subdirectory should now be displayed.

9. Click OK to accept your changes.

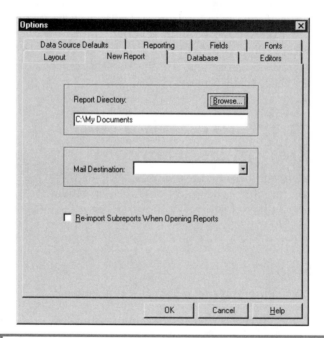

Figure 3-11 You can set the default directory for your reports

Project Summary

You can customize the Crystal Reports design environment to meet your needs and preferences. This project showed you how to set two global options for Crystal Reports: turning on autosave and specifying a default directory for your reports.

Understanding Field Objects

Crystal Reports reports include a number of different fields, from database fields, to parameter fields, to fields that hold text that you enter directly into your report. Chances are that you will need to use all of these types of objects to achieve the results that you desire. The following sections describe the common field objects, how to identify them, and their use within your reports.

Database Fields

Database fields are fields that are drawn from the tables, views, or stored procedures used in your report. Database fields are represented with the designation {*TableName.FieldName*}. This information can be seen by clicking the field and looking in the lower-left corner at the status bar. For example, if you were looking at a Phone Number field from a Customer table, the designation would be {*Customer.Phone*}. Database fields are used to display information from your database and are most commonly used in the Details section of your report, but they can also appear elsewhere.

Formula Fields

A formula field is a calculated field that can be inserted onto your report and displayed the same as any other field is displayed. Backed by a powerful formula language that looks like a cross between Excel's formula language and Visual Basic, formulas can incorporate database fields, parameter fields, and so on to perform complex calculations and string, date, and time manipulations. Formula fields are always prefixed with an @ symbol and are enclosed in curly braces: for example, {@commission}. Formula fields can be inserted anywhere on your report and have a wide range of uses, including mathematical calculations, string manipulation, and execution of complex logical statements and outcomes. A formula field can be used just about anywhere you need a calculated or derived field.

Parameter Fields

Parameter fields are used to prompt report users for information. Parameter fields are prefixed by a question mark and are enclosed in curly braces: for example, {?EnterState}. Parameter fields can be used with record selection, formulas, and so on, and can be inserted anywhere on your report.

Special Fields

Special fields are generated by Crystal Reports and include page numbers and summary information fields. Special fields are designated only by their field name, and all of the field names are reserved words. Special fields contain system-generated information and can be inserted anywhere they are needed in your report.

Running Total Fields

A running total field is a specialized summary field that can be used to create running totals, averages, and so on, and display this information on your report. A running total field is prefixed by a hash symbol and is enclosed in curly braces: for example, {#TotalSales}. Running totals frequently appear on the page footer or in the Details section with the detail data, but they can be placed in any section of your report.

SQL Expression Fields

A structured query language (SQL) expression field is similar to a Crystal Reports formula field in that a SQL expression field can be used for calculations. However, with a SQL expression field, these calculations occur on the database server itself and take advantage of the server's advanced processing power. A SQL expression field is prefixed by a percent sign and is enclosed in curly brackets: for example, {%CalcSummary}. A SQL expression field can be inserted anywhere in your report.

Summary Fields

A summary field can be used for calculations as simple as a subtotal or average, or as complex as a standard or population deviation. At first glance, summary fields and formulas may appear to do the same thing, but the major difference is that a summary field does not require any coding. A summary field can be identified by the use of the summary type (Sum, Average, and so on), the word "of," and the field that is being summarized: for example, Sum of Sales. A Summary field is generally placed in the group, page, or report header or footer, but it can be placed anywhere in your report that you like.

3

Group Name Fields

A group name field is generated by Crystal Reports to label any group that you have inserted into your report. All group name fields can be identified by the same label—Group #*n* Name—where *n* is the number of the group that you are working with, such as Group #3 Name. Group names are generally inserted in their corresponding group header or footer. When a group name field is displayed on the Preview tab of your report, it will appear as the actual name of a group you have inserted. For example, if you inserted a grouping by state, the group name field might read Alaska, Alabama, and so on.

Inserting Field Objects

When inserting fields onto your report, you will be using the Field Explorer, shown in Figure 3-12.

Tip
You can resize the Field Explorer by dragging the lower-right corner of the Field Explorer window.

The Field Explorer displays all of the different types of fields that you can insert into your report, broken down by the field type. You can see the fields that are available in each category by clicking the plus sign beside the category name to expand the group. If you click the plus sign beside the field type Database Fields, this may display a list of all of the database tables you have selected; to find the field you need, you may need to expand the contents of each table to find your field. For the rest of the field categories, you can simply expand the category to see all of the fields contained within.

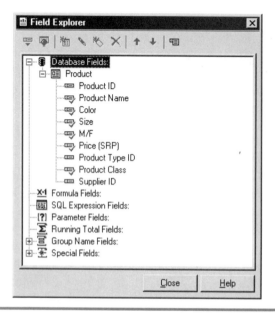

Figure 3-12 The Crystal Reports Field Explorer

Tip

If you have a large number of tables and fields, you may want to consider sorting alphabetically either on the table name, field name, or both. You can find this option under File | Options | Database.

As most of your time will be spent adding and arranging fields in your report, Crystal Reports tries to make this process as intuitive as possible. Fields can be dragged directly from the Field Explorer onto your report, or you can highlight a field and use the ENTER key to attach the field to the tip of your mouse—then position it where you want using your mouse and click once to release it; it's that simple.

Tip

When you insert fields into the Details section of your report, you will notice that a text object appears in the page header as well, to label the field you have inserted. This works only with fields that are inserted into the Details section. This feature can be turned off from the dialog box that appears when you choose File | Options.

Working with Field Objects

Once a field has been inserted into your report, you will probably want to control the way the field looks: its properties, size, font, and so on. One way you can control the way a field looks and behaves is by editing its properties.

Formatting Field Objects

Every field object within Crystal Reports has properties associated with it. From the font that is used to display the field contents, to the format of numbers contained within the field—you name it; there is a property to control it. To view the properties of a particular field, right-click directly on top of the field and select Format Field from the right-click menu that appears, shown here in Figure 3-13.

This will open up the property pages for this object. In our example, we have selected a string field, so there are tabs for Common, Border, Font, and Hyperlink property pages. The property pages that appear depend on the type

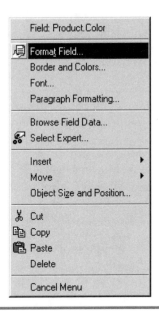

| **Figure 3-13** | You can format a field by right-clicking on top of the field and selecting Format Field. |

of field you select. For example, all field objects within Crystal Reports will display the property pages for Common, Border, Font, and Hyperlink as all of these objects have these properties in common.

But when you compare a numeric field to a date field, you will notice some differences. A numeric field will have an additional tab with properties that relate only to numeric fields; likewise, a date field will have an extra tab with properties that can be set for date fields.

The following sections describe some of the most common object formatting properties.

Common Formatting Options

All of the different types of field objects within Crystal Reports have a Common set of properties, as shown in Figure 3-14. There properties include the following:

- **Suppress**   Click to enable suppression so that the object does not appear on your report. (The object will remain in your report design, but will not appear when the report is previewed or printed.)

- **Horizontal Alignment**   Select from the drop-down list provided to left-align, center, right-align, or justify (in the figure, the default) the contents of the object. The default setting varies by type of field.

- **Keep Object Together**   Enable this option to attempt to keep large objects on the same page.

- **Close Border on Page Break**   Set this option for objects that have a border to ensure that the border extends to the edge of the page, and that the border closes before the next page begins.

- **Can Grow**   For multiline objects, select this option to ensure that the object can grow as needed, whether 2 lines or 20 are used. To control the maximum size of any object, you can also set the maximum number of lines. By default, this is set to zero to indicate no limit.

- **Tool Tip Text**   Set this to enable tool tip text to appear when the user moves the mouse over a particular object. Enter the text using the X+2 formula button located on the right side of the dialog box.

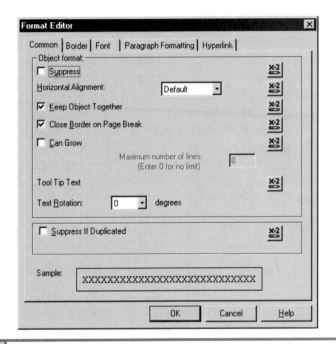

3

Figure 3-14   Common formatting properties

Note

You need to enter the tool tip text in quotation marks (for example, "This is tool text") in the formula and click Save and Close when finished with the formula editor. The X+2 icon turns from blue to red to indicate that tool tip text has been entered.

- **Text Rotation**   Use this to rotate the text in an object either 90 or 270 degrees.

- **Suppress If Duplicated**   Use this option to suppress a field if the contents are duplicated exactly. The object still appears in your report design, but the data itself does not appear when previewing or printing.

Formatting Numbers and Currency

For formatting numbers and currency, Crystal Reports also offers a number of specific properties. To make things easier, you can set these properties and formatting options by example, as shown in Figure 3-15. Instead of actually setting all of the properties, you can just pick a format that looks similar to what you want.

To add a currency symbol, use the options at the upper right of the dialog box to enable a currency symbol. You can also specify whether the symbol should be fixed in one position or floating beside the numbers.

To specify a custom numeric format, click the Customize button at the bottom of the dialog box. These options are available for customization on the Currency Symbol and the Number tabs:

● **Enable Currency Symbol** Specifies whether the symbol will be shown or not.

● **Fixed/Floating** Specified whether the currency symbol is fixed in place in the left margin of the field or floats next to the first digit.

● **One Symbol per Page** Places one symbol at the top of each page.

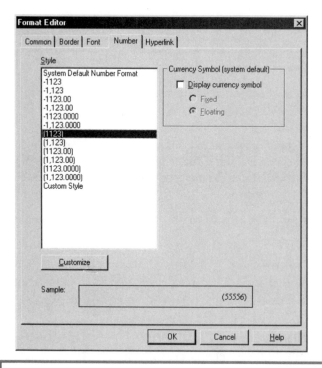

Figure 3-15 Selecting a numeric format by example

- **Position** Determines where the currency symbol will be displayed.

- **Currency Symbol** Specifies the currency symbol that will be used with numeric fields.

- **Use Accounting Format** Fixes the currency symbol at the left and displays negative amounts as dashes.

- **Suppress If Zero** Suppresses the display of a field if that field's value is zero.

- **Decimals** Specifies the number of decimal places, by example, to 10 decimal places of accuracy.

- **Rounding** Specifies the number of places to round to, from 10 to 1,000,000 decimal places.

- **Negatives** Displays a negative symbol before or after the number or uses parentheses to indicate negative numbers.

- **Reverse Sign for Display** Reverses the sign that would normally appear beside a value—for example, displays a negative sign for positive numbers and a positive sign for negative numbers.

- **Allow Field Clipping** Specifies whether field clipping is performed. Field clipping occurs when a field frame is not large enough to hold the entire contents of the field. In situations where this occurs, Crystal Reports clips the field by default and shows only part of the field. If you uncheck this option, Crystal Reports displays number signs (#####) to indicate that a field is longer than the space allotted to it. To get rid of the number signs, you need to drag the field frame so that it is large enough to accommodate the entire contents.

- **Decimal Separator** Changes the decimal separator. By default, Crystal Reports uses a period to mark the place between a whole number and the numbers after the decimal point.

- **Thousands Separator** Changes the thousands separator and symbol. By default, Crystal Reports uses a comma to indicate the thousands place in a number.

3

- **Leading Zero** Adds a leading zero to any numbers displayed as a decimal.

- **Show Zero Values As** Displays zero values in the default format, which is zeros or a dash (–).

Tip

Any custom formats that you create cannot be saved and must be re-created each time you want to use them.

Formatting Date Fields

Date fields can also be formatted by example. Crystal Reports gives you a number of predefined formats to serve as a starting point. If you locate the date or time field that you want to format, right-click the field, and select Format Field, you'll notice that the properties include a Date/Time tab, which allows you to choose a date format by example (just like you did for numbers), as shown in Figure 3-16.

To select a custom style, click Customize at the bottom of the dialog box and specify a custom numeric format. Options available for customization are as follows:

- Date/Time Order

- Separator

- Date Type

- Calendar Type

- Format (Month, Day, Year)

- Era/Period Type

- Order

- Day Of Week Type

- Separator

- Enclosure

- Position

- Separators

3

- 12/24 hour

- AM/PM Breakdown

- Symbol Position

- Format (Hour, Minute, Second)

- Separators

Resizing Fields

All of the fields you can insert onto your report can be resized. If you click a
field object, you'll notice that four handles (or little blue boxes) appear on each
side of the object. By moving these handles, you can resize the object.

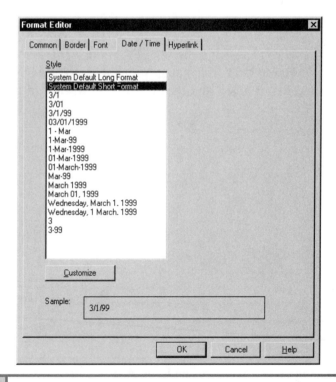

| Figure 3-16 | Choosing a date field format by example |

Tip

Resizing objects in Crystal Reports works like resizing objects in other Microsoft Office applications, such as Word and PowerPoint.

As a timesaving feature, Crystal Reports lets you select multiple objects (even different types of objects), and when you resize one, all are resized in proportion. Locate the objects that you want to resize in your report and multiple-select them. You perform a multiple-select operation by drawing a marquee box (sometimes called a stretch box) around the objects or by clicking each while pressing SHIFT or CTRL.

Choose one of the objects and resize its frame using the handles (or boxes) that appear on each side. Each object is resized proportionate to the object that you selected, as shown in Figure 3-17. Click anywhere outside the selected fields to finish the operation.

If you need to resize a field with some precision, you can also specify the exact size and position of an object. Locate the object that you want to resize or position and right-click directly on top of it. From the menu that appears, select Object Size and Position. Using the dialog box shown in Figure 3-18, select the X and Y positions of your object and the object's height and width.

Tip

Again, the height and width settings use the measurement unit defined in your Windows setup.

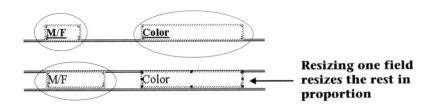

Resizing one field resizes the rest in proportion

Figure 3-17   An example of resizing multiple objects at once

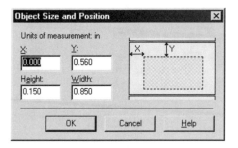

Figure 3-18   You can specify the exact size and location of objects in your report

Moving Field Objects

When moving field objects around, you have a couple of choices. The first, dragging and dropping, is more of a Windows skill than a Crystal Reports technique. By clicking an object, holding the mouse button, and moving the mouse, you can drag field objects around and drop them where you like by releasing the mouse button. If you have used other Windows applications, chances are you have used this technique many times. While it is the easiest way, it can also be the most time consuming, as you have to move each individual field and field heading, and so on. A much easier method is to use guidelines.

Tip

Another way to move field objects in the Design view of your report is to click the object to select it and then nudge the object around using the arrow keys.

Guidelines

Guidelines, shown in Figure 3-19, are invisible objects that can be used to align and move fields.

Tip

Guidelines are invisible when you print your report. When working with the report design or preview, guidelines can appear as a dashed line in your report.

The easiest way to think of a guideline is as a piece of string; you attach objects to that string, and when the string moves, everything attached to it moves as well.

Guidelines can be added to your report by clicking anywhere in the ruler. A small icon (sometimes called a caret), shown here, will appear, indicating that you have created a guideline.

Tip

Guidelines are also created with each new field that you add to the Details section of your report.

Once you have created a guideline, you can then snap objects to it by moving them close to the guideline; you should see them jump a bit as you get closer. This appearance of jumping can be likened to the effect of a magnet; the object seems to want to stick to the guideline as you move it closer.

When you move the guideline caret, the guideline and all of the objects attached to it move, too.

Design	Preview						
Report Header							
Page Header		**Product Listing** Print Date **Product Class**	**Product Name**		M/F	Color	
Group Header #1: Product.Product Class - A		Group #1 Name					
Details		Product Class	Product Name		M/F	Color	
Group Footer #1: Product.Product Class - A		Group #1 Name					
Report Footer		Grand Total:					
Page Footer							

Figure 3-19   Guidelines can appear on both the report Design and Preview tabs

─┼─*Tip* ────────────────────────────────────

To remove a guideline from your report, drag the caret off of the ruler.

Moving or Aligning Multiple Objects

An alternative to using guidelines is to move or align multiple objects at the same time. The first thing you will need to do is locate the objects that you want to align in your report and then multiple-select them. You perform a multiple-select operation by drawing a marquee box around the objects or by clicking each while pressing SHIFT or CTRL.

─┼─*Tip* ────────────────────────────────────

A standard Windows' shortcut is to use the SHIFT key to select contiguous items in a list and the CTRL key to select distinct items.

After you have selected all of the objects that you want to align, right-click directly on top of one of the objects and, from the menu that appears, select Align, as shown in Figure 3-20.

Select one of the eight options to align your fields and then click anywhere outside the selected fields to finish.

Ask the Expert

Question: Is there any way to automatically arrange your report?

Answer: Yes, Crystal Reports does have a feature called the Auto Arrange Expert, but it is not frequently used. To see the results for yourself, be sure to save your report before you start. Then select Format | Auto-Arrange Report. Crystal Reports will issue a warning message that says "Impossible to Undo This Command." Click OK to proceed. Your report will be arranged according to Crystal Report's own internal guidelines, and you will be returned to the Design or Preview environment. Unfortunately, the arrangement that results is seldom pretty, and most users resort to manually adjusting the arrangement of objects in their report.

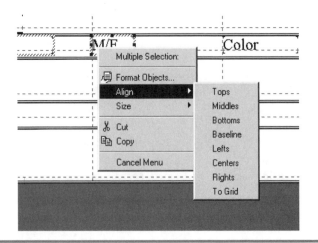

| **Figure 3-20** | Alignment options can be found on a right-click menu |

Controlling Object Layering

Crystal Reports uses transparent object layering; that is, objects can be placed directly on top of one another. To control where objects sit within a layer, locate the object on your report that you want to use and right-click directly on top of the object. From the shortcut menu that appears (shown in Figure 3-21), select the layering option to control where the object is positioned.

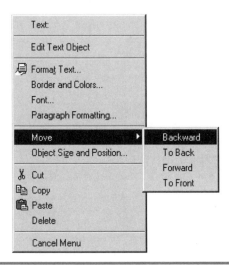

| **Figure 3-21** | You can control object layering using this menu |

Project 3-2: Working with Fields

Using the techniques learned in this section, we are going to add a database field to the report used in Module 2 and set a few properties and formatting options for existing fields within the same report.

Step-by-Step

1. Open the Product Listing report you were working on in Module 2 (Product Listing Ch2-1.rpt).

2. Choose Insert | Field Object and expand the section marked Database Fields.

3. Expand the Product table (see Figure 3-22) and then select the M/F field from the listing; this will identify whether the product is for a male or a female.

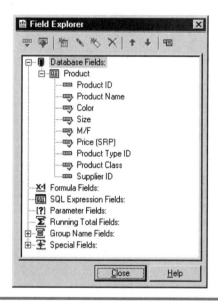

Figure 3-22   Database fields can be inserted from the Field Explorer

Tip

If you are unable to locate the field that you want to insert, start typing the name of the field, and the dialog box will jump to matching fields.

4. Press ENTER to attach the M/F field to the tip of your mouse pointer.

5. Use the mouse pointer to position your field, and click to place the field on your report beside the product name field in the Details section.

Tip

If you select the wrong field, you can remove a field that is attached to your mouse pointer by pressing ESC. An alternate method of inserting a database field is to drag and drop the field from the list directly onto your report.

6. Move and resize the fields surrounding this field to correct report spacing and style.

7. Save your report as **Product Listing Ch3-2.rpt**.

Project Summary

Most of your time in the Crystal Reports designer will be spent working with individual fields. In this project, you got a feel for how to insert, move, resize, and format field objects. As you work with Crystal Reports, your confidence in these new skills will grow, and working with fields will become almost second nature.

1-Minute Drill

● How do you show the guidelines in your report?

● How can you align multiple objects in your report?

Text Objects

Text objects enable you to type text directly into your report. Text objects are simply labeled "Text" on the status bar and can be combined with database

---

● Right-click in any free space and select either Show Guidelines in Design or Show Guidelines in Preview from the menu that appears.
● By selecting the multiple objects and right-clicking directly on top of your selection; there will be an option in the right-click menu for Aligning objects.

fields or formatted as paragraph text. Preformatted text, such as rich text format (RTF) and hypertext markup language (HTML), can be inserted directly into text objects. Text objects are used for report titles, field headings, and any text that needs to be inserted into your report.

Tip

By default, text objects are inserted as column headings when you insert a field into the Details section.

Working with Text Objects

Text objects can be inserted anywhere on your report through the Insert menu. When you choose Insert | Text Object, an empty text object is attached to the tip of your mouse; position the mouse where you want to place the object and click once to release. Crystal Reports will immediately place the text object in Edit mode and place the tip of your mouse pointer inside the text object so you can start typing text. When you are finished editing the text, click anywhere outside the text object to leave Edit mode.

Once inserted on your report, text objects behave just like the field objects we looked at earlier: they can be moved, resized, formatted, and so on. If you need to change the text you have entered in a text object, you can double-click the object to put it back into Edit mode, or you can right-click directly on top of the object and select Edit Text Object from the menu, shown in Figure 3-23.

For more control over a text object, you can also set paragraph formatting, including indentation, line spacing, character spacing, and tab stops, bringing some word processing features to Crystal Reports.

Although text objects are most often used for report titles, column headings, and the like, they also can be combined with database and other fields where these formatting features come in handy.

Combining Text Objects and Other Fields

When working with Crystal Reports, you are eventually going to have a situation in which you are moving a field around in your report and suddenly (and unexplainably) the field merges with a text object. Believe it or not, this is a feature. You can combine text objects with other fields to create form letters, statements, and so on within Crystal Reports. Imagine that you are writing a

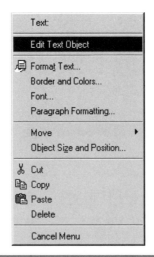

Figure 3-23 You can edit a text object from the right-click menu

letter; you could merge the text "Dear:" with the database field containing the first name of your customer to create a personalized letter generated by Crystal Reports.

The mechanics of combining a text object with another field are simple—as mentioned earlier, you may have already done it by accident. Simply locate the text object where you want to insert your other field and drag that field on top of the text object. Your cursor will change to the one shown in Figure 3-24, indicating the insertion point where you can place your field within the text object. If you release the mouse while this cursor is shown, your field will be placed inside the text object.

It may take some time to get the hang of the technique, but once you do, it is a handy trick to have up your sleeve.

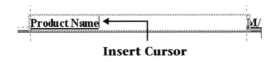

Insert Cursor

Figure 3-24 The insert cursor

Inserting Preformatted Text

When working with text objects and form letters or statements, you probably don't want to have to enter all of the text directly into Crystal Reports: Crystal Reports does not have a spell check or grammar facility, and it is difficult to type and format large amounts of text directly into a text object. To help you, Crystal Reports allows you to use your favorite word processor to create form letters and text and then bring that preformatted text directly into Crystal Reports.

   If you are editing a text object and right-click the object, you will see the option Insert from File (shown in Figure 3-25), which allows you to insert a text, RTF, or HTML file into your text object.

Project 3-3: Working with Text Objects

Continuing with the report we were working with in the last project, we are going to add a text object to show the report author and combine the File Name and Path field with a text object to identify where the report is stored.

Step-by-Step

1. Open the Product Listing report you created in Module 2 and have used in earlier projects in this chapter.

2. Choose Insert | Text Object. This attaches a blank text object to your mouse pointer.

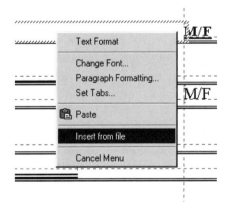

Figure 3-25   You can insert preformatted text into your text object

3. Position the pointer in the page header on the left side of the page and click to drop the blank text object onto your report.

Tip

If the mouse pointer displays the black circle with a line through it, you cannot place a text object in the area that you have specified.

The text object is displayed as a box outline, and a flashing cursor appears inside, indicating that the text object is now in Edit mode, and that you can enter text.

4. Enter the text **This report created by *Your Name***.

5. After you have finished entering the text for your text object, click anywhere outside of the text object to finish.

Tip

When working with an existing text object, you can double-click the text object to place it in Edit mode.

6. Choose Insert I Text Object again to attach an empty text object to your mouse pointer.

7. Position the pointer in the page header on the right side of the page this time and click to drop the object onto your report.

8. Within the text object outline, enter the text **Report File Name:** .

9. Choose Insert I Field Object.

10. The Field Explorer opens. If the Field Explorer window is obstructing your text object, reposition it by dragging it by the title bar, so that you can clearly see the text object. Then locate the File Path and Name field in the Special Fields section and drag the field onto your report.

11. As you drag the database field close to the text object, your cursor should change to the insert cursor, shown in Figure 3-26. The line cursor within the text object indicates the object placement.

12. When you are satisfied with the field placement, click to insert the field.

13. Save your report as **Product Listing Ch3-3.rpt**.

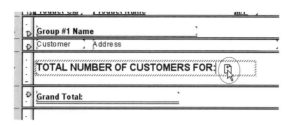

| **Figure 3-26** | You know that you have a field positioned correctly for insertion when your mouse pointer changes to the cursor shown here |

3

14. Click outside of the object to complete the process. The text object remains in Edit mode and displays the field name until you click anywhere outside of the object itself. After you are out of the Edit mode and preview your report, the file name and path should be displayed, as shown in Figure 3-27.

Project Summary

Combining text objects with other types of fields gives you more options when creating page and column headings, form letters, statements, and more. Using the skills learned in this project, you should be able to start using this technique to apply advanced formatting to your reports.

Product Listing
10/18/01 This report created by David McAmis   Report File Name: c:\my reports\productlist.rpt

Product Class	Product Name	M/F	Color	Size	Price (SRP)
Accessory					
Customer	Address		black		33.90
Customer	Address				21.90
Customer	Address			sm	13.50
Customer	Address			med	13.50
Customer	Address			lrg	13.50
Customer	Address			sm	15.50
Customer	Address			med	15.50
Customer	Address			lrg	15.50
Customer	Address		white	sm/med	33.90
Customer	Address		green	sm/med	33.90
Customer	Address		red	sm/med	33.90
Customer	Address		white	med/lrg	33.90
Customer	Address			xsm	14.50
Customer	Address		red	med/lrg	33.90
Customer	Address				17.50
Customer	Address		red		33.90
Customer	Address				11.90
Customer	Address				9.98
Customer	Address				37.90
Customer	Address				14.50

| **Figure 3-27** | The finished report |

☑ *Mastery Check*

1. What are the four methods you can use to navigate through a report preview?

_____

_____

2. How many toolbars are available within Crystal Reports?

_____

_____

3. The autosave feature is enabled by default:

A. True.

B. False.

4. What is meant by "format by example"?

_____

_____

5. Which of the following can be combined with text objects?

A. Database fields.

B. Parameter fields.

C. Special fields.

D. All of the above.

Module 4

Organizing Your Report

Goals

- Understand how to use grouping and sorting in your report
- Create specified groups
- Learn how to create drill-down and summary reports
- Change page layouts and margins

Among the key goals of report design are the extraction and organization of data, turning it into information that people can use to make better decisions. Grouping and sorting both play key roles in organizing your report and in adding value to the information presented. In this chapter, you learn how to use these techniques and others to increase the effectiveness of the information presented.

Inserting Groups into Your Report

A group, simply put, is a collection of related records. When used in a report, groups allow you to put records together, in order, to analyze the information that they contain. If you were creating an international sales report, for example, you would want to group your customer records by the countries where the customers reside, as shown in Figure 4-1. For an analysis of orders you have received, you may want to group the orders by the customers who placed them.

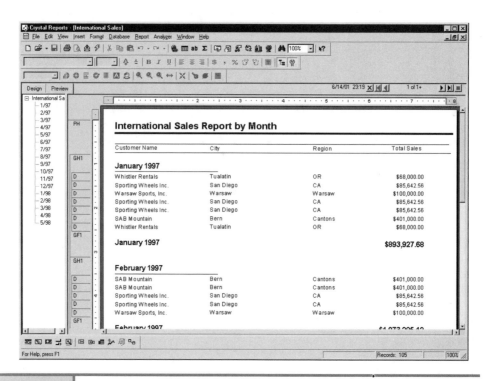

Figure 4-1 An international sales report

4

For each group that you create in Crystal Reports, a group header and footer are created, as shown in Figure 4-2. The group header or footer is usually where you put the name of the group, as well as any summaries that are created from the group's data.

If you have worked with different types of reports before, you may notice that groups in Crystal Reports closely resemble control breaks in other reporting tools and platforms. Both groups and control breaks share the same concept of putting like items together and placing space between the like items to indicate where one group ends and the next begins.

Groups can be based on any of the database fields, parameter fields, or SQL expressions that appear in your report. Select Insert | Group; using the dialog box shown in Figure 4-3, you can select a field to be used to sort and group the records in your report.

Tip

An SQL expression is similar to a Crystal Reports formula, except that it is written using Structure Query Language (SQL) code. Creating SQL Expressions is outside the scope of this book, but you can find out more about the topic in *Crystal Reports 8.5: The Complete Reference*, also from McGraw-Hill/Osborne.

To create a simple group, all you will need to do is select a field and a sort order and click OK—Crystal Reports does the hard work for you and sifts

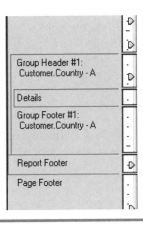

Figure 4-2   A group header and footer

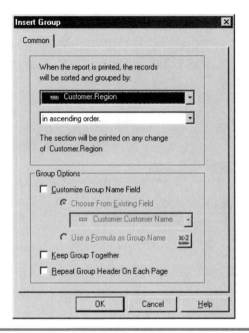

Figure 4-3   Options for inserting a group

through your data, finding like values and grouping them together. When it is finished with this process, it will create the group header and footer mentioned earlier, as well as a group name and a group tree that will appear on the left-hand side of the preview tab. The group tree will show all of the groups within your report, and you can click on a group name to go directly to that page.

Tip

You may notice that when you move your mouse over a group name, the cursor turns into a magnifying glass icon—if you double-click the group name, a separate Drill Down tab will be opened, displaying just the data for that group. Drill-down functionality is covered a little later in this chapter.

Grouping Options

With grouping in Crystal Reports, the groups are not only separated by the field criteria that you specify; they are also arranged in the order that you specify.

You can choose to sort groups in ascending or descending order (A through Z, 1 to 9 or Z through A, 9 to 1), use the original sort order from the database, or specify your own order and groupings.

Grouping on a Date or Date-Time Field

Grouping on a Date field requires you to specify how the dates are grouped. To create a group based on a Date field, you would simply insert a group as you normally would, by selecting Insert | Group, and then selecting a date or date-time field (Database, Formula, or Parameter) to be used to sort and group the records in your report.

You will need to select a sort order for your group (ascending, descending, specified, or original), and you will notice that Crystal Reports has added an additional option box for selecting the interval at which the group should be printed, shown in Figure 4-4. The interval options are slightly different for date and time fields. Here are your options:

For dates:

- For Each Day
- For Each Week
- For Each Two Weeks
- For Each Half Month
- For Each Month
- For Each Quarter
- For Each Half Year
- For Each Year

For times:

- For Each Second
- For Each Minute
- For Each Hour
- For Each AM/PM

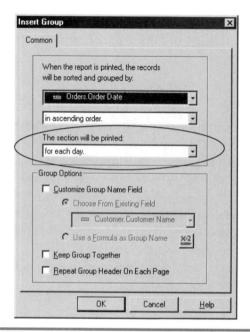

Figure 4-4 Group options for date and date-time fields

You can set any group options for customizing the group name, keeping the group together, and so forth. Once you have clicked OK and your group has been created, check out the Design tab, and you should see the group that you inserted represented by a group header and footer that appear in the gray area on the left side of the page.

When you preview your report, the group name is generated from the interval that you picked when creating your group, as shown in Figure 4-5. If you selected the option For Each Day, Crystal Reports would group all of the dates that share the same date together—you can format this group name just like any other time- or date-time-type field.

Tip

Crystal Reports usually uses the last date in the interval to create a group name. If you selected a grouping by week, it would display the last day of each week as the group name.

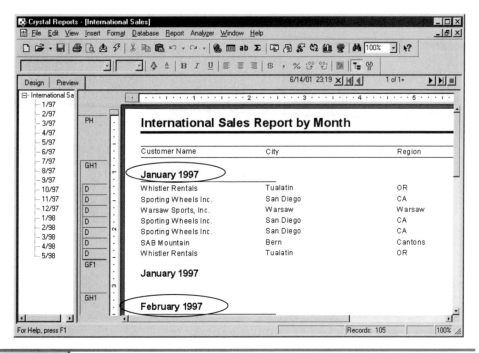

Figure 4-5   A typical group name generated for a group based on a date or date-time field

Hierarchical Grouping

When working with groups and sorting, you sometimes make assumptions about the design of your database. For a report on international sales, for instance, you might assume that separate fields for the customer's country, region, and city are in the database. To create a hierarchical group based on these fields, you would then simply insert three groups: one for the country, one for the region, and one for the city.

What about the instance where the data that comprises the hierarchy is all stored in one table in one single field? That is when you need to use hierarchical grouping. A common example of where you need to use this feature is when working with employee data. Imagine that you have an employee table that contains all of the details for the employees that work at your company. In this table, a field indicates the manager of each employee, using the managers' employee IDs, as shown in Figure 4-6.

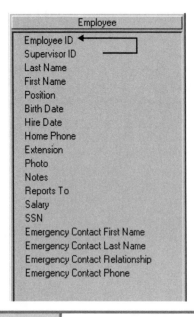

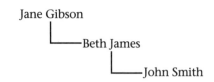

Employee ID	Supervisor ID	Last Name
1	—	Gibson
2	1	James
3	2	Smith

Figure 4-6 An example of a hierarchical relationship

How would you show this relationship on a report? If you attempted to use a simple group, you could produce a report that has a separate group for each manager, listing his or her employees. Unfortunately, that method would not show the hierarchical relationship among all of the employees (that is, John works for Beth who works for Jane and so forth).

If you use hierarchical grouping in this situation, you can specify a parent field for your group, and the report produced will display the complete hierarchical view of your employee data. Although it sounds complex, setting up a hierarchical group requires only one extra step.

When creating a hierarchical group, insert a group as you normally would by selecting Insert | Group and choosing the field that represents the link to the next step in the hierarchy.

For example, if you are working with an employee table that has a Supervisor ID field and you want to show the hierarchy of which employees work for whom, you would select the Supervisor ID field for your group. Then you would select Report | Hierarchical Grouping Options to open the dialog box shown in Figure 4-7.

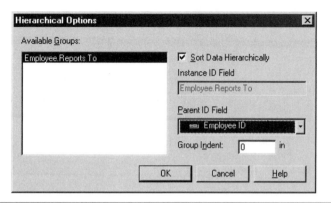

Figure 4-7 Hierarchical Options dialog box

From this point, you would select the Sort Data Hierarchically option, and from the Available Groups list, you would select the group that you want to group hierarchically. You can then select the parent ID field that this hierarchy is based on. In the example here, the field is the Employee ID field.

Finally, you can set the indentation size for when your group is displayed and click OK to accept your changes. The group that you have inserted should now reflect the hierarchy that you created.

Tip

A sample report (hierarch.rpt) that uses hierarchical grouping is available in the module for this chapter; it can be downloaded from the Osborne Web site at www.osborne.com.

Specified Grouping

Specified grouping is a powerful feature that allows you to regroup data based on criteria that you establish. For example, suppose you have sales territories composed of a number of states. You can use a specified group to create a separate group for each sales territory and to establish your own criteria (for example, North Carolina plus South Carolina is Bob's territory). To create a specified group, you start to insert a group as you normally would; then in the Insert Group dialog box, you change the sort order to In Specified Order.

A second tab, labeled Specified Order, should appear in the Insert Group dialog box, as shown in Figure 4-8.

From this point, there are two steps: the first is to define a group name, and the second is to specify the group criteria. I usually start by typing all of the group names I want to create, pressing ENTER after each, to build a list of group names.

Once you have all of the group names defined, you can highlight each one and click the Edit button to specify the criteria. To establish the criteria for records to be added to your group, use the drop-down menu to select an operator and value(s).

Note

These are the same operators as used with record selection.

From our earlier example with Bob's Territory, we could select the operator Is One Of and then select the values for NC and SC (for North and South Carolina, respectively).

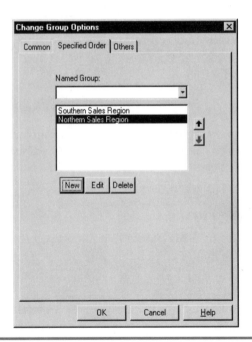

Figure 4-8   The Specified Order option page

You can add other criteria by clicking the New tab, and use the operators to specify additional selection criteria, which are evaluated with an Or statement between the criteria that you specify (but always using the same field that your group is based on).

Tip

Make sure you delete any groups you may have added by accident; even if you set the criteria to Any Value, adding additional criteria can still have an effect on report performance.

4

After you have entered a single group, another tab appears with options for records that fall outside of the criteria that you specify. By default, all of the leftover records are placed in their own group, labeled Others. You can change the name of this group by simply editing the name on the Others tab, which is shown in Figure 4-9. You also can choose to discard all of the other records or to leave them in their own groups.

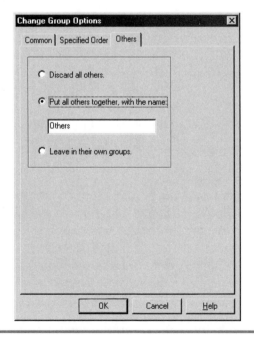

Figure 4-9   Options for dealing with other records

After you have defined your specified groups and criteria and have reviewed the settings for other records, click OK to accept the changes to the group. Your specified grouping is now reflected in your report, as shown in Figure 4-10.

1-Minute Drill

- How do you insert a group into your report?
- What are the four sort orders available for groups?

Changing Groups

Once you have a group inserted onto your report, you can change the options for the group without having to remove and add the group back again. You may want to change the group field or sort order, or just have a look at the options you have set. In any case, you will want to get to know the Change Group Expert.

Using the Change Group Expert

The Change Group Expert can be used for changing groups and group options. To invoke the expert, select Report | Change Group Expert. As shown in Figure 4-11, select the group that you want to change and then select Options.

The standard Change Group Options dialog boxes appear, and they allow you to make changes to the group field, sort order, and so forth. Click OK to accept your changes. They should be reflected in the report design immediately.

Reordering Groups

When working with groups, it is easy to get the hierarchy out of order (for example, by inserting a group for the country inside a group for the state). To reorder the groups that appear in your report, you can simply drag and drop the sections.

In Design mode, locate the group headers and footers in the gray area on the left side of the page. Locate the groups that you want to reorder and move these up

---

- Select Insert | Group, select a field, and click OK.
- The sort orders are Ascending, Descending, Specified, and Original order.

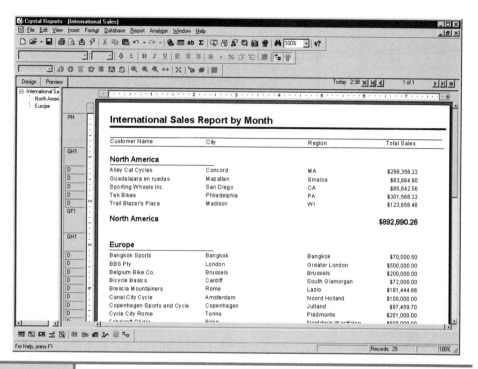

Figure 4-10   You can use the Change Group Expert to change group criteria

or down by dragging the appropriate section of the report. When you have a group selected, your mouse pointer displays a hand cursor, as shown in Figure 4-12,

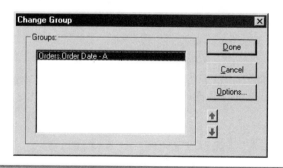

Figure 4-11   An example of specified grouping within a report

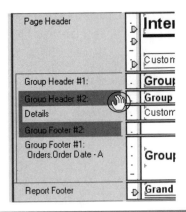

| Figure 4-12 | The cursor changes to indicate that you are dragging an entire group or section of the report |

which indicates that you have attached to a group. While you are moving the group up and down, a thick bold line indicates where in the group hierarchy your group will appear.

After you are satisfied with the group location, drop the group into position by releasing the mouse button.

Changing the Group Selection Formula

When a group is created, Crystal Reports automatically creates a group selection formula. Editing this formula gives you more control of the data that appears in each group. You can edit the group selection formula by selecting Report | Edit Selection Formula | Group. This opens the Crystal Reports formula editor. You can then use the formula editor to enter your group selection formula.

Tip

If you are interested in writing your own formulas, you may want to skip ahead to Module 8, "Formulas and Functions."

Project 4-1: Inserting a Group

In this project, we are going to create a new report from the Customer table. To help us get started, we are going to use the Standard Report Expert to create a simple listing report. Once we have a preview of our report, we are going to insert a group on the Country and Region fields, to split our customers into geographic groups.

Step-by-Step

1. From the Start I Programs menu, start Crystal Reports 8.5.

2. From the Welcome dialog box, select Create a New Crystal Report Document, and from the next dialog box, select Using the Report Expert.

3. From the Crystal Report Gallery, select the Standard Report Expert.

4. Click the Database button to open the Data Explorer and navigate to the Xtreme Sample Database under the ODBC node of the tree.

5. From Xtreme Sample Database, select the Customer table and click the Add button. A green check mark should appear next to the table, and the Data tab should reflect your selection. Click Close to close the Data Explorer and to return to the report expert.

6. On the Fields tab, select the fields that you want to see in your report. For this project, we are going to select the following fields:

   ● Customer Name
   ● Contact First Name
   ● Contact Last Name
   ● City
   ● Region
   ● Country

   To select a field, highlight it from the list on the left and click the right arrow button to move it to the list on the right.

7. At this point, you have completed the Data and Fields tabs of the expert; click the Finish button to see a preview of your report.

8. Select Insert I Group.

9. Using the dialog box shown in Figure 4-13, select the Customer.Region field, which will be used to sort and group the records in your report.

10. Select a sort order of Ascending (A-Z).

11. Set any group options for customizing the group name, keeping the group together, and so forth.

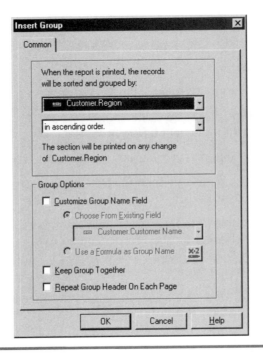

Figure 4-13   Options for inserting a group

12. Click OK to create your group.

13. Click the Design tab, and you should see the group that you inserted represented by a group header and footer that appear in the gray area on the left side of the page.

14. Repeat the process to add a group based on the Country field. Your report should look like the one shown in Figure 4-14.

15. Save your report as **Customer by Country Ch4-1.rpt**.

Project Summary

When you have a large amount of information to show in a report, you will need to help the user by adding some organization to the information. With the two groups you have inserted, your report should now be easier to read and navigate.

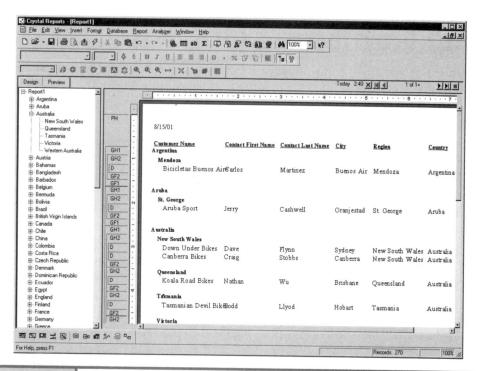

Figure 4-14   The Customer by Country report with the two groups inserted

Ask the Expert

Question: The groups and fields I have inserted make my report look crowded—is there any way I can get more information on the page?

Answer: By default Crystal Reports will set up your report as a letter-sized page, with the default margins and portrait orientation. You can change the margins under File | Page Setup. You can also change the orientation of your page from portrait to landscape by selecting File | Printer Setup and using the radio buttons that appear.

Group Formatting Options

With any group you insert onto your report, you are going to want to control how that group looks and the formatting options applied. Using the tips and tricks in the next section, you should be able to make a group do just about anything you need it to do!

Inserting Group Names

Group names are generated by Crystal Reports and are used to label the groups you create. You have already seen them in action—Crystal Reports automatically inserts them whenever you insert a group, and they usually appear in both the group header and footer.

There will be instances when you want to insert group names manually, and Crystal Reports lets you do this as well. Before you start to insert a group name, to make it easier to see where you are going to place the field, switch the design view of your report by clicking the Design tab in the upper-left corner. Then select Insert | Field Object. This opens the Field Explorer, shown in Figure 4-15. Click the plus sign to open to the section for Group Name fields.

A list of all of the different group names in your report will appear. Select the field that you want to insert into your report and press ENTER. This attaches the field to the tip of your mouse, and as you move your mouse around the page, you should see the outline of the field follow.

Position your mouse in the area where you want to place the Group Name field and click once to insert the field in your report. When your report is previewed, this field will be replaced with the name of the group it represents.

Customizing the Group Name Field

Group Name fields can be customized in a number of different ways. You can access the group options to customize a group name when you first insert a new group or when you are changing a group's properties.

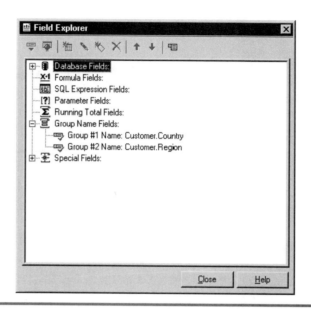

4

Figure 4-15   The Field Explorer is used to insert fields into your report

Tip

To change an existing group, you can use the Change Group Expert by selecting Report I Change Group Expert.

As shown in Figure 4-16, you can choose a group name for an existing field by selecting Choose From Existing Field and then selecting a field name. A common example of when you would use this is when you have grouped on a company ID and want to display the company name.

You can also choose a group name based on a formula by clicking Use a Formula as Group Name and entering a formula using the X+2 button. This opens the Crystal Reports formula editor and allows you to enter a formula that returns a group name. An example of when you would use a formula-based group name is when you have grouped by a country code and want to display the country name. The formula in this situation is as follows:

```
If {Customer.Country_Code} = 61 then "Australia"
```

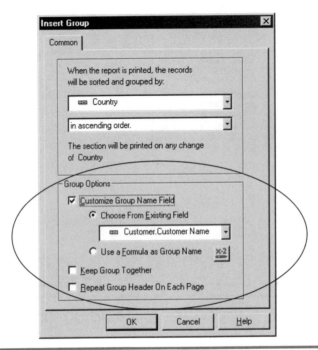

Figure 4-16 You can customize the Group Name field based on an existing field, formula, and so forth

After you have entered a custom formula for your group name and exited the editor, you'll notice that the X+2 button, shown here, changes from blue to red to indicate that you have entered formula text.

Tip

Again, if you are itching to get into the formula language, check out Module 8.

Changing Group Criteria

After a group has been inserted, you may need to change the group criteria, and there is a handy little trick to help you out. In Design mode, locate the group header or footer for the group that you want to change. After you have located the group that you want to change, right-click directly on top of the group header or footer that appears in the gray area and select Change Group. You can then make any changes to the group using the Change Group Options dialog box, shown in Figure 4-17.

Click OK to accept your changes. The changes should be immediately reflected in the Report Design or Preview window.

Keeping a Group Together Across Multiple Pages

The option for keeping a group together attempts to prevent one section of the group from being orphaned on a separate page. Where possible, Crystal Reports tries to display the complete group on the same page. You can access the options to keep a group together when you first insert a new group or when you are

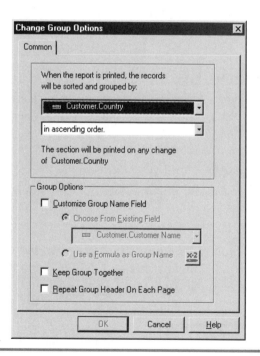

| **Figure 4-17** | Change Group options |

changing a group's properties. From either the Insert Group dialog box or the Change Group Options dialog box, select Keep Group Together. Click OK to accept your changes. When your report is previewed or printed, Crystal Reports attempts to move all of the group records to a single page.

Note

In any case where Crystal Reports is unable to fit all of the records on the same page, it places the records on separate pages, even with this setting turned on.

Repeating a Group Header on Each Page

For long reports, a group header may be required on each page to identify each group because the group header and footer may be 10 or even 20 pages apart. To repeat a group header on each page, choose the group option Repeat a Group Header when you first insert a new group or when you are changing a group's properties. When your report is previewed or printed, the Group Header section is printed at the top of each page immediately under the Page Header section, as shown in Figure 4-18.

Creating a Page Break Between Groups

For readability, you may want to consider inserting a page break between the groups that appear in your report. If you select Format | Section, the Section Expert will open.

Tip

If the process here is a bit confusing, don't worry—the Section Expert is covered in Module 10.

Locate the group footer of the group that you want to use as a page break. Highlight the group by clicking directly on top of it. From the options that appear on the right side of the page, select New Page After.

Tip

Alternatively, you could have selected the group header and picked New Page Before.

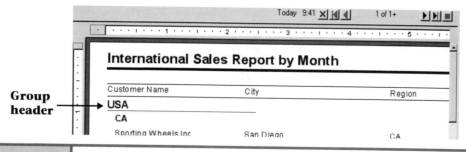

Group header →

Figure 4-18   The group header can be printed at the top of each page

Your report should now have a page break at the end of each group, making it a bit easier to read.

Record-Level Sorting

Another tool that you have to help organize your reports is record-level sorting. Record-level sorting is similar to grouping in that it orders the records according to the criteria that you specify (for example, alphabetically by country). However, the difference is that record-level sorting leaves the records in one big group. In the earlier example of grouping, the records were grouped by country and put in order so that each country had its own group, group header and footer, and so forth. If we had just performed a sort on those same records, they would have been ordered, but left in one large list.

Record-level sorting can be found on the Report menu under Sort Records, which will open the dialog box shown in Figure 4-19.

Record-level sorting is used to sort simple listing reports and records that appear within groups. Locate and select the field that you want to use for your sort and move it from the list on the left to the list on the right by highlighting the field and clicking Add.

Note

In the Record Sort Order dialog box, note that group sorts take precedence and cannot be changed from this dialog box. To remove a group sort, you need to delete the group itself.

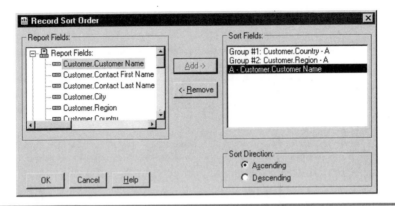

Figure 4-19   Options for record-level sorting

To change the sort order, highlight the field in the list on the right and choose between the two radio buttons for sort direction: Ascending or Descending.

Tip

To remove a sort field, simply move it from the list on the right back to the list on the left.

1-Minute Drill

● Which takes precedence: group-level sorting or record-level sorting?

● How can a group name be inserted into your report?

Drill-Down and Summary Reports

Creating meaningful information from large volumes of data can be difficult. If a report is too long, report consumers generally tune out before they get to the section of data that is relevant to them. One trick for the concise presentation of information is to use a drill-down or summary report.

● Group-level sorting always takes precedence.
● A group name is inserted by default when you insert a new group, or you can select Insert I Field Object and drag a group name into your report from the Group Name section of the Field Explorer.

Drill-down and summary reports are similar because they contain a summary of information from your data. For a sales report, you may want to summarize a particular salesperson's sales for a given month, showing the total sales figure, but not the details that comprise it.

Although drill-down and summary reports of this information look similar, one difference does exist. A drill-down report allows you to double-click the salesperson's name or any of the summary fields to display all of the details that make up that summary. In a drill-down report, the details are simply hidden away from view, but are still available when a user needs them. With a summary report, the details are suppressed from view and are not available to be seen by the user.

Each type has specific uses. If the report that you have created is likely to raise questions such as "Why are John's sales up this month?" or "Why is that number negative?" a drill-down report can provide report consumers with the information they need to answer these questions without having to have another report created.

4

Ask the Expert

Question: Is there any way I can make a report that uses groups run faster?

Answer: Although Crystal Reports features a powerful report-processing engine, you can achieve significant performance gains by pushing as much of the processing as possible back onto the database server itself. To insert a group that can be processed on the database server, follow these steps:

● Select File | Report Options.

● From the Report Options dialog box, click Use Indexes or Server for Speed.

● Click Perform Grouping on Server.

● Click OK to accept your changes and return to your report design or preview.

Note that this feature applies only to client-server databases that support the SQL Group By operator and reports that are created with the Details section suppressed.

Drill-down reports can be used to drill down into the data as many times as required, and with each additional query, users open a separate Preview tab. This information can be printed independently of the main report and can be exported as well. For report consumers, this provides a significant ad hoc capability. Instead of having to ask for a new report to be created for each request, they may be able to navigate through an existing comprehensive report and extract the information that they need. For this situation, a drill-down report is ideal.

On the other hand, if you are distributing a report that is a summary of expenses, including payroll figures that are confidential, you may not want to give users the ability to drill down into that information.

Regardless of which type of report you choose, both drill-down and summary reports can be used to add real value to the information that you present in your report.

Project 4-2: Creating a Drill-Down Report

Using the Customer by Country report we created earlier in the chapter, we are going to create a drill-down report. When we are finished, our report will show only the countries represented within the database, as shown in Figure 4-20.

When a user double-clicks a country, a list of regions within that country will appear, and from that point, the user can double-click the region to drill down to the detailed customer information.

Step-by-Step

1. Open the Customer by Country report you created in Project 4-1.

2. Switch to the Design view of your report and locate the group header and footer for the Region group.

3. Right-click directly on top of the header in the gray area on the left side of the page and select Hide from the right-click menu, as shown in Figure 4-21.

4. Repeat the same process to hide the footer for both the Region group and the Country group.

5. Choose File | Report Options and select Show All Headers on Drill-Down. Click OK to accept your changes.

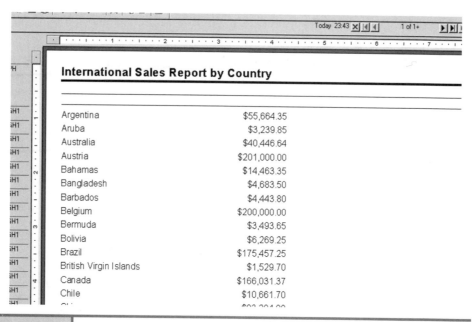

Figure 4-20   The Customer by Country report as a drill-down report

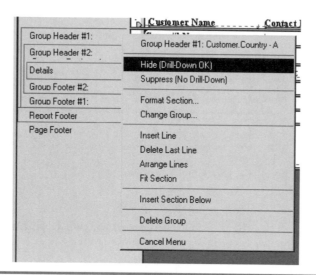

Figure 4-21   You can hide a section using the right-click menu

6. Click the Preview tab. Your report should now be displayed in summary form as shown in Figure 4-22.

7. To test the drill-down capabilities, move your mouse to any country, and the mouse should turn into a magnifying glass pointer. Double-click the country name to display the regions; double-click a region name to display all of the customers within that region.

8. Save your report as **Customer by Country Drill Down Ch4-1.rpt**.

Tip

A separate tab appears showing you the drill-down report you have selected. You can use the red X that appears on the navigation bar to close any drill-down tabs that you have opened.

Project Summary

Drill-down reports are the best means of quickly displaying an overview of the information contained within your report. Drill-down tabs can be printed individually, allowing a user to use one report for many sets of information. When combined with summary fields (covered in Module 5), drill-down reports offer a powerful analysis function, allowing users to see the details that make up a particular sum or total.

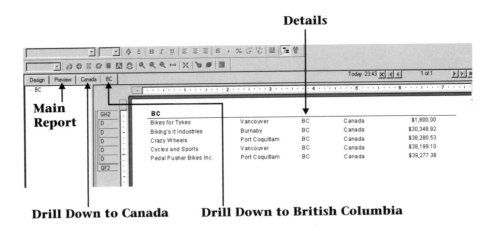

Figure 4-22 An example of a drill-down report

☑ *Mastery Check*

1. Which type of field cannot be used when inserting a group?

   A. Database fields

   B. Formula fields

   C. Parameter fields

   D. Running total fields

2. How many groups can you have inserted in your report?

   _____

   _____

3. When grouping on a date or date-time field, what is the default period that will be used?

   A. Group by day

   B. Group by week

   C. Group by month

   D. Group by quarter

4. Where can you find the setting to repeat the group header on every page?

   _____

   _____

5. What is the difference between *hiding* the details and *suppressing* them?

   _____

   _____

6. How do you create a page break between groups?

   _____

   _____

Module 5

Analyzing Report Data

Goals

- Understand how to use record selection to filter your report
- Add summary fields to your report
- Use other analysis features (TopN, Running Totals, and so on) in your report

With the basic skills of report creation out of the way, it's time to look at how to enhance the reports you have created by analyzing the information presented. From filtering the records that are shown to adding statistical summaries, running totals, and conditional formatting, you can use Crystal Reports to add value to the data that you extract from your database. In this module, you learn how to use these analysis features to create information-rich reports that provide insight into the data your organization has collected.

Using Record Selection to Filter Your Report

When creating a report, chances are good that you don't want to use all of the records that are stored in your database. You may want to use a subset of records for a particular state, region, date range, and so on. The process used to cut down the number of records returned is called record selection. Record selection uses the Crystal Reports formula language to create a logical statement that records are evaluated against. A record selection formula might look something like this:

```
{customer.country} = "USA"
```

As records are read from the database, this formula is evaluated, and, where it is true, those records are returned to Crystal Reports from the database. When the report is printed, you will see only records of customers within the United States.

If formulas make you squeamish, you are in luck—you don't have to write complex formulas to use record selection (although you can if you want to). Crystal Reports features a Select Expert that will do most of the work for you. The Select Expert, shown in Figure 5-1, is actually a set of specialized dialog boxes designed to help you quickly create record selection criteria without writing your own formulas.

The Select Expert can be used to apply record selection to a single field or multiple fields with a number of different record selection operators. Regardless of how many fields or how complex the criteria, the Select Expert can take the choices you make and actually write the selection formula for you. The sections that follow describe some of the most common uses of record selection.

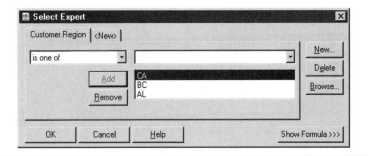

Figure 5-1   The Crystal Reports Select Expert

5

Applying Record Selection to a Single Field

Basing your record selection on a single field is the easiest way to see how the Select Expert works. Our earlier example showed a record selection formula created on a single field that returned only customers within the United States ({customer.country} = "USA"). We could enter this formula directly, but we are going to let the Select Expert do the work for us.

To get started, select Report | Select Expert. This will open a list of fields that are available for you to use for record selection, as shown in Figure 5-2.

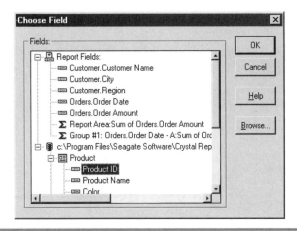

Figure 5-2   You need to choose the field that your record selection will be based on

Tip

If you don't see this list of fields, you may have had a field selected before you selected Report | Select Expert. In this case, Crystal Reports will assume you want to perform record selection using this field.

Select the field that will be used for your record selection criteria and click OK. Using the Select Expert, choose a record selection operator and enter the required criteria. Click OK to accept your changes.

The record selection operators can be used to narrow your report records to display only the records you need. Table 5-1 describes these operators.

Operator	Description
Is any value	Default option for record selection, allowing all records to be returned, regardless of the value.
Is equal to	Looks for an exact match to the criteria entered.
Is not equal to	Looks for all records except those matching the criteria specified.
Is one of	Is used to build a list of criteria, allowing you to select multiple values from one field (for example, is one of USA, Canada, and Mexico).
Is not one of	Is used to build a list of criteria you *don't* want (for example, is not one of Australia, New Zealand, and Japan).
Is less than	Brings back any records less than the criteria entered.
Is less than or equal to	Brings back any records less than or equal to the criteria entered.
Is greater than	Brings back any records greater than the criteria entered.
Is greater than or equal to	Brings back any records greater than or equal to the criteria entered.
Is between	Used to specify inclusive values as criteria. Any records between the two inclusive criteria are returned.
Is not between	The opposite of Is between. Any records outside the two inclusive criteria are returned.
Formula:	Used to enter a record selection formula directly without using the Select Expert.

Table 5-1   Record Selection Operators

Applying Record Selection to Multiple Fields

The Select Expert can also be used to apply selection criteria to multiple fields. To establish criteria for multiple fields, you perform the same process as for a single field: select Report | Select Expert. Then click the New button, shown in Figure 5-3.

After you have clicked the New button, a field list will appear, from which you can choose the second field you want to use in your record selection; then a second tab will appear, and you can specify the operator, values, and so on.

Tip

Whenever you use multiple fields for record selection, Crystal Reports makes the relationship between these two criteria an AND relationship (that is, Condition1 and Condition2 must be true for Crystal Reports to return a record). For more information on record selection, see Module 9.

To delete criteria, click the tab for the field you want to delete and use the Delete button to remove that tab.

Applying Record Selection Based on Date Fields

For date fields, an additional record selection operator is available, called In the Period. This operator addresses some of the common types of record selection based on dates.

To make your life easier, Crystal Reports has a number of predefined periods that can be used for record selection. These periods each generate their

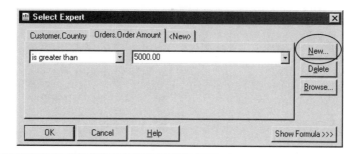

Figure 5-3   You can click the New button to add criteria for multiple fields

own internal list of dates based on each period's definition and the current date. For example, if you select the period MonthToDate, Crystal Reports builds a list of all of the dates that have passed since the first of the month and subsequently uses that list to select records from the database.

One of the most frequently asked questions about periods is "Can I add periods to this list or change the definitions?" The answer is no. The periods reflected in the list are hard-coded within Crystal Reports. You can, however, create your own user-defined functions and include similar functionality.

Note

For more information on creating user-defined functions, check out *Crystal Reports 8.5: The Complete Reference* by George Peck (McGraw-Hill/Osborne).

For now, let's take a look at the periods available for use when performing record selection on dates:

- WeekToDateFromSun
- MonthToDate
- YearToDate
- Last7Days
- Last4WeeksToSun
- LastFullWeek
- LastFullMonth
- AllDatesToToday
- AllDatesToYesterday
- AllDatesFromToday
- AllDatesFromTommorow
- Aged0to30days
- Aged31to60days
- Aged61to90days

- Over90Days
- Next30days
- Next31to60days
- Next61to90days
- Next91to365days
- Calender1stQtr
- Calendar2ndQtr
- Calendar3rdQtr
- Calendar4thQtr
- Calendar1stHalf
- Calendar2ndHalf
- LastYearMtd
- LastYearYtd

To use these periods with a date field in your report, choose Report | Select Expert. From the Choose Field dialog box, select the date field that you want to use in your record selection and then click OK. This brings up the Select Expert. Using the first pull-down list, shown in Figure 5-4, select either Is in the Period or Is Not in the Period. This opens a second pull-down list with the periods listed.

Select the period you want to use for record selection. Click OK to accept your changes to the record selection criteria and to return to your report, which should now reflect only the data from the period you specified.

1-Minute Drill

- Which record selection operator is used to select a list of values?
- With the period LastFullWeek, which day does Crystal Reports count as the start of the week?

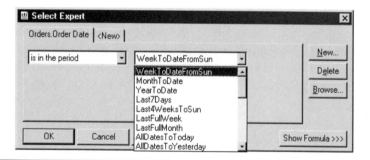

Figure 5-4   When you use Is in the Period for record selection, a second pull-down box appears showing all of the available periods

- Is One Of
- Sunday

Writing Record Selection Formulas

In addition to the Select Expert, Crystal Reports provides a second method of record selection by allowing you to edit the record selection formula directly. When looking at the Select Expert, you may have noticed a button in the bottom-right corner marked Show Formula. When you click the Show Formula button, you can view the formula that the Select Expert has created. By looking at the formula that Crystal Reports has created, you can pick up clues about how record selection formulas work. To write your own selection formula, select Report | Edit Selection Formula | Record. This opens the Crystal Reports Record Selection Formula Editor.

Note

You may be warned that you will not be able to keep any drill-down tabs that are open. Click OK to acknowledge this message and to continue writing your record selection formula.

Using the formula editor, you can create a record selection formula that results in a Boolean value (meaning it can be evaluated as either true or false). Use the X+2 button on the toolbar to check the syntax of your record selection formula. When you are finished working with the selection formula, click the save and close icon (the disk with an X) in the upper-left corner to save your formula. Your report should now reflect the record selection criteria you created.

Tip

If all this is just a bit too much, check out Module 8 for more information on working with the Crystal Reports formula language and then revisit this section with those new-found formula skills.

Project 5-1: Using Record Selection

In this project, we are going to take the report we created in Module 4 (Customer by Country) and apply record selection to limit the number of records that are returned. The report originally returned records for all countries within the database; now we are going to limit the report to just North American countries: Canada, Mexico, and the United States.

Step-by-Step

1. From the Start I Programs menu, start Crystal Reports 8.5.

2. From the Welcome dialog box, select Open an Existing Report, click More Files, and click OK; then, in the next dialog box, open the Customer by Country report you created in Module 4.

Tip

If you can't find the report you created or didn't get a chance to finish the project; a copy of this report is available in the folder for this module that can be downloaded from the Osborne Web site at www.osborne.com.

5

3. Select Report I Select Expert.

4. In the Choose Field dialog box, locate the {Customer.Country} field, click to select it, and then click OK.

5. In the Select Expert dialog box, use the operator list to select Is One Of; a second drop-down list appears.

6. From the second drop-down list, select the values for "Canada", "Mexico", and "USA". Alternatively, you could type each value (without the quotation marks), pressing the Enter key after each.

Tip

If you make a mistake selecting a field, highlight the field and click the Remove button.

7. When you are finished entering the values, click OK to return to your report. Your report should now reflect only those customers in Canada, Mexico, or the United States.

Note

You may be prompted with the message "Use saved data or Refresh?" Select the option for Refresh to go back to the database and apply your record selection criteria to the entire database (as opposed to just to the saved records that Crystal reports has read before).

8. Save your report as **Customer by Country Ch5-1.rpt**.

Project Summary

Using record selection is an easy way to add analysis to your report by showing only a subset of the records within your database.

Summaries Versus Formulas

When it comes to adding calculations to your report, you have two choices. You can either insert a summary field or write a formula. The difference between the two is that summary fields are designed to eliminate the need to write formulas for common calculations, including sums, averages, counting records, and others.

The ease of use offered by summary fields also has limitations. Summary fields are not as flexible as formulas that you write, and they are limited to the 19 summary operators currently available. Summaries are also tied to a particular group or the grand total for your report. If you need full control of how a calculated field is derived or where it is placed, you probably need to create a formula field. If you are looking for a quick and easy standard calculation based on some grouping you have inserted into your report, summary fields may be for you. Here is a list of the most popular summary fields and how they are used:

- **Sum**   Provides a sum of the contents of a numeric or currency field

- **Average**   Provides a simple average of a numeric or currency field (that is, the values in the field are all added together and divided by the total number)

- **Minimum**   Determines the smallest value present in a database field and is for use with number, currency, string, and date fields

- **Maximum**   Determines the largest value present in a database field and is for use with number, currency, string, and date fields

- **Count**   Counts the values present in a database field and is for use with all types of fields

- **Distinct Count**   Counts the values present in a database field, but counts any duplicate values only once.

A number of statistical functions are also available for use, including:

- Correlation
- Covariance
- Weighted average
- Median
- Pth percentile
- Nth largest
- Nth smallest
- Mode
- Nth most frequent
- Sample variance
- Sample standard deviation
- Population variance
- Population standard deviation

Tip

A primer on these statistical functions and their use can be found at http://www.nsns.com/Syllabits/stat/.

Adding Summary Fields to Your Report

Simple summary fields include sum, average, minimum, maximum, and other calculations that do not require any additional criteria. To create a simple summary field, click the field that you want to summarize and select Insert | Summary. In the dialog box is shown in Figure 5-5, from the Insert a Field Which Calculates The box, select the summary operation you want to use.

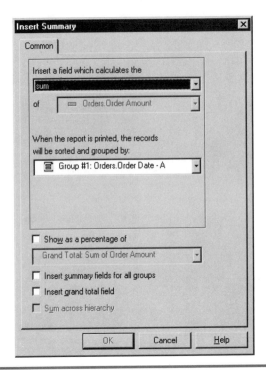

Figure 5-5 | Options for inserting simple summary fields into your report

Click OK to accept your changes. Your summary field is inserted in the group footer for the group you have selected.

Inserting Summary Fields for All Groups

When working with summary fields, chances are that you will want to insert them for each group you have inserted into your report. You could create these fields individually, but it is much easier to let Crystal Reports do the difficult part for you. To insert a summary field for all of the groups in your report, click the field that you want to summarize and select Insert | Summary. From the Insert Summary dialog box, select the Insert Summary Fields for All Groups check box, as shown in Figure 5-6.

Click OK to accept your changes. A summary field is added for each group you have inserted into your report.

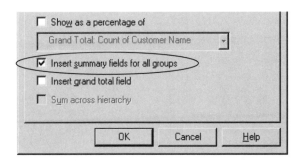

| Figure 5-6 | Select this option to insert a summary field for each group you have inserted into your report |

5

Changing Summary Field Operations

After a summary field has been inserted into your report, you can change the summary operation by locating the summary field that you want to change on your report, clicking to select the field, and selecting Edit | Change Summary. In the Change Summary dialog box, use the drop-down list provided to change the summary operation and then click OK to accept your changes. The operator change should immediately be reflected in your report.

Note

An important point to remember is that selecting a different summary operator may mean specifying additional parameters, depending on the summary operator you choose.

Inserting Summary Fields Shown as Percentages

The information in a summary field can be shown as a percentage of a grand total. For example, you may want to see what percentage a certain customer contributes to your total business. If you insert a summary field shown as a percentage of the grand total of your report, that information is readily available.

To insert a summary field to be shown as a percentage, select Insert | Summary. In the dialog box, from the Insert a Field Which Calculates The box, select the summary type you want to insert.

Next, choose the field you want to summarize and select a field for the sort and group order. At the bottom of the dialog box, check Show as a Percentage Of. Using the pull-down box under Show as a Percentage Of, select the grand total

field that you want to use to calculate the percentage, as shown in Figure 5-7.
Click OK to accept your changes and to add the summary field to your report.

Tip

The show-as-percentage feature is especially handy when used alongside sums
and averages. For instance, if you were creating a report on international sales,
you could show the dollar amount (sum) for each country and the average sales,
as well as a percentage representing that country in the total sales.

Inserting Correlation, Covariance, and Weighted Averages

For the statistical functions available for use within summary fields, you may
want to pull on a pair of boots, as we will be wading into deeper water. If you
work with statistics, this information will make more sense, but if you are just
starting out, check out the Web site mentioned earlier (http://www.nsns.com/
Syllabits/stat/) for a detailed explanation of all of the statistical terms.

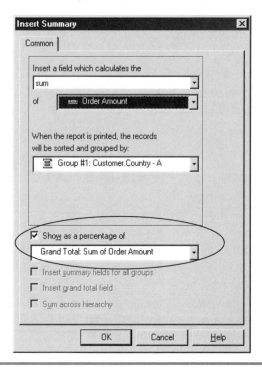

Figure 5-7 Options for showing a summary field as a percentage

Correlation, covariance, and weighted averages are all related because they require a field to serve as the basis of the summary, as well as a second field that is related. To insert a correlation, covariance, or weighted average summary field, locate and select the field that will serve as the basis for your correlation, covariance, or weighted average. Right-click directly on top of the field and select Insert | Summary. In the dialog box shown in Figure 5-8, select the summary function you want to use from the Insert a Field Which Calculates The drop-down menu.

When you select correlation, covariance, or weighted average, a With pull-down box should appear. Use this pull-down box to select the field to be used when calculating your summary field.

Tip

For a correlation or covariance, this will be the field you want to compare against. For a weighted average, choose the field that contains the values that will weight the average denominator. (In a normal average, this defaults to 1 for each value, but for a weighted average it can be any number you specify.)

Select the field that you want to sort and group by when creating this summary field. Click OK to accept your changes and return to your report. Your summary field is inserted into the group footer you specified.

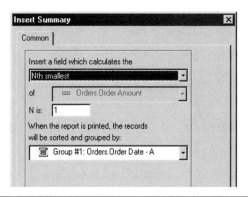

Figure 5-8 For certain types of summaries, additional information may be required

Calculating the Pth Percentile

The Pth percentile summary function can be used to determine the value of P in a numeric or currency field. For example, suppose you want to see where an employee's age falls within your company's distribution. If you enter **50** for the P value in your summary, Crystal Reports will return a value from the 50th percentile (for example, 42, meaning that 50 percent of your employees are younger than 42). To insert a Pth percentile summary, locate the field that will serve as the base field, click to select the field, and select Insert | Summary.

In the Insert Summary dialog box that opens, select the Pth percentile summary function. When you select Pth percentile, a P Is text box should appear, as shown in Figure 5-9. Use this text box to enter the value for P.

Select the field that you want to sort and group by when creating this summary field. Click OK to accept your changes and to return to your report. Your summary field is inserted into the group footer you specified.

Calculating Nth Largest, Nth Smallest, and Nth Most Frequent

When creating a report, you may want to know what is the largest, smallest, or most frequent data item. Although you can use TopN/BottomN/Sort All analysis to obtain similar information from your report, it is much easier to use a summary field. To insert one of these summary fields onto your report, locate and select the

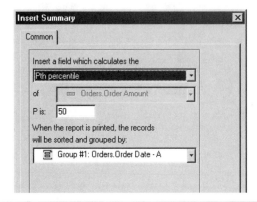

Figure 5-9 You will need to enter a value for *P*

field that will serve as the base field. Right-click directly on top of the field and select Insert | Summary. In the Insert Summary dialog box that opens, select the Nth Largest, Nth Smallest, or Nth Most Frequent Summary function.

When you select any of these summary operators, an N Is text box should appear. Enter a value for N in the box, as shown in Figure 5-10.

Select the field you want to sort and group by when creating this summary field. Click OK to accept your changes and return to your report. Your summary field is inserted into the group footer you specified.

Inserting Grand Total Fields

Grand total fields appear in the report footer at the end of your report and are used to summarize the contents of your report. To insert a grand total field, locate and select the field you want to summarize with a grand total and select Insert | Grand Total. Using the Insert Grand Total dialog box, select a summary type for your grand total and click OK to accept your changes. A summary field is inserted into your report footer representing the grand total.

5

—*Tip* —————————————————————————

The term *grand total* is a little misleading. A grand total within Crystal Reports can be a value calculated with any of the summary operators, including Sum, Average, and so on.

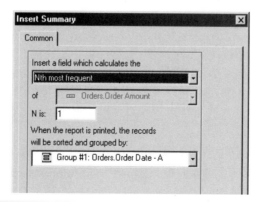

| **Figure 5-10** | Options for inserting an Nth summary field |

1-Minute Drill

● Which operator is used to find the number in the data set that occurs most frequently?

● What is the difference between count and distinct count?

Project 5-2: Using Summary Fields

Summary Fields can be used to provide quick and easy analysis of the information contained within a group. In this project, we are going to continue working with the Customer by Country report and add summary fields for each group.

Step-by-Step

1. From the Start | Programs menu, start Crystal Reports 8.5.

2. From the Welcome dialog box, select Open an Existing Report, select More Files, and click OK. Using the next dialog box, open the Customer by Country Drill Down Ch4-2.rpt report we have been working with in this module.

3. To make navigation a bit easier, switch to the Design view of your report by clicking the Design tab in the upper-left corner.

4. Select Insert | Field Object and drag the field {Customer.Last Years Sales} onto your report in the Details section; this is the field we are going to summarize.

5. Right-click directly on top of the {Customer.Last Years Sales} field and select Insert | Summary.

Tip

Make sure you right-click the field itself and not the field heading—it is easy to get confused. If you click a particular field, you can see the field type in the lower-left corner of your screen in the Crystal Reports status bar.

6. From the Insert Summary dialog box, select the summary operator Sum.

7. At the bottom of the dialog box, select the option Insert Summary Fields for All Groups.

● Mode
● Count is used to count all records; distinct count only counts unique records.

8. Click OK to return to your report's design.

9. Preview your report; the sum for each country and region should now appear as shown in Figure 5-11.

10. Save your report as **Customer by Country Ch5-2.rpt**.

Hint

When you insert a summary field, Crystal Reports automatically places the field in the group header. Because we are using our Customer by Country report, which shows multiple drill-downs, you may want to move the summary field from the group footer to the group header in your report to avoid the spacing problems you may encounter.

5

Project Summary

Summary fields offer a quick and easy alternative to creating formulas and can provide insight into the data that has been placed in groups.

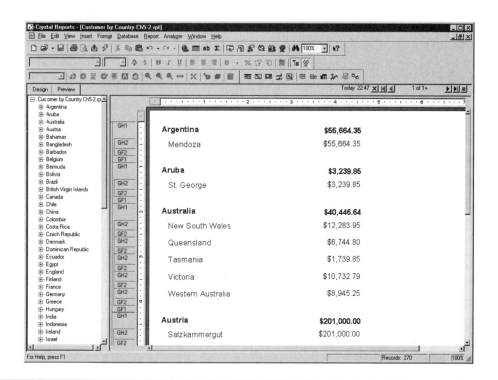

Figure 5-11 An example of the completed report

Analysis Options

In addition to calculated fields like summaries and formulas, Crystal Reports also includes a number of other options for analyzing information that appears in your report. Analysis methods range from simply reordering the data to presenting running totals alongside the data to highlighting areas of your report based on preset criteria. Regardless of which analysis options you choose to use in your report, you can quickly see the value they add.

Using TopN/BottomN Analysis

TopN/BottomN is a function of Crystal Reports used to sort groups according to a summary field that has been created based on that group. Most often, this function is used to determine the top 20 customers or the top 5 products (or the bottom 5). Before you can use TopN/BottomN analysis in your report, you need to make sure that you have two things inserted onto your report: a group and a summary field. Without both of these present, you cannot use TopN/BottomN analysis.

To add TopN/BottomN analysis to your report, verify that your report has at least one group and summary inserted and then select Report | TopN/Sort Group Expert. From the dialog box shown in Figure 5-12, select either Top N or Bottom N.

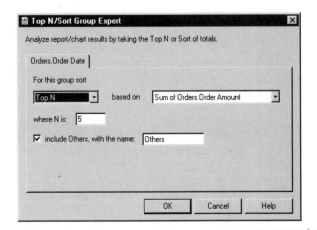

| **Figure 5-12** | Options for TopN/BottomN analysis |

Using the drop-down list of available summary fields, select the field that your analysis will be based on (you'll notice that this list is limited to the summary fields you have inserted into your report). As the final step in creating your TopN/BottomN analysis, you will need to enter a value for N.

By default, the other groups in your report are included in a group called Others. If a group is not included in the Top (or Bottom) N you specify, it will get lumped into this group. To suppress this functionality, click the check box at the bottom of the dialog box. If you would like to keep the Others group but just change the name of the group, you can enter a new name in the text box beside the Include Others box. Click OK to accept your changes and to apply TopN/BottomN analysis to your report.

Sorting Groups by Subtotal or Summary Fields

When working with groups, you may sometimes want to sort the groups according to some summary field that you have inserted in your report. This functionality is similar to TopN/BottomN analysis, except that it isn't limited to just a certain number of groups. Using the Sort All functionality within Crystal Reports, you can order *all* of the groups by a summary value.

To sort the groups in your report by the value of a summary field, verify that your report has at least one group and summary inserted. Select Report | TopN/Sort Group Expert; then in the dialog box that is shown in Figure 5-13, from the For This Group Sort drop-down menu, select All.

Ask the Expert

Question: How do I turn TopN/BottomN Analysis off?

Answer: This has to be one of the most frequently asked questions in relation to TopN/BottomN analysis, and the procedure is pretty easy, once you know the trick. To turn off TopN/BottomN analysis and return your report to returning all records, choose Report | TopN/Sort Group Expert and select the Sort All option, but do *not* select a summary field from the second drop-down list. Click OK; your report should now reflect all of the groups.

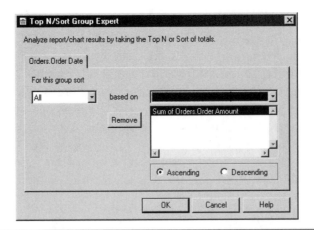

Figure 5-13 You can sort groups by a summary field that you have inserted into your report

Using the drop-down list of available summary fields, select the field that your analysis will be based on. Select a sort order (Ascending or Descending) and click OK to accept your changes and to apply TopN/BottomN analysis and Sorting to your report.

Running Totals

Running totals provide an at-a-glance look at cumulative values in your report and display a running summary beside each record. With each release of Crystal Reports, running totals have grown in functionality and can now be used for a wide range of summary and analysis tasks. Running totals also feature a flexible evaluation and reset function that makes complex analysis easier.

Inserting Running Totals

By using running totals in your report, you can quickly give users the information they need without have to wade through the report to get to a summary field or end of a section. For example, suppose you want to create a running total that runs alongside a list of your customers and their last year's orders. With each record, you want this last year's orders figure added to the running total, as shown in Figure 5-14.

Regional Sales Report - 1998

Customer Name	City	Region	Order Amount	Running Total
Tek Bikes	Philadelphia	PA	$10,384.96	$10,384.96
Extreme Cycling	Clearwater	FL	$10,472.41	$20,857.37
Crank Components	Champaign	IL	$10,605.18	$31,462.55
The Great Bike Shop	Huntsville	AL	$10,662.75	$42,125.30
Backpedal Cycle Shop	Philadelphia	PA	$10,798.95	$52,924.25
Blazing Bikes	Eden Prairie	MN	$10,877.46	$63,801.71
Psycho-Cycle	Huntsville	AL	$11,081.41	$74,883.12
Rowdy Rims Company	Newbury Park	CA	$11,099.25	$85,982.37
Hooked on Helmets	Eden Prairie	MN	$11,156.00	$97,138.37
Feel Great Bikes Inc.	Eden Prairie	MN	$11,316.60	$108,454.97
The Biker's Path	DeKalb	IL	$11,465.42	$119,920.39
Road Runners Paradise	Kingston	RI	$11,621.52	$131,541.91
C-Gate Cycle Shoppe	Winchester	VA	$11,759.40	$143,301.31
Wheels and Stuff	Clearwater	FL	$11,867.20	$155,168.51
Trail Blazer's Place	Madison	WI	$12,323.10	$167,491.61
The Great Bike Shop	Huntsville	AL	$12,913.80	$180,405.41
Rockshocks for Jocks	Austin	TX	$14,039.10	$194,444.51

Figure 5-14	An example of a report with a running total

Hint

You also can insert running totals from the Insert | Field Object menu. Locate the section for running totals in the Field Explorer, right-click, and select New.

The first step in creating a running total is to locate and select the field that will serve as the base field. Right-click directly on top of the field and select Insert | Running Total, which opens the dialog box shown in Figure 5-15.

The first thing you need to do is type a name for your running total in the Running Total Name box. It can be any name you like, as long as it makes sense to you.

Tip

Crystal Reports will put the pound symbol (#) in front of your running total name so you can easily identify this field as a running total when it is inserted into your report.

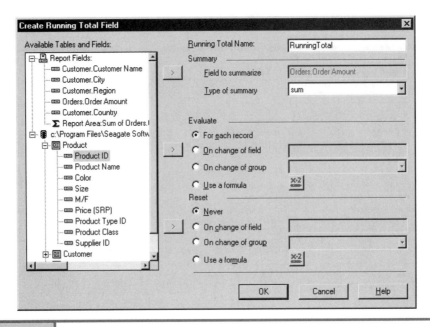

Figure 5-15 Running total options

The next step in creating a running total is selecting a field to summarize and then choosing a summary option, as shown in Figure 5-16. To select a field, locate it in the list on the left and then click the top-right arrow to move the field to the text box on the right.

From the pull-down box immediately below the summary field, you need to select a summary operator. All of your old favorites are here: Sum, Average, and so on.

In this example you are inserting a running total that will run down the page, so you don't need to worry about the Evaluate and Reset options for the running total. Click OK to accept your changes and return to your report's design or preview. You'll notice that your running total field has been inserted into your report in the Details section.

As you created your first running total field, you may have noticed two sections in the Create Running Total Field dialog box, marked Evaluate and Reset. These sections are for setting the options related to when your running

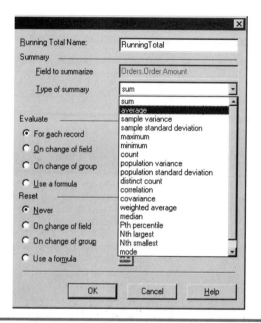

Figure 5-16 You need to select a field to summarize and a summary operator for your running total

total will be evaluated and when the total will be reset. For evaluation times, you can select a calculation time for your running total from the following options:

- For Each Record
- On Change of Field
- On Change of Group
- Use a Formula

For example, you would want to use these options if you were creating a running total to sum all of the international sales in a report. You could select the Use a Formula option and enter this criterion:

```
{Customer.Country} <> "USA"
```

The resulting running total field would be evaluated only for those customers who are not in the U.S.

Likewise, you can reset your running total field using the following options:

● Never

● On Change of Field

● On Change of Group

● Use a Formula

For example, you could reset the running total for each change of the country field within your list. By using the evaluation and reset options, you can create running total fields for just about any use you can imagine.

Note

To use these options, in most cases you will need to select the option and the corresponding field or group. For the Use a Formula option, you will need to select the option and then click the X+2 button to open the Crystal Reports formula editor and enter your criteria. Just as with record selection, the formula you create here needs to return a Boolean value: either true or false. If the value is true, then the record will be evaluated or the running total reset (depending on the option you are working with); likewise, if the condition evaluates to false, the action will not take place.

Inserting Running Totals for a Group

In addition to setting running totals for a list of fields, you can set running totals for a group, allowing you to quickly summarize the contents of multiple groups in your report. To insert a running total for a group, select the field you want to summarize, right-click directly on top of the field, and select Insert | Running Total.

Because you are inserting a running total for a group, select the For Each Record evaluate option, and, under Reset, select On Change of Group and select the group you want to use, as shown in Figure 5-17.

Click OK to accept your changes, and your new running total should appear in your report in the group footer of the group you specified earlier.

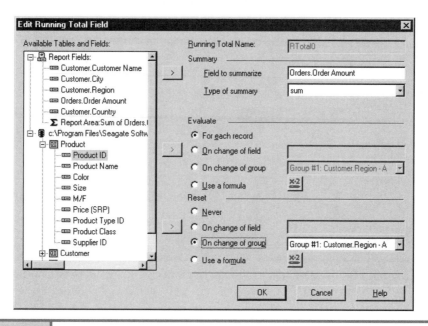

Figure 5-17 | An example of creating a running total on a group

Highlighting Expert

Just like a highlighter could be used to physically mark up a report, indicating
values to be scrutinized, the Crystal Reports Highlighting Expert can do the
same thing by changing the font, background colors, and borders when criteria
are met. Created through a simple interface, multiple highlighting criteria can
be established to mark problem areas that need to be addressed or data to be
further reviewed. You may want to highlight customers whose sales have been
under expectations or customers who have had exceptionally large sales in the
past year. The criteria you specify are completely up to you.

To use the Highlighting Expert in your report, locate and select the numeric
field that you want to highlight. Right-click directly on top of the field and, from
the menu that appears, select Highlighting Expert. This opens the Highlighting
Expert, shown in Figure 5-18.

5

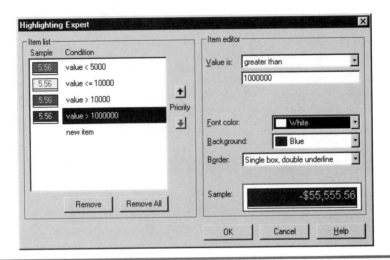

Figure 5-18 Using the Highlighting Expert, you can quickly identify values in your report that meet some criteria you have established

The Highlighting Expert is easy to use. You simply enter a condition on the right side of the dialog box and then specify the formatting options that you want used when that condition is true. If you would like to enter multiple criteria, click New Item in the item list. To change the order of precedence for highlighting criteria (items), use the up and down arrows. After you have finished entering all of your criteria, click OK to accept your changes. The field that you originally selected should now reflect the options set in the Highlighting Expert.

Tip

You may want to review Module 8, "Formulas and Functions," before attempting to use Conditional Formatting.

Conditional Formatting

Conditional formatting provides more functionality than the Highlighting Expert, but the concept behind this type of formatting is very simple. If some condition is true, a formatting option is applied. Conditional formatting can be applied to most of the formatting options within Crystal Reports, and these options generally fall into two categories.

The first category includes those formatting options that can have multiple outcomes. When establishing the criterion to change the font color when an invoice is more than a certain amount, the criterion has to be considered, but color (blue, red, orange, or another) to be used when the criterion is met also needs to be considered.

When using conditional formatting with these type of fields, you are required to create an If-Then statement with the criteria and outcomes. For example, if we want to flag every invoice that is more than $10,000, the formula would look like this:

```
If {Invoice.InvoiceAmount} > 10000 then BLUE
```

An easy way to tell when we need to write an If-Then statement for conditional formatting is when the property is represented in the property pages by a pull-down or multiple selection box.

When creating a conditional formatting formula of this type, Crystal Reports displays a number of specialized functions in the function list of the Formula Editor, as shown in Figure 5-19. These functions include Current Field Value, Default Attribute, and, in this case, a list of color constants that are related to the field that we are working with. (If you were working with the border, for example, a different set of constants would appear.)

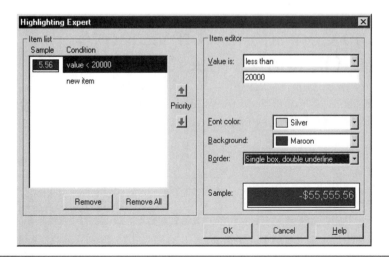

Figure 5-19 Specialized functions are associated with each multiple-outcome property.

The second category of formatting options involves those properties that are Boolean—either they are on or they are off. A good example of this type of property is the Suppress option; a field is either suppressed or it is not suppressed.

When working with conditional formatting and Boolean properties, we can simply enter a Boolean statement in the Formula Editor. If that statement is true, the formatting option is turned on. For example, if we wanted to suppress all invoice amounts that are less than $500, the conditional formula related to the Suppress property would look like this:

```
{Invoice.InvoiceAmount} < 500
```

When that condition is met, the field is suppressed. The criteria established can be as complex as you like, but must result in either a true or false outcome.

Note

Another question that frequently arises is "Between the Highlighting Expert and conditional formatting, which takes precedence?" The answer is that conditional formatting will *always* take precedence over any highlighting you have in your report. This means that if you have used the Highlighting Expert to turn a field green if a certain criterion is met, and conditional formatting is also on the same field with criterion to turn the font color yellow, the font color will always be yellow. Highlighting is applied first, and then conditional formatting is applied on top of that.

Applying Conditional Formatting to Multiple-Outcome Properties

When using conditional formatting with multiple-outcome properties (colors, borders, and so forth), you need to write an If-Then statement to indicate that, when some criterion is true, some formatting option occurs, such as

```
if {customer.sales} < 10000 then RED
```

To use conditional formatting with multiple-outcome properties, you first need to locate and select the field that you want to highlight. Right-click directly on top of the field, and from the menu that appears, select Format Field. This should open the object's property pages.

For this example, we are going to conditionally format the font color, although the same technique could be applied to any multiple-outcome property. Go to the Font tab and click the X+2 button beside the font color selection to open the Crystal Reports Formula Editor (shown in Figure 5-20).

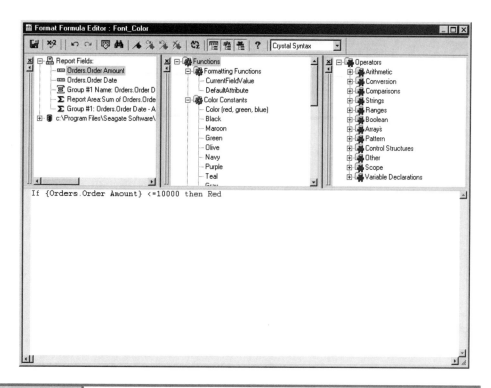

Figure 5-20 | The Crystal Reports Formula Editor

┼Tip

A good way to tell the difference between a multiple-outcome property and a Boolean property is that a multiple-outcome property usually has a pull-down box associated with it, but a Boolean property usually has just a checkbox or option to select.

Enter an If-Then statement to indicate when the font color should be changed and which font color to use. An example is

```
if {Invoice.InvoiceTotal} < 1000 then Red
```

Click the Save and Close button on the Formula Editor to return to the Font tab. Click OK to accept your formatting changes and to return to your report. The conditional formatting you established should now be reflected on your report.

Applying Conditional Formatting to Boolean Properties

Working with conditional formatting and Boolean properties (suppress, for example) is much easier than multiple-outcome properties. With Boolean properties, you simply need to create a Boolean formula. If the formula is true, the formatting option is set.

To use this type of conditional formatting, first locate and select the field that you want to format. Right-click directly on top of the field and, from the menu that appears, select Format Field. This should open the object's property pages in the Format Editor.

For this example, we are going to suppress an invoice total if it is less than $10,000 using the suppress property. Locate the Suppress check box on the Common tab.

Tip

Do not click the Suppress button. It suppresses every occurrence of the field, regardless of the condition that we enter.

Click the X+2 button immediately to the right of the Suppress option. Enter a Boolean formula to indicate when the field should be suppressed. An example is

```
{Invoice.InvoiceTotal} < 10000
```

Click the Save and Close button on the Formula Editor to return to the Common tab. Click OK to accept your formatting changes and to return to your report. The conditional formatting you established should now be reflected on your report.

Project 5-3: Using the Highlighting Expert

The Highlighting Expert lets you, the report developer, call attention to certain areas of a report if a condition is met. Using the Highlighting Expert, we will identify the customers in the Customer by Country report that have had sales of less than $20,000 and turn the values for those customers red.

Step-by-Step

1. From the Start | Programs menu, start Crystal Reports 8.5.

2. From the Welcome dialog box, select Open an Existing Report; then, in the next dialog box, open the Customer by Country Ch5-2.rpt report we have been working with in this module.

3. To make things a bit easier, switch to the Design view of your report by clicking the Design tab in the upper-left corner.

4. Locate the {Customer.Last Years Sales} field, right-click directly on top of the field, and select Highlighting Expert from the right-click menu. This opens the Highlighting Expert dialog box.

5. On the right side of the dialog box, use the first drop-down list to select the less-than operator.

6. Using the text box immediately below the operator, enter a value of **20000** (no dollar signs or decimal points).

7. Using the formatting controls at the bottom-right of the dialog box, select a different font color, background, and border.

8. Click OK to accept your changes. When you preview your report, you should see this conditional formatting.

Tip

You may need to drill down to the details of your report to see it in action.

9. Save your report as **Customer by Country Ch5-3.rpt**.

Project Summary

The Highlighting Expert can be used to change the formatting attributes of a particular numeric field based on criteria you enter and provides an easy way to get the attention of anyone reading a report you have created.

☑ *Mastery Check*

1. Which record selection operator allows you to select a list of values to be included?

_____

_____

2. When you use the Select Expert to create record selection on more than one field, what is the default relationship between these criteria?

    A. OR

    B. AND

    C. NOT

    D. None of the above

3. Why can you *not* enter a value when using the operator In the Period?

_____

_____

4. What is the difference between a summary field and a formula?

_____

_____

5. Why might you want to use the Highlighting Expert?

_____

_____

Module 6

Using Parameter Fields

Goals

- Understand how parameter fields can be used in a report
- Create parameter fields
- Insert parameter fields into a report
- Use parameter fields with record selection

One of the goals of good report design is creation of a single report that delivers information to a number of people, without the need to create multiple reports that basically show the same information. One method for creating reports that fit many different types of situations is to use parameter fields. In this module, you will learn about parameter fields, how they are created, and how they can be used to enhance your report's design and usefulness.

Parameter Field Overview

Parameter fields enable you to create reports that can be used in a variety of ways, prompting the user for various kinds of information, including values to be used in record selection, sort order, report titles, comments, and more. Parameter fields also give you a quick and easy way to create reports that can serve many users and purposes.

Parameter fields can be used in your report in a number of ways. The simplest use of a parameter field is to display some text in your report. The text could be the report title, a brief explanation of the report, your name, or just about any text that you want to add to your report at runtime.

A second use for parameter fields is in conjunction with formulas. You may want to prompt the user for the sales tax percentage, which will then be calculated; or a particular type of shipping (for example, two-day or overnight), which could then be used to calculate shipping cost; or even a discount amount when printing invoices.

The third and most popular use of parameter fields is for record selection. By using parameter fields, you can create a single report that can be sliced many different ways, depending on the values the user enters for the parameter fields. These fields are then used in the record selection formula to determine what data is brought back from the database.

Parameter Field Attributes

The first step in creating a parameter field is specifying a name for that field. Once you have created your parameter field, Crystal Reports will enclose this field name in brackets, preceded by a question mark to indicate that it is a parameter field: for example, {?ParamFieldName}. You can also enter prompting text that will appear whenever the Parameter Field dialog box appears, as shown in Figure 6-1.

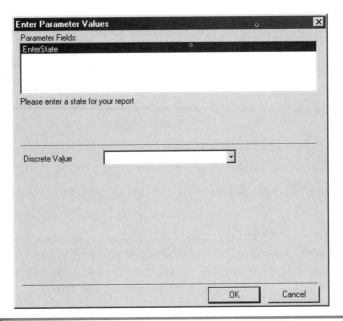

Figure 6-1   Prompting text can be used to help the user understand what values to enter

Prompting text should help the user understand what to enter in the value field of the dialog box (for example, "Please enter a state for your report").

By default, any parameter you create will have a default type of string, but there are actually seven field types you can use:

- **String**   For entering alphanumeric text.

- **Currency**   For prompting users to enter an integer with two decimal places.

- **Date**   For entering a standard date in the format *Month/Day/Year*.

- **Date Time**   For prompting for a date/time string, in the format *Month/Day/Year Hour/Minute/Second*/A.M. or P.M.

- **Time**   For entering the time in the format *Hour/Minute/Second*/A.M. or P.M.

- **Number**   For entering a number with variable decimal places.

- **Boolean**   For prompting users for a true or false response.

Which field type you choose depends on how you are going to use the field in your report. Other attributes that can be set when creating a parameter field are:

- **Allow Multiple Values**   Allows you to enter a list of values for your parameter field.

- **Discrete**   Allows you to enter a single value.

- **Range**   Allows you to specify an inclusive range, using start and end values.

- **Discrete and Range**   Allows a combination of discrete and range specifications.

- **Allow Editing of Default Values**   Allows the editing of any default values you may have given the user to assist in completing the parameter field (for example, if you give users a list of states to choose from, this option would let them edit one of the states from the list to enter their own variation).

Most of the attributes discussed here are optional. To create a parameter field, the only requirement is that you give your parameter field a name and choose a field type.

Creating a Simple Parameter Field

To create a simple parameter field to be used in your report, select Insert | Field Object. This will open the Crystal Reports Field Explorer, shown in Figure 6-2.

Right-click Parameter Fields and select New from the menu that appears. In the Create Parameter Field dialog box, type a name for your parameter field. For example, in Figure 6-3, the parameter field is named EnterState.

Next, enter any prompting text you want to appear when the user is prompted for information (for instance, "Please enter an employee ID for this report"). From the Value Type box, select a data type for your parameter field. The following types are available:

- Boolean
- Currency
- Date
- Date Time
- Number

● String

● Time

Click OK to accept your changes. Your parameter field should now appear in the Field Explorer, ready to be used in your report.

Inserting a Parameter Field into Your Report

To insert a parameter field you have created, you can simply drag it from the Field Explorer to your report's design or preview.

Hint
When placing fields on your report, it is usually easier if you do so in Design view.

6

Once you have dragged a parameter field onto your report, you will be prompted to enter a value for the parameter the next time the report is previewed, as shown in Figure 6-4.

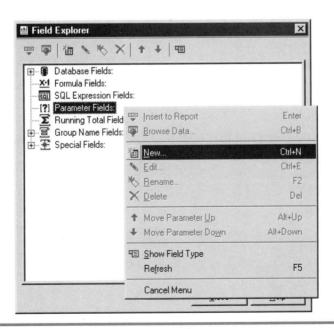

| **Figure 6-2** | The Crystal Reports Field Explorer |

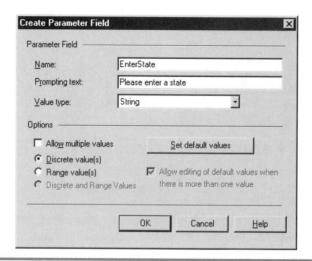

Figure 6-3 You can create a parameter field using this simple dialog box

After you have entered a value for your parameter field, that value will be displayed in the report preview until you refresh your report and specify that you want to prompt for a new parameter value.

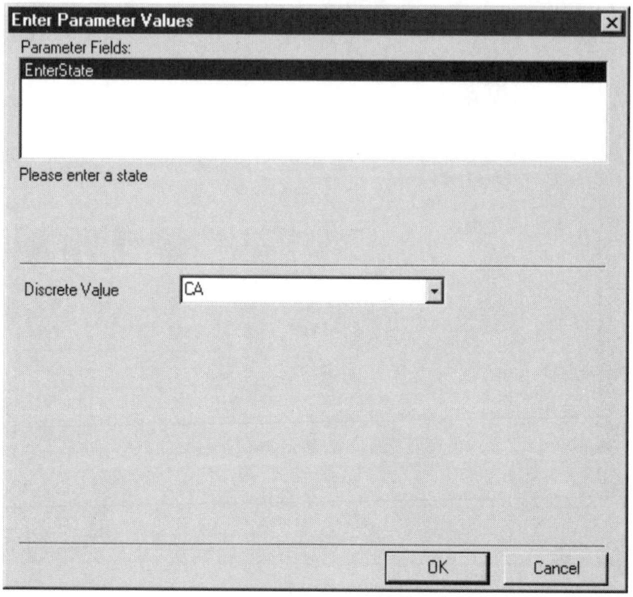

Figure 6-4 A typical parameter prompt dialog box

Project 6-1: Inserting a Parameter Field

In this project, we are going to create a brand-new report from the information contained in the Employee table of our fictional Xtreme Mountain Bike Company. On our report, we want to show each employee's first and last name, position, and salary. We will then use a parameter field to enter the name of the person who ran the report. This parameter field will then be displayed in the page header.

Step-by-Step

1. From the Start | Programs menu, start Crystal Reports.

2. From the Welcome dialog box, select Create a New Crystal Report Document. Then select Using the Report Expert from the Create a New Crystal Report Document section of the Welcome dialog box and click OK

3. From the Crystal Report Gallery, select the Standard Report Expert and click OK.

4. Click the Database button to open the Data Explorer and navigate to Xtreme Sample Database under the ODBC node of the tree.

5. From Xtreme Sample Database, select the Employee table and click the Add button. A green check mark should appear next to the table, and the Data tab should reflect your selection. Click Close to close the Data Explorer and to return to the Standard Report Expert.

6. On the Fields tab, select the fields that you want to see in your report. For this project, select the following fields:

   - First Name
   - Last Name
   - Position
   - Salary

   To select a field, highlight it in the list on the left and click the right arrow button marked Add to move it to the list on the right.

7. This is all the information the Standard Report Expert needs to create your report. Click the Finish button to preview your report, which should look something like Figure 6-5.

8. Switch to the Design view of your report by clicking the Design tab in the upper-left corner.

9. Select Insert | Field Object to open the Crystal Reports Field Explorer.

10. Locate the section for parameter fields. Right-click directly on the heading and select New from the menu that appears.

6

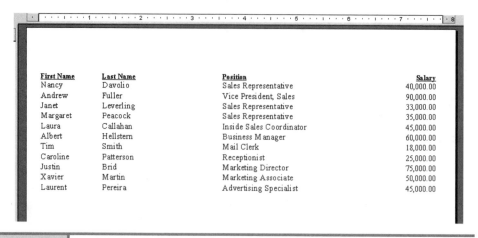

First Name	Last Name	Position	Salary
Nancy	Davolio	Sales Representative	40,000.00
Andrew	Fuller	Vice President, Sales	90,000.00
Janet	Leverling	Sales Representative	33,000.00
Margaret	Peacock	Sales Representative	35,000.00
Laura	Callahan	Inside Sales Coordinator	45,000.00
Albert	Hellstern	Business Manager	60,000.00
Tim	Smith	Mail Clerk	18,000.00
Caroline	Patterson	Receptionist	25,000.00
Justin	Brid	Marketing Director	75,000.00
Xavier	Martin	Marketing Associate	50,000.00
Laurent	Pereira	Advertising Specialist	45,000.00

Figure 6-5   Your finished report should look similar to the one shown here

11. The Create Parameter Field dialog box opens, as shown in Figure 6-6. Enter a name for your parameter field. In this case, we'll call our parameter field ReportUser.

12. In the Prompting Text box, enter some text that will appear when the user enters a value for this parameter field. This could be something like "Please enter your name."

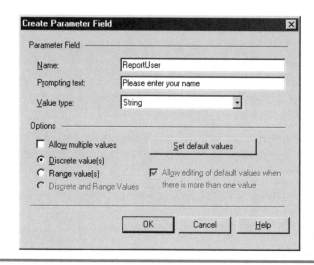

Figure 6-6   The Create Parameter Field dialog box

13. Click OK to accept your changes. You now should see the parameter field you have created in the Field Explorer.

14. Drag and drop your parameter field from the Field Explorer to the page header of your report. By default, Crystal Reports automatically adds a report date field as well, so you can either remove this field or place your parameter field beside it.

15. Click the Preview tab, and you should be prompted for your parameter field, as shown in Figure 6-7.

16. Enter a value and click OK; this value should appear in your report's page header.

17. Save your report as **Employee List Ch6-1.rpt**.

6

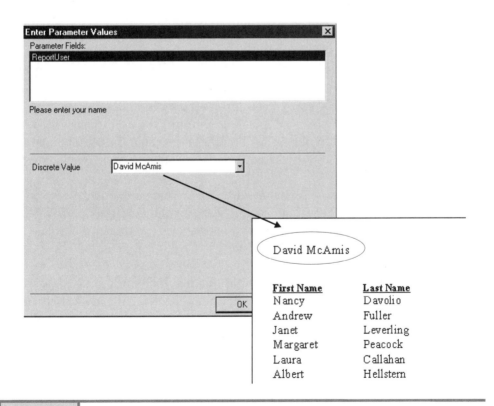

Figure 6-7 A typical parameter prompt dialog box

Project Summary

Parameter fields have many uses, the simplest being to display information on your report. In the sections that follow, you'll learn more about parameter fields, including how to use them in record selection.

Working with Special Parameter Types

When working with parameter fields, there are a couple of special types of fields that we can use in our reports, including Boolean parameter fields (for entering true-or-false values), parameter fields that allow the entry of multiple values (similar to using the One Of operator), and parameter fields that allow a range of values (like the Is Between operator). Sound confusing? The information on the next few pages should help you sort things out in no time.

Creating Boolean Parameter Fields (True/False)

Boolean parameter fields can be used to prompt users for a true or false response and can be used to control report formatting, summary levels, and more. For example, you may want to create a report that prompts the user to answer the question "Show Negative Numbers?" and then use the value the user entered in a record selection formula to filter out any negative numbers that may otherwise appear in the report.

Creating a Boolean parameter field is just like creating any other parameter field. To start, select Insert | Field Object. This opens the Crystal Reports Field Explorer. Right-click the section of the explorer labeled Parameter Fields and select New from the right-click menu. Using the Create Parameter Field dialog box, type a name for your parameter field.

Next you would need to enter any prompting text that you want to appear when the user is prompted for information (for example, "Would you like to print totals for this report?"). As a final step, change the value type to Boolean and click OK to accept your changes (see Figure 6-8).

When a user is prompted for a Boolean parameter field, a dialog box similar to the one shown in Figure 6-9 will appear, and the user can enter a selection of True or False.

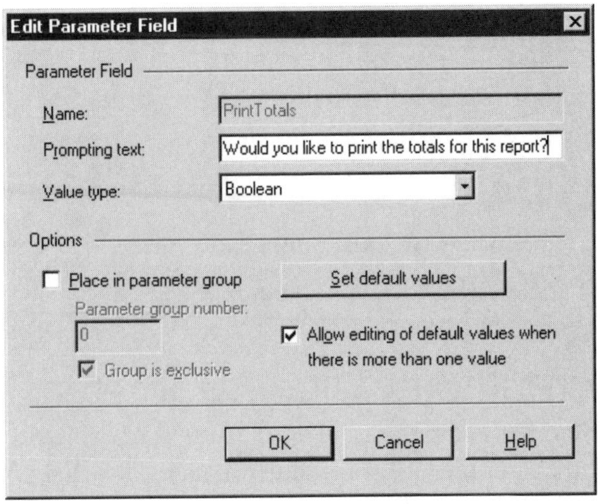

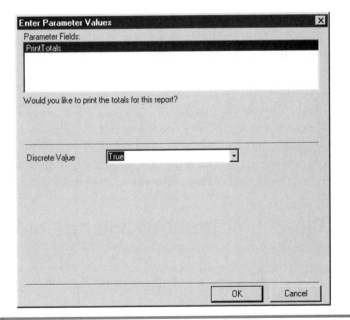

Figure 6-8   Options for Boolean parameter fields

Figure 6-9   A typical Boolean parameter field

If you are not really fond of true and false, you can specify how the Boolean value is entered (True/False, Yes/No, or On/Off) by using the Set Default Values button that we will talk about a little later in the module.

1-Minute Drill

● What is the difference between a number and currency type parameter field?

● How are parameter fields marked in your report?

Creating a Multiple-Value Parameter Field

In addition to fields that accommodate single and range values, parameter fields can also enable users to enter multiple values. This means that you can create one parameter field that can accept from one value to as many as you like. You can create a parameter field for Country, for example, and then let the user pick which countries to run the report for—from 1 country to 3 to 30—it is their choice.

Tip

The only downside of using a multiple-value parameter field is that the values you enter can't be displayed on your report, which makes sense as there isn't enough room in the field to display the extra values.

To create a multiple-value parameter field, create a parameter field as you normally would, only this time click the check box marked Allow Multiple Values. Click OK to accept your changes and return to the design or preview of your report. When a user is prompted for a parameter field, a dialog box similar to the one shown in Figure 6-10 will appear and allow the user to build a list of values.

Limiting Parameter Input to a Range of Values

When using parameter fields, you can give users the option of entering start and end values, allowing them to use the fields in record selection. Again, insert a parameter field as you normally would, only this time use the radio buttons

---

● Parameters defined as number can have a floating decimal; currency is limited to two.
● Parameter fields are marked with a question mark, like {?ParameterName}, for example.

Figure 6-10   Users can enter multiple parameter field values using the dialog box shown here

in the Options section of the dialog box to select range values. When your parameter field is inserted into your report or used with record selection and this setting is in effect, you will be prompted for a range of values using the dialog box shown in Figure 6-11.

Note

A little later in the module, we will talk about how to use this type of field with record selection.

Setting Default Parameter Values

An easy way to help users complete parameter field prompts is to give them some default values to choose from. You may have noticed when working with parameter fields up to this point that there is a button marked Set Default Values that we haven't discussed. If you have a parameter field for which you want to

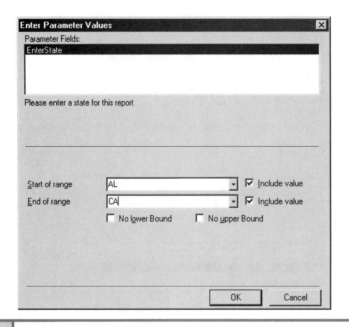

Figure 6-11 You can define a parameter to accept a range of values, a discrete value, or both

set some default values, click this button to open the Set Default Values dialog box, which is described in more detail next.

Setting Default Values for a Parameter Field

A list of default parameter values can be read from your database or entered manually, giving users a list of values to choose from. An important concept when working with default parameter values is that this is a manual process that can occur only when you are designing the report.

While it would be preferable to have a direct connection to the database when you are running the report to provide this information, Crystal Reports allows you to populate this list only when designing your report. To set up default parameter values for your users and make data entry a bit easier, you may want to choose from the following selections that appear in the Set Default Values dialog box, shown in Figure 6-12:

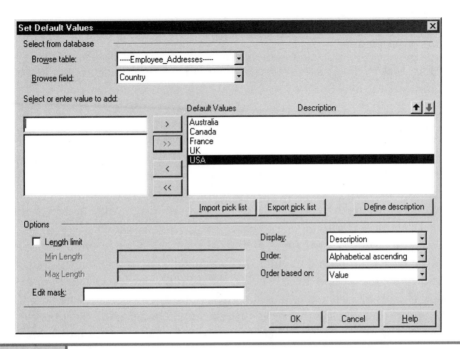

| **Figure 6-12** | Default field values can be included to give users a list of values to select from |

- **Browse Table**   This is the table that contains the default parameter values.

- **Browse Field**   This is the specific field within that table that contains the default values.

- **Default Values/Description/Display**   Specify the list of values that is displayed when the user is prompted to enter a value, a description for each value (optional), and whether to display just the value or the value and description.

- **Pick Lists**   Once you have established a list of default values and descriptions, this information can be exported to a text file and reused in other reports by importing the text file.

- **Order**   You can select the sort order that determines how the default values are displayed.

- **Order Based On**   You can specify whether the order of the default values is to be based on the Default Values or Description field.

- **Length Limit**   You can specify a minimum and maximum length limit for your parameter field.

- **Edit Mask**   You can specify a template that is used for entering data to indicate the appropriate format.

Adding Descriptions to Default Values

In addition to displaying a default value, Crystal Reports can also display a description of the value to help users select the correct value (for instance, the description field can display "North Carolina" when the field value is NC). To add descriptions to default field values, highlight each value and click the Define Description button.

Using the dialog box shown in Figure 6-13, enter a description to be displayed when the user is prompted to enter the parameter value.

In the pick list located directly below the default values, you will also need to choose whether to display the value and description or just the description. Click OK to accept your changes to the default values and OK again to accept the changes you have made to the parameter field itself. From that point forward, users should see either the value or description (or both) that you have specified.

Tip

Remember that regardless of whether users select a description or a value, it is the value that is passed through to appear on your report in record selection and so on.

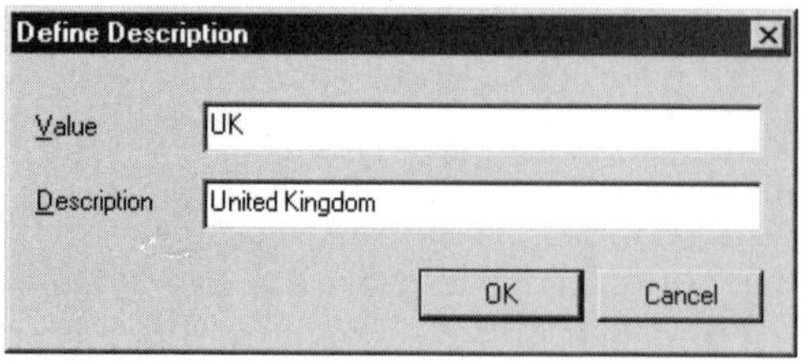

Figure 6-13   A description can be added to values to make them easier to understand

Sorting Parameter Field Default Values

To make looking through these default values a little easier, you can sort the
contents of the drop-down boxes of values that the user sees. When working with
the default values, select a sort order from the Order field at the lower right, as
shown in Figure 6-14.

Seven sort options are available:

- No Sort

- Alphabetical Ascending

- Alphabetical Descending

- Numeric Ascending

- Numeric Descending

- Date/Time Ascending

- Date/Time Descending

6

Tip

If you do not choose a sort type that matches the parameter field value type,
no sorting will occur.

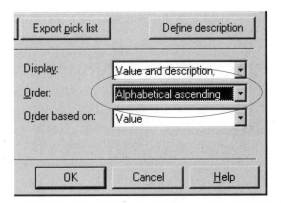

Figure 6-14 You can select a sort order for the default values in your report

With a sort order in place, users will have an easier time selecting the values they want.

Importing or Exporting a Parameter Field Pick List

When working with parameter fields and default values, you may have multiple reports that use the same default values and descriptions. Typing these values and descriptions each time you want to use them is time consuming, but Crystal Reports provides an easy way to work around this problem. If you frequently use the same parameter fields, you can export and import field pick lists, eliminating the need to establish default values and descriptions each time. The pick list files themselves are simply text files and can be used with any report you create.

To import or export a parameter field pick list, create a list of default values for your parameter, highlight each value, and click the Define Description button. Enter a description for this field to be displayed when the user is prompted to enter the parameter value.

Once you have entered all of the descriptions for your values, select Export Pick List and choose a file name and location for your pick list file. Click Open to export the values and descriptions to this file. You can then use Notepad to open the file to verify that the process ran correctly.

Tip
You can also use the Import Pick List button to import an existing pick list.

Controlling Parameter Field Input

An edit mask can be applied over parameter input to help users understand what type of value should be entered and the format that should be used. For example, a phone number made up of a 3-digit area code and 7 numbers could be displayed as (704) 555-1212. When using an edit mask for parameter entry, the mask characters will appear to guide the user, but the actual value returned does not include the mask characters (in our example, the value returned would be 7045551212).

Using the text box at the bottom of the Enter Parameter Values dialog, enter the edit mask for your parameter field, using the operators listed in Table 6-1.

Ask the Expert

Question: How can I change the order in which my parameters appear?

Answer: Select Insert | Field Object. Click the section of the Field Explorer marked Parameter Fields to expand this node and list all of the parameter fields available. Highlight the field you want to move and right-click directly on top of it. From the right-click menu shown here, select the direction to move the field. Once you are finished changing the order of the parameter fields, click Close to exit the Field Explorer and return to your report's design or preview page.

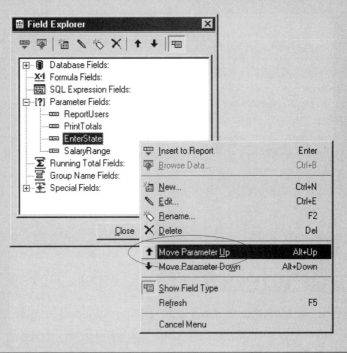

6

Note

There is also the option of specifying the edit mask option of "Password"—this will cause any data entry that is performed within the parameter field text box to appear as asterisks (i.e. "*********").

Operator	Description	Input Required
0	Digit from 0 to 9	Yes
9	Digit from 0 to 9 or a space	No
#	Digit from 0 to 9, space or plus/minus sign	No
A	Any alpha-numeric character	No
L	Character from A to Z	Yes
?	Character from A to Z	No
&	Any alpha-numeric character or space	Yes
C	Any alpha-numeric character or space	No
. , : ; - /"	Separator characters	No
<	Change all of the following characters to lowercase	No
>	Change all of the following characters to uppercase	No
\	Display following field as literal	

Table 6-1 Parameter Mask Characters

To verify that your parameter mask works correctly, insert the parameter field onto your report or use it in record selection (which will be covered next). When you preview your report and are prompted to enter a parameter field value, the edit mask should appear in the input box.

Parameter Fields and Record Selection

Using parameter fields for record selection is a popular way to give users more control over the report at runtime. Setting up this functionality is quick and easy; there are two steps involved.

The first step is to actually create the parameter field used to prompt the user for information using the techniques learned earlier in the module. You will want to make sure that this parameter field is created with the same type as the field you want to use for record selection. (It will do you no good to create a string-type parameter field when you want the user to enter an invoice number.)

The second step is to set your record selection formula using this parameter field. In its simplest form, your record selection formula might look something like this:

```
{Customer.Country} = {?EnterCountry}
```

Note

If formulas are not your thing, you can use the Select Expert to do most of the work for you.

In this example, {?EnterCountry} is the name of the parameter field you have created. Whenever the report is run, a dialog box will pop up and ask for a country to be entered, such as USA. Once this data entry has occurred, the record selection formula will replace the parameter name with the actual value and make a request to the database to retrieve the correct records for companies in, say, the United States.

To make matters a little more complicated, parameter fields can also be created with the ability to accept multiple values. In this case, the formula looks exactly the same:

```
{Customer.Country} = {?EnterCountry}
```

When the dialog box pops up for entering information for this parameter field, as shown in Figure 6-15, you can pick a list of values to be used, such as USA, Canada, and Mexico. These values are then used in the record selection formula, and the appropriate records are returned.

This is often confusing to new report developers, as the proper record selection operator for multiple values is Is One Of. Crystal Reports stores these multiple values in memory and is smart enough to make the translation when processing occurs. Unfortunately, as was mentioned earlier, you cannot display the contents of this array in your report; you can use it only for record selection.

The same concept also applies when you specify that a parameter field can accept a range of values, as shown in Figure 6-16. You will be prompted for start and end values, but Crystal Reports stores these values in its own internal memory and allows you to use the same record selection formula:

```
{Customer.Country} = {?EnterCountry}
```

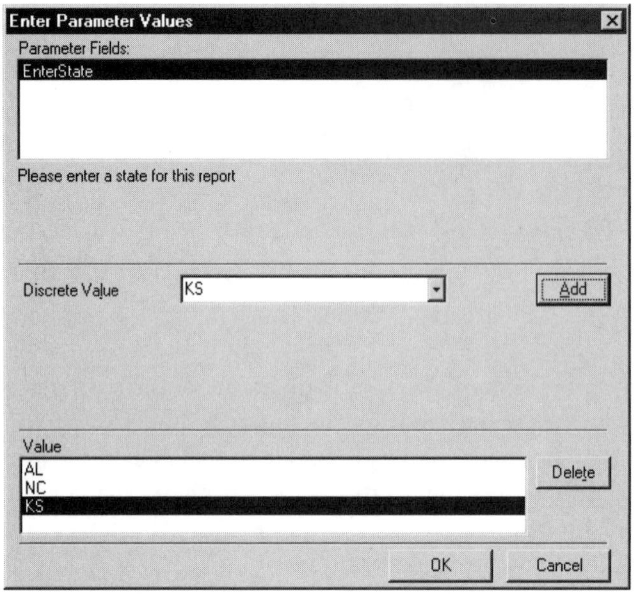

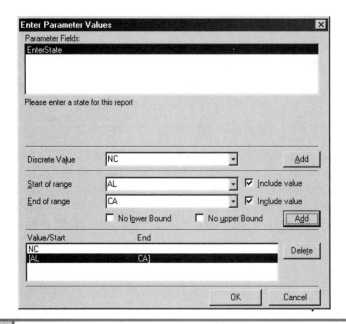

Figure 6-15   You can enter multiple values for parameters using the dialog box shown here

Figure 6-16   A parameter field can also accept a range of values

Now, with that said, it does not mean that Is Equal To is the only record selection operator you can use with parameter fields. Parameter fields are treated just like any other field, so you can use any record selection operator or logic to achieve the desired results.

Using a Parameter Field in Simple Record Selection

Parameter fields can be used in a number of different ways, but the most common use of parameter fields is in conjunction with record selection, prompting a user for a value that will be used to narrow the results of a particular report.

To use a parameter field with record selection, determine which field from your database you want to use for record selection and note the type and length of the field. You will then need to create a parameter field with the same field type as your database field. To use this field with record selection, select Report | Select Expert. A list of fields will appear. Choose the field from your database that you want to use for record selection. This opens the Select Expert, where you can choose a record selection operator (Equal To, Is Not Equal To, Is One Of, and so on).

Once you have selected an operator, a second dialog box will open, as shown in Figure 6-17, where you can select or enter a value to be used in your record selection. Use the pull-down list to locate and select the parameter field you have created.

Click OK to accept your changes to your report's record selection and return to the report design or preview. When you next preview or refresh your report, a dialog box will open prompting you for the parameter field you created.

6

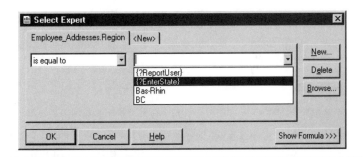

Figure 6-17   A second pull-down list appears, where you can select the parameter field you have created

After you enter this value, it will be used in the record selection formula and subsequently passed to the database.

Parameter Field Limitations

Finally, here is a word about the limitations of parameter fields. One of the first questions from report developers concerning parameter fields is "Can I change the default dialog box that pops up?" The answer is no; you can control the way it looks based on the features you select for your parameter field (for example, whether it accepts a range of values, multiple values, and so on), but other than that, the dialog box will always remain the same.

Another question frequently asked is "Can I make the parameters mandatory?" Again, the answer is no. If a user wanted to, the user can click OK without entering any parameter field values at all.

One more common question is "Can I go back to the database for default values at runtime?" Once again, the answer is no. You can collect these values only when you are designing your report, through browsing a table for the information, importing a pick list, or entering this information by hand.

Although there may be some characteristics that you would like to change about parameter fields, they still represent the best way to create one report that can be displayed in many different ways for different users.

Project 6-2: Using Parameter Fields with Record Selection

Parameter fields can be used in a number of ways, but the most common use of parameter fields is in conjunction with record selection, to prompt a user for a value that will be used to narrow the results of a particular report. In this project, we are going to build on our Employee Listing report and use a parameter field to prompt the user for a salary threshold. Only employees with salaries higher than the value entered will be shown.

Step-by-Step

1. From the Start | Programs menu, start Crystal Reports.

2. From the Welcome dialog box, select Open an Existing Report, select More Files, and click OK. Then in the next dialog box, locate the report from Project 6-1 that you saved as Employee List Ch6-1.rpt.

3. Select Insert | Field Object.

4. Locate the section for parameter fields and right-click directly on top of the section heading. Select New from the right-click menu.

5. Enter the name **SalaryThreshold** for your parameter field and enter some prompting text such as **Please enter a salary threshold for this report.**

6. For the type of parameter field, select Number and then click OK.

7. Select Report | Select Expert.

8. Locate the {Employee.Salary} field, click to select it, and click OK.

9. In the Select Expert that opens, you can choose from record selection operators (Equal To, Is Not Equal To, Is One Of, and so on). In this example, choose the operator Greater Than.

10. Once you have selected the operator, a second drop-down list opens that allows you to select or enter a value to be used in your record selection. Use the pull-down list to locate the parameter field you created, {?SalaryThreshold}, and select it.

11. Click OK to accept your changes to your report's record selection and return to the report design or preview.

12. When you next preview or refresh your report, a dialog box will open prompting you for the parameter field you created. Once you enter this value, it will be used in the record selection formula and subsequently the request that is passed to the database.

13. Save your report as **Employee List Ch6-2.rpt**.

Project Summary

In this project, you saw how a parameter field can be used with record selection. Try experimenting with multiple parameters and record selection fields. You will find that once you get the hang of it, almost every report you create can benefit from a parameter field (or two!).

☑ *Mastery Check*

1. What are some of the uses for parameter fields?

_____

_____

2. Which of the following is *not* a valid value type for a parameter field?

   A. Boolean

   B. String

   C. Binary

   D. Date

3. How do you get Crystal Reports to prompt for a new parameter value?

_____

_____

4. Do you have to enter the descriptions for default values every time (even when you are using the same descriptions in other reports)?

_____

_____

5. How can you tell whether a field in your report is a parameter field?

_____

_____

Module 7

Distributing
the Results

Goals

- Understand available export formats
- Optimize report design for a specific export format
- Distribute report results

Now that you have learned how to create reports and add features and functionality to your reports, it is time to look at how you are going to deliver this information to other users. In this module, you will learn about the export formats available, as well as the distribution methods available to distribute your exported report to users.

Report Distribution Overview

When designing reports, an important consideration is how you are going to deliver these reports to users. It does no good to create a killer report if your users can't access the report you have created. An easy solution to this problem is to purchase a copy of Crystal Reports for every user. This would give your users complete control over the report design and allow them to refresh the report whenever they need to, but it may be more economical to export your reports to a format that others can use without having to purchase any additional software licenses.

Crystal Reports 8.5 includes over 16 different export formats that cover a wide range of applications and uses, including formats for use with word processing programs, spreadsheet applications, and just about everything in between.

With this release of Crystal Reports, you can also export your report to Adobe Portable Document Format (PDF), enabling users to view reports using the free Acrobat Reader program available online from Adobe Systems.

Note

In addition to being able to export reports, Crystal Reports includes a scalable Web server and delivery framework as part of Crystal Enterprise Standard, which ships with the product. Using the Crystal Enterprise framework, you can view reports with live data in a Web browser, using a number of smart viewers or a zero-administration DHTML client. For more information on Crystal Enterprise, check out www.crystaldecisions.com/products/crystalenterprise.

In addition to export formats, Crystal Reports also includes a number of distribution methods. For instance, you can send the exported file as an e-mail attachment or put the file in a Microsoft Exchange folder or Lotus Notes database. But before we get into distribution of the exported reports, let's take a look at the formats that are available.

Exporting to WYSIWYG Formats

If you want to distribute your report to users exactly as you have created it, you will probably want to consider using one of Crystal Report's WYSIWYG formats. WYSIWYG is an acronym for "what you see is what you get." Using Crystal Reports, you have two options for getting a true WYSIWYG copy of your report.

Saving Your Report with Data for Distribution

If your users have a copy of Crystal Reports 7.0 or later, one option you have is to save your report with data and distribute the report file with the saved data inside. The Save Report with Data option is actually a setting that Crystal Reports turns on by default, and it provides an easy method for distributing your report to other Crystal Reports users without having to give them access to your data source.

To save your report with data, verify that the option Save Data with Report is checked by selecting File | Save Data with Report. From that point, all you need to do is refresh your report data (using F5) and save your report using File | Save, specifying a file name and location for the report. Once you have saved the .rpt file, you can send it to other Crystal Reports users, and they can view and print both the report and the data contained within.

┤*Tip* ─────────────

If you are sending a report with saved data to someone who is using Crystal Reports 7.0, you will need to select File | Save As and select Crystal Reports (version 7.0) in the Save as Type box at the bottom of the dialog box. You will lose any formatting or other features that are specific to the Version 8.0 file format.

7

Exporting to an Acrobat PDF File

Crystal Reports 8.5 includes the ability to export to Adobe's Portable Document Format, which provides a true WYSIWYG representation of your report.

Tip

The PDF files created by Crystal Reports can be read using the free Acrobat Reader available at http://www.adobe.com/products/acrobat/readstep.html.

To export your report to Acrobat format, select File | Print | Export to open the Export dialog box, shown in Figure 7-1.

In the Export dialog box, select the format Acrobat Format (PDF) and the destination Disk File and click OK. In the Export Options dialog box that appears, enter the page range to be exported and click OK to proceed.

At this point, you will need to enter a file name and location for the exported file and click OK. A progress dialog box, shown in Figure 7-2, will appear while the records are being exported, and you will be returned to your report's design or preview page when the export is finished.

If you have already installed the Adobe Acrobat Reader, you should be able to locate the file you just exported and double-click to view the report.

Tip

As with the majority of export formats, you will not be able to use any of the native Crystal Reports features such as drill-down and record selection when you export to PDF.

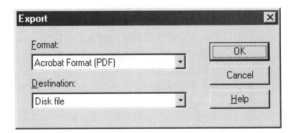

Figure 7-1 The Crystal Reports Export dialog box

Figure 7-2   A progress dialog box appears while the report is being exported

Exporting to Text File Formats

Text file formats are popular because most word processing, spreadsheet, and database applications can read them. To make life easier, there are a number of text file formats to choose from when exporting your report; which format you choose will probably be based on the target application or platform for the exported file. With all of these file formats, there are some report design considerations that need to be taken into account to successfully export your report.

First, if you are considering creating a report for export to text-only format, keep in mind that Crystal Reports will attempt to export all of the elements of the report to the text file. This means that if you have page numbers at the bottom of every page, these numbers could end up in the text file as values, as shown in Figure 7-3. If you were to import this file into a spreadsheet or database application, the page numbers would be treated as values and imported as well.

For reports that are specifically created for export to a text file, it is a good idea to remove any unnecessary fields that you may have inserted, including the report title, page numbers, special fields, and comments. Another consideration is that all of the column headings and fields should be relatively the same size and aligned in your report.

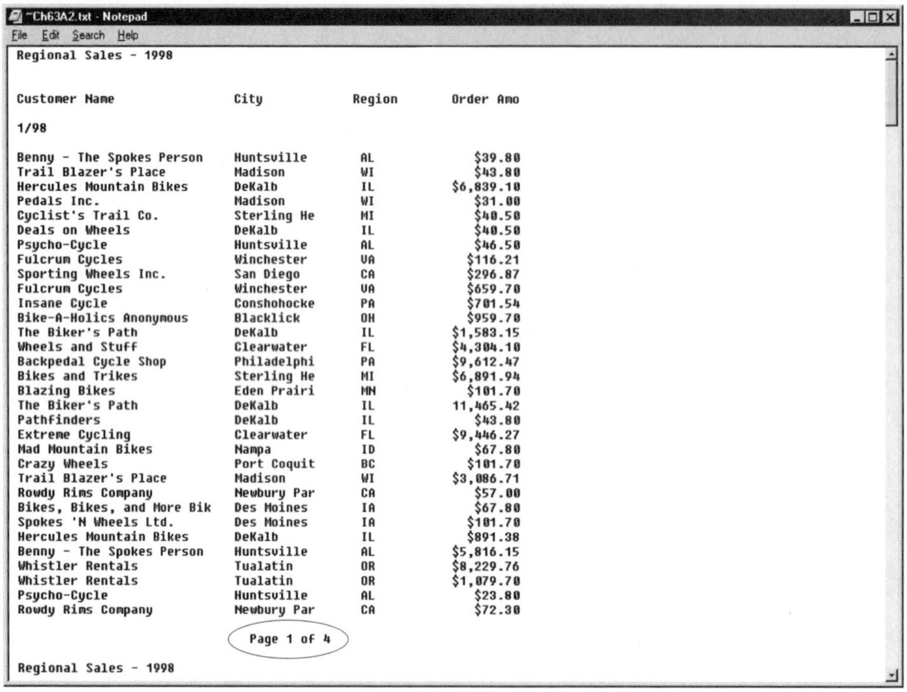

Regional Sales - 1998

Customer Name	City	Region	Order Amo
1/98			
Benny - The Spokes Person	Huntsville	AL	$39.80
Trail Blazer's Place	Madison	WI	$43.80
Hercules Mountain Bikes	DeKalb	IL	$6,839.10
Pedals Inc.	Madison	WI	$31.00
Cyclist's Trail Co.	Sterling He	MI	$40.50
Deals on Wheels	DeKalb	IL	$40.50
Psycho-Cycle	Huntsville	AL	$46.50
Fulcrum Cycles	Winchester	VA	$116.21
Sporting Wheels Inc.	San Diego	CA	$296.87
Fulcrum Cycles	Winchester	VA	$659.70
Insane Cycle	Conshohocke	PA	$701.54
Bike-A-Holics Anonymous	Blacklick	OH	$959.70
The Biker's Path	DeKalb	IL	$1,583.15
Wheels and Stuff	Clearwater	FL	$4,304.10
Backpedal Cycle Shop	Philadelphi	PA	$9,612.47
Bikes and Trikes	Sterling He	MI	$6,891.94
Blazing Bikes	Eden Prairi	MN	$101.70
The Biker's Path	DeKalb	IL	11,465.42
Pathfinders	DeKalb	IL	$43.80
Extreme Cycling	Clearwater	FL	$9,446.27
Mad Mountain Bikes	Nampa	ID	$67.80
Crazy Wheels	Port Coquit	BC	$101.70
Trail Blazer's Place	Madison	WI	$3,086.71
Rowdy Rims Company	Newbury Par	CA	$57.00
Bikes, Bikes, and More Bik	Des Moines	IA	$67.80
Spokes 'N Wheels Ltd.	Des Moines	IA	$101.70
Hercules Mountain Bikes	DeKalb	IL	$891.38
Benny - The Spokes Person	Huntsville	AL	$5,816.15
Whistler Rentals	Tualatin	OR	$8,229.76
Whistler Rentals	Tualatin	OR	$1,079.70
Psycho-Cycle	Huntsville	AL	$23.80
Rowdy Rims Company	Newbury Par	CA	$72.30

Page 1 of 4

Regional Sales - 1998

Figure 7-3 A standard text file exported without considering the report format

Each of the export formats listed here may have additional options that allow you to control the file's contents. Here is a rundown of all of the text file formats, the additional options they present, and the output they return:

- **Character-Separated Values (CHR)** Allows you to pick a separator and delimiter for your text file and choose the date and number formats for the resulting text file.
- **Comma-Separated Values (CSV)** Standard CSV file format, with values enclosed in quotation marks and separated by commas. CSV allows you to choose the date and number formats.
- **Data Interchange Format (DIF)** Standard DIF file format. DIF allows you to choose the date and number formats.

- **Tab-Separated Text (TTX)**   Creates a tab-delimited text file, with text and values in quotation marks.

- **Tab-Separated Values (TSV)**   Creates a tab-delimited file, with text in quotation marks and values shown as is. TSV allows you to specify the date and number formats.

- **Paginated Text (TXT)**   Close representation of the report's layout in text format, using spaces and page breaks to match the report's design.

- **Record Style (Columns of Values) (REC)**   Presents distinct columns of text. REC allows you to choose the date and number formats.

- **Text (TXT)**   A simple text file export representing the report's design as closely as possible.

Exporting to a Text File (TXT, CSV, DIF, and So On)

7

To export your report to a text file, select File | Print | Export to open the Export dialog box and select from one of the text file formats: Text File, Comma Delimited (CSV), and so on.

Tip

Keep in mind that some of these export formats may require additional information, such as how you want the numbers or text to appear.

Select a destination of Disk File and click OK. Enter a file name and location for the exported file and click OK. A progress dialog box should appear while the records are being exported, and you will be returned to your report's design or preview page when the export is finished.

From that point, you should be able to open your text file using Notepad or any other software application that is capable of opening text files. If the resulting file is not what you expected, try changing your report's design (removing page numbers, headings, and so on) to optimize the text file produced.

1-Minute Drill

● What does PDF stand for?

● Which text file format would export a report to a column-based format?

Exporting to Office File Formats

Crystal Reports includes a number of export file formats for Microsoft Office, Lotus SmartSuite, and WordPerfect Office. For each of the primary application in these suites, there is an export format that should give you the majority of the information required for distribution and further analysis.

Note

Where Crystal Reports does not provide an export format targeted specifically for the application listed, the most compatible formats are listed.

Microsoft Excel (XLS)

Crystal Reports can export to Microsoft Excel using two methods. The first, called the regular or WYSIWYG method, takes your report's design and translates it into an Excel file, attempting to match the report's layout and design as best as it can, as shown in Figure 7-4. While this method of Excel export captures all of the spacing and information contained within the report, it can be frustrating for users who have to perform additional clean-up on the resulting Excel spreadsheet, removing extra columns and rows, before they can use it for analysis.

The second method of Excel export is preferred. This is called the extended method. Using the extended method and the options associated with it, you can control how the report is exported to Excel. You can also set the column widths with the extended Excel format, making it the best choice for Excel output. Compare the report in Figure 7-5, which was exported using extended Excel export format, to the same report in Figure 7-4.

● Portable Document Format
● Record Style (.REC)

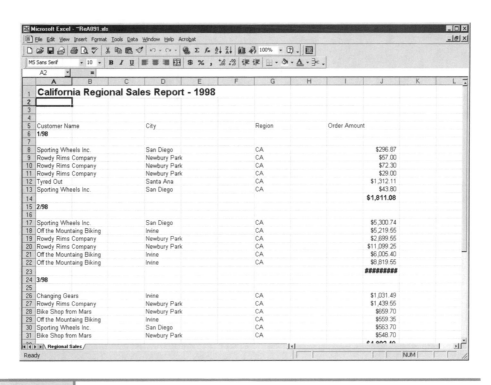

Figure 7-4 A report exported using the standard Excel export format

Note

When exporting to a recent version of Excel, there is a limit to the amount of data you can export—generally around 65,000 rows and 256 columns.

In addition to keeping an eye on the number of row and columns, you will also want to design your report with exporting in mind, following these suggestions for better output:

● Make column headings and fields the same width and height.

● Leave a small gap of white space between columns in your report.

● Remove any unnecessary fields or headings.

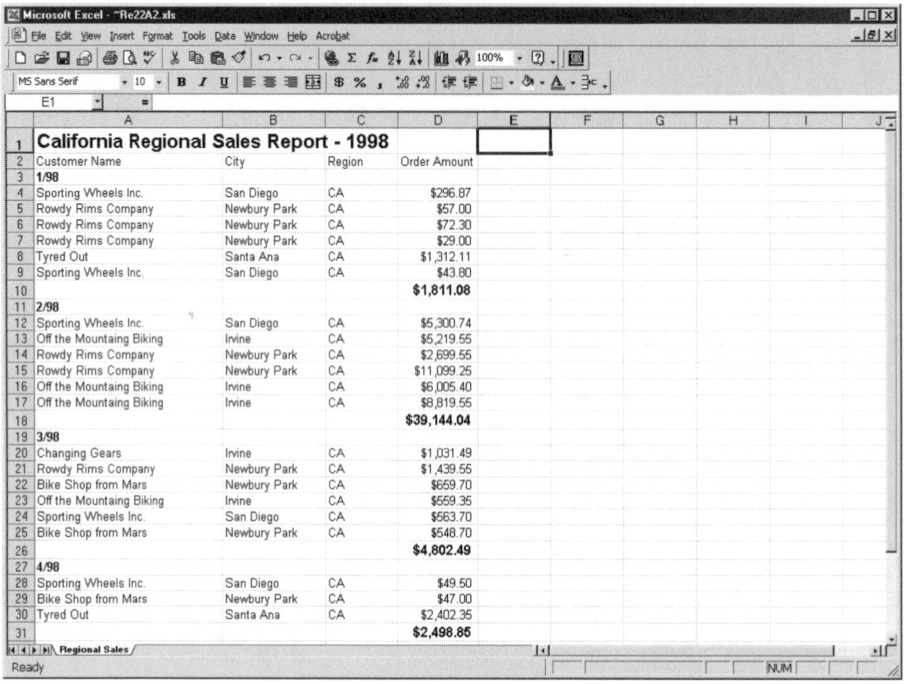

Figure 7-5 A report exported using the extended Excel export format

When the report is exported using a columnar format, Crystal Reports should have no problem determining which field or column should go where.

Note

Even with these suggestions, there will be elements of your Crystal Reports design that will not be exported, such as lines, boxes, rotated text, and maps. A complete list of export formats and supported features can be found at http://support. crystaldecisions.com/communityCS/TechnicalPapers/cr85_exportlimitations.zip.

To export your report to Excel, select File | Print | Export. Then in the Export dialog box, select Excel 8.0 (XLS) (Extended) and a destination of Disk File.

+Tip

If you want a WYSIWYG export of your report to Excel, choose one of the Excel export formats not marked Extended.

From the dialog box shown in Figure 7-6, select the options for your export, including:

- **Column Headings**   Includes column headings from the report in your spreadsheet.

- **Use Worksheet Functions to Represent Subtotals in the Report**   Tells Crystal Reports to attempt to convert the subtotals in your report to Excel formulas, meaning that when a user changes a value in the spreadsheet, the subtotals will be dynamic and change accordingly.

- **Constant Column Width**   Allows you to specify the column width for the columns that are exported to Excel.

- **Column Width Based on Objects in Area**   Allows you to select a section that defines the boundaries of your columns.

- **Non-Tabular Format**   Provides a WYSIWYG representation of your report without your having to put individual fields in separate columns.

- **Tabular Format**   Places each column in your Crystal Report in a separate column within your exported Excel spreadsheet. Crystal Reports will attempt to place the columns of your report in adjacent Excel columns with this option.

Click OK to accept the options you have selected. In the dialog box that follows, choose a file name for your exported file and click OK to start the report export.

A progress dialog box should appear while the records are being exported, and you will be returned to your report's design or preview page when the export is finished. From that point, you should be able to locate and open the Excel spreadsheet you have created. Again, if the results are not what you expected, go back to the report's design and try to troubleshoot any problems by aligning columns, reducing the font size, and so on, and then try your export again.

7

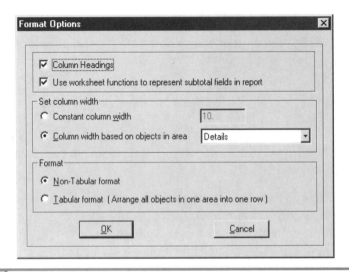

Figure 7-6 Options for the extended Excel format

Microsoft Word (DOC, RTF)

There are actually two different file export formats available for Microsoft Word. The first, Word for Windows, was originally designed as an export format specifically for Word. The Word for Windows export format will try to reflect the design and content of your report within a Word document, with mixed results, as shown in Figure 7-7.

A much better choice is to export your report using the Rich Text Format export option. A significant amount of development work has been put into the RTF format export to ensure that most formatting options from your report design will be exported. Figure 7-8 shows the same report as in Figure 7-7, but exported in RTF format.

Lotus 1-2-3 (WK1, WK3, WKS)

Crystal Reports includes output options for three different versions of Lotus 1-2-3, including files with the extension .wk1, .wk3, and .wks. With Lotus 1-2-3, only 8,192 rows can be exported from Crystal Reports. You can also use alternative text formats such as CHR, CSV, and TXT if required.

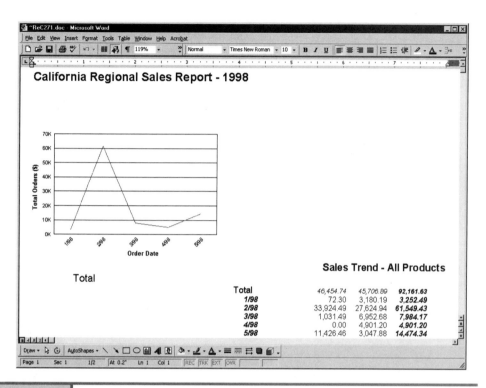

Figure 7-7 | A report exported to the Word for Windows export format

Lotus WordPro, WordPerfect (RTF)

There is not an export format specifically for Lotus WordPro or WordPerfect, but Crystal Reports can export to Rich Text Format, which can be read by WordPro and will allow your exported report to retain most of its formatting features.

QuatroPro (XLS, CHR)

Again, there is not a specific export format for QuatroPro, but the latest release of the product can read Microsoft Excel files, or you may want to consider exporting your report to a text file (such as a CHR file), which QuatroPro can read.

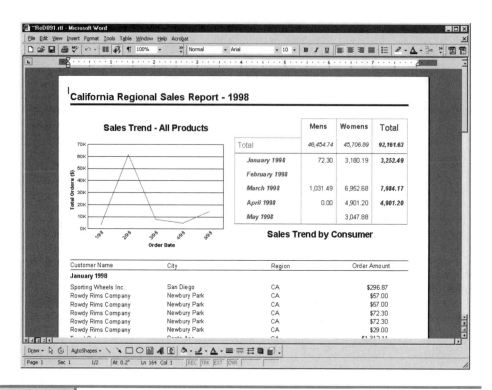

Figure 7-8 A report exported to the Rich Text Format

Exporting to Other Formats

In addition to the formats listed, Crystal Reports also supports some unusual export options that may come in handy.

Exporting Your Report's Definition

If you ever need to document a Crystal Report you have created, you will be delighted at how easy it can be. Using the export options within Crystal Reports, you can generate a text file that describes and documents the structure and layout of your Crystal Report.

This file is called the Report Definition and it is one of those hidden gems within Crystal Reports. Shown in Figure 7-9, it contains a detailed description of your report, broken into logical sections. This description includes not only the fields, formulas, groups, and record selection in your report, but also a summary of the formatting options applied to each field, object, or section to give you the precise details of how the report was created.

To export your report's definition, select File | Print | Export to open the Export dialog box. In the Export dialog box, select the Report Definition format and a destination of Disk and click OK. Once you have selected a file location and name, a progress dialog box should appear while the records are being exported; you will be returned to your report's design or preview page when the export is finished.

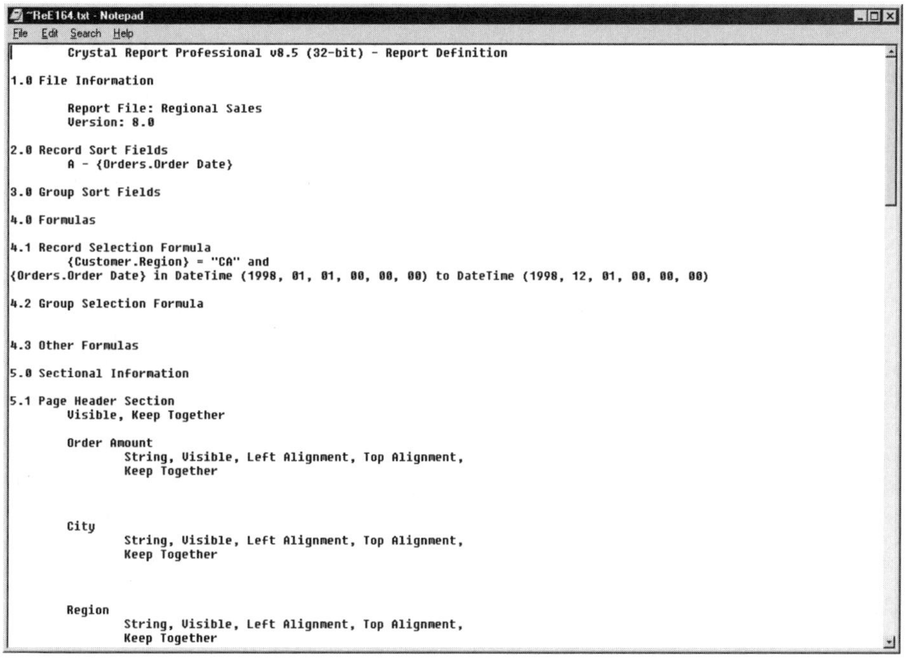


```
        Crystal Report Professional v8.5 (32-bit) - Report Definition

1.0 File Information

        Report File: Regional Sales
        Version: 8.0

2.0 Record Sort Fields
        A - {Orders.Order Date}

3.0 Group Sort Fields

4.0 Formulas

4.1 Record Selection Formula
        {Customer.Region} = "CA" and
{Orders.Order Date} in DateTime (1998, 01, 01, 00, 00, 00) to DateTime (1998, 12, 01, 00, 00, 00)

4.2 Group Selection Formula


4.3 Other Formulas

5.0 Sectional Information

5.1 Page Header Section
        Visible, Keep Together

        Order Amount
                String, Visible, Left Alignment, Top Alignment,
                Keep Together


        City
                String, Visible, Left Alignment, Top Alignment,
                Keep Together


        Region
                String, Visible, Left Alignment, Top Alignment,
                Keep Together
```

Figure 7-9 A sample report definition file

7

You can then locate the text file that has been created and open it using Notepad or some other word processing application.

Note

This report definition is for documentation purposes only. It does not control or drive the report's design and cannot be modified to change the report's design. The report definition is also for export only, meaning that you can generate it at any time, but Crystal Reports cannot read a report definition file or create a new report from it.

Exporting to an ODBC Database

Another option frequently overlooked is the ability to push a report's contents directly back into an ODBC database as a new table. This functionality is available for most ODBC drivers and requires that you have create permission on the database in question. (Your database administrator should be able to help you with this.) When you choose this option, Crystal Reports will ask you for a table name. Then Crystal Reports creates a table using the report's definition and exports the data from your report into the same table.

To get started, you will need to configure an ODBC data source name that points to the database where you want to export your report contents.

Tip

Before you get started, make sure you verify with your database administrator that you have create and update rights on the database you want you use.

Select File | Print | Export to open the Export dialog box, and in the Export dialog box, select the format ODBC-*dsn name* (where *dsn name* is the name of the ODBC data source you have created) and click OK. In the dialog box that appears, shown in Figure 7-10, enter a table name for your exported report.

Note

By default, this table name is CREXPORT, but you can change it to anything you like within your database's naming constraints.

Figure 7-10 You will need to specify a name for your exported table of report information

A progress dialog box should appear while the records are being exported, and you will be returned to your report's design or preview page when the export is finished. Your report contents should now be exported to the table you specified in your database. If the results are not as you expected, modify the report design to optimize it for exporting to a database table. The most common culprits are page headings, page numbers, and report titles because these elements are also placed in your database table.

1-Minute Drill

- Which export format allows you to format your Excel output?
- Which format would you choose for exporting to a word-processing program?

Exporting to Web Formats

Crystal Reports includes export formats for both HTML 3.2 and HTML 4.0 (DHTML), allowing you to export your report for viewing in a Web browser without any additional plug-ins. The HTML 4.0 (DHTML) format is the better of the two as it can translate more of the report's design into HTML using some of the features introduced with HTML 4.0, as shown in Figure 7-11.

With either export format, you can choose whether you want the report displayed as a single page or multiple pages, as well as whether the exported

7

- Excel (Extended)
- Rich Text Format (.RTF)

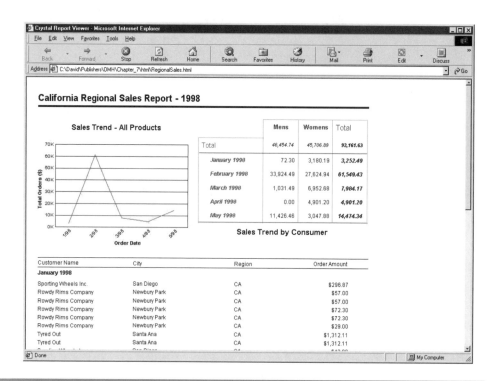

Figure 7-11   A Crystal Report exported to HTML

report has built-in page navigation. You can also specify the page range to be exported and the base file name and subdirectory where the files are stored.

Exporting to HTML provides a static view of your report, as all of the pictures, graphs, and maps in your report are created as static JPEG files and stored in the same directory structure as the HTML files generated. If you need a live, dynamic report within a Web browser, you may want to consider adding your report to the Crystal Enterprise framework, which allows you to view your report in a preview window provided by any number of smart viewers or plug-ins for the Web.

Most of the smart viewers included with the Crystal Enterprise framework give you a live, dynamic view of the report, allowing you to refresh the data contained; drill down into charts, graphs, and summary fields; search for fields; and more.

When you are working with Web reporting, the Crystal Enterprise framework provides a better solution for deploying reports to an intranet or Internet site, but exporting can also be helpful for one-off exports or for cases when you need to manually edit the HTML before it is published.

To export your report, select File | Print | Export to open the export dialog box. In the export dialog box, select the format HTML 4.0 (DHTML) and the destination Disk File and click OK. In the dialog box that appears, shown in Figure 7-12, select a directory name and location for storing your HTML and related files.

Select a base file name for your report and use the check boxes to specify whether you want a page navigator to appear and whether you want the report exported to a single HTML document.

7

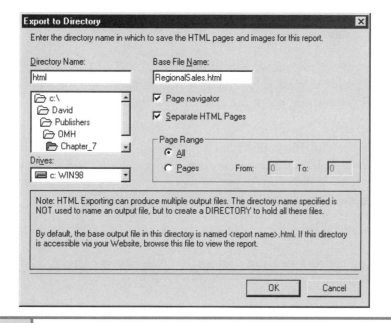

Figure 7-12   You can select a directory name and file location for storing your HTML files

Finally, select a page range to be exported and click OK to start the export. A progress dialog box should appear while the records are being exported; you will be returned to your report's design or preview page when the export is finished.

From that point, you can view your report using Internet Explorer or Netscape Navigator by locating the folder where your HTML files were created and viewing the base file. At the bottom of each HTML page will be links to navigate between pages (if specified), and you can print each of the report pages independently.

Distributing Your Report

In addition to various file formats, Crystal Reports 8.5 also includes a number of methods for distributing these exported files. These methods range from simply saving a file to disk to placing a report in a Lotus Notes database or Exchange folder to sending the exported file as an e-mail attachment. Here are the destinations available:

- **File Export**   You can save an exported report directly to a file, using any of the export formats listed earlier. Once you specify a file name, Crystal Reports adds the appropriate extension to the file name.

- **Application**   If you specify a destination of Application, Crystal Reports will save a temporary file in the format you specify and launch the associated application. For example, if you select Adobe Acrobat (PDF) and specify Application, Crystal Reports will create the PDF file and then immediately launch Acrobat Reader to display the file.

- **Lotus Notes, Domino**   You can push an exported report back into a Lotus Notes or Domino database file (NSF) using any of the supported Crystal Reports format. In addition, Crystal Reports can be run from within Lotus Notes or Domino using LotusScript.

- **Lotus cc:Mail (VIM)**   Reports can be sent as e-mail attachments using Lotus cc:Mail version 3.0.

┤Note

If you are using cc:Mail 4.0+, note that Lotus switched to a MAPI interface, and the Microsoft Mail (MAPI) option can be used instead.

- **Microsoft Exchange** A report can be placed in an Exchange public folder and shared with Exchange and Outlook users. These reports can be exported to any format, and when they are launched from within a public folder, the associated application will be launched.

- **Microsoft Mail (MAPI)** Reports can be sent as e-mail attachments using a simple Microsoft MAPI hook. Mail clients supported include Outlook, Outlook Express, and any other MAPI-compliant mail program.

- **Crystal Enterprise** Crystal Enterprise is a scalable report scheduling and distribution solution from the makers of Crystal Reports. A copy of Crystal Enterprise Standard is included with every copy of Crystal Reports 8.5 and provides the Web reporting framework for Crystal Reports.

- **Application Integration** Crystal Reports includes a number of integration methods for popular programming languages, including Visual Basic, Visual C++, Delphi, and Java, allowing you to integrate Crystal Reports design and viewing functionality without your application.

7

⟩Ask the Expert

Question: Can I still use compiled reports with Crystal Reports 8.5?

Answer: Previous versions of Crystal Reports allowed you to compile a report into a stand-alone executable file and compile and distribute all of the runtime files required to run this executable. With the release of Crystal Reports 8.0, this functionality was available through a separate download only, and with Crystal Report 8.5 and its tighter Web integration using Crystal Enterprise, this option is no longer available.

Saving Your Report Directly to a Microsoft Office Web Folder

Crystal Reports can save reports directly to a Microsoft Office Web folder. Select File | Save As. In the dialog box that appears, shown in Figure 7-13, select the Web Folders icon on the left. This opens a list of available Web folders for you to use.

Choose an existing folder or create a new one and specify the file name for your report.

Tip

To add a new Web folder, click the Create New Folder icon on the toolbar and specify a Web server folder name and alias.

Once you have selected a location and file name, click OK to accept your changes and save your report file.

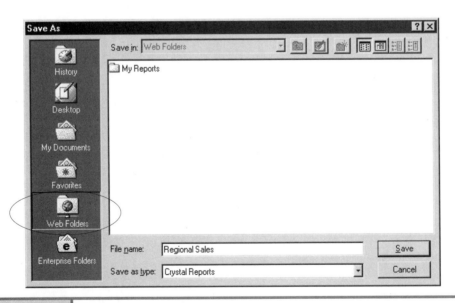

Figure 7-13 You can save a report file directly to a Microsoft Office Web folder using the dialog box shown here

Sending Your Report as an E-mail Attachment (MAPI)

A simple MAPI hook has been included with Crystal Reports to send an e-mail message and attachment from directly within Crystal Reports. To send your exported report as an attachment, you need to verify that you have a working MAPI mail client (such as Outlook or Outlook Express) installed on the computer from which you want to export your report, and that you can send and receive e-mail successfully using this client.

Once you have verified those requirements, select File | Print | Export to open the Export dialog box. In the Export dialog box, select the export format and the destination Microsoft Mail (MAPI) and click OK. If Microsoft Mail does not appear as an option, your e-mail client may not be correctly installed and configured as the default mail application on your computer. See your e-mail administrator to correct this problem.

Tip

You will not be prompted for a file name when sending a file by e-mail. The file name will be determined by the report name and will have the correct extension for the format you use (for example, MyReport.xls for an Excel export of a report named MyReport.rpt).

7

A blank e-mail form will appear, allowing you to enter the e-mail address where this report will be sent as well as a subject and message. Use the Address button to select e-mail addresses from your address book and the Check Names button to check the names you have manually entered against your address book.

When you are finished, click the Send button to send your e-mail. Your exported report will be attached to the e-mail message you have composed and sent through the default mail client installed on your machine. A progress dialog box should appear while the records are being exported, and you will be returned to your report's design or preview page when the export is finished.

Sending Your Report as an E-mail Attachment (VIM)

Crystal Reports can also send your exported report as an e-mail attachment through a VIM connection to older versions of cc:Mail.

Again, just as with the other mail clients, you will need to verify that you have a working Lotus cc:Mail client installed on the computer from which you want to export your report, and that you can send and receive e-mail successfully using this client.

Tip

If you are having problems sending an e-mail message with a report as an attachment, make sure that the location of your VIM.DLL file is included in your computer's path.

To attach and send your report, select File | Print | Export to open the Export dialog box. In the Export dialog box, select the export format and the destination cc:Mail (VIM). A blank e-mail form will appear, allowing you to enter the e-mail address where this report will be sent as well as a subject and message.

Use the Address button to select e-mail addresses from your address book and the Check Names button to check the names you have manually entered against your address book. When you are finished, click the Send button to send your e-mail. Your exported report will be attached to the e-mail message you have composed and sent through the default mail client installed on your machine.

A progress dialog box should appear while the records are being exported, and you will be returned to your report's design or preview page when the export is finished.

Sending Your Report to an Exchange Public Folder

Exchange public folders can be used to disseminate a wide range of information to Outlook users, and exported reports can be place directly into Exchange public folders without leaving the Crystal Reports interface.

Before you get started, you will need to verify that Microsoft Outlook has been installed and configured correctly on your machine. You should be able to open Outlook and view the public folder where you want to place your exported report. Also, check with your Exchange administrator to ensure that you have write access to the Exchange public folder where you want to place your report.

To place a report in an Exchange public folder, select File | Print | Export to open the Export dialog box. In the Export dialog box, select the export format and the destination Exchange Folder and click OK. A dialog box will open and allow you to choose an Exchange public folder for storing your report. Click to select the folder and then click OK to accept your selection. A progress dialog box should appear while the records are being exported, and you will be returned to your report's design or preview page when the export is finished.

Using Your Report with Seagate Info 7.5

Seagate Info 7.5 is a powerful scheduling and distribution method for Crystal Reports version 7.0 and 8.0 reports. It has been superceded by Crystal Enterprise 8.0, but to support users who are still using Seagate Info 7.5, you can add Crystal Reports to the Info desktop by selecting File | Save As. In the Save As dialog box, change the Save as Type value to Crystal Reports (Version 7.0) and select a file name for your report. Click OK to save your file in this format. From the Start menu, select Programs | Seagate Info 7.5 | Info Desktop. Using the credentials supplied by your Seagate Info administrator, log on to the Seagate Info desktop, using the dialog box shown in Figure 7-14.

7

Once you are logged on to the Seagate Info desktop, you will see a number of folders available for storing reports. Locate the folder where you want to place your report file and click to select the folder.

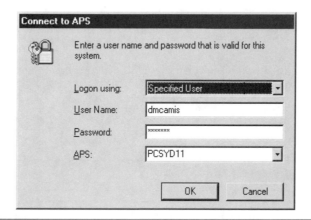

Figure 7-14   You need to log on to place objects on the Info desktop

Select File | New and, from the dialog box that appears, choose Report and click OK. Using the browse button in the dialog box shown in Figure 7-15, select your report file name and click OK to accept it.

Note

Another option is to open the location of the report in Windows Explorer and drag and drop the report file directly on top of the Info folder where you want to place it.

Set any other report properties that are required (default database logons, security, and so on) and click OK. Your report should now appear on the Seagate Info desktop in the folder you selected.

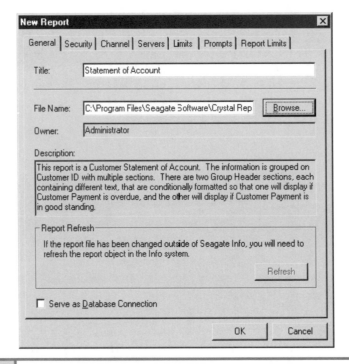

Figure 7-15 You can browse to your report location to place it on the Info desktop

Using Your Report with Crystal Enterprise

Crystal Enterprise provides a scheduling and distribution method for Crystal Reports. You can save your report directly to a Crystal Enterprise folder by selecting File | Save As. In the Save As dialog box, the option for Enterprise Folders is located in the bottom-left corner. Select this option to open the Connect to APS dialog box. Enter the username, password, and APS name provided by your Crystal Enterprise administrator and click OK.

Once you have successfully logged on to the Crystal Enterprise APS, use the Choose Folder dialog box to select the folder where you want to place your report, enter a name and description for your report, and click OK.

Tip

To verify the save process, you can open Crystal Enterprise e-Portfolio and look for your report in the folder you specified.

Export Limitations

7

When exporting a Crystal Report to another file format, keep in mind that the features you see in Crystal Reports have been created specifically for Crystal Reports. While the export formats attempt to push as many of these features as possible to the target application, you will still lose some formatting with almost all of the export formats.

If your users require their reports to have a specific, unchanging format, you may want to use the Adobe Acrobat export format to give them a read-only copy of the report, exactly as you created it. Another option is to place the report in Crystal Enterprise and allow users to run it themselves.

In any case, be prepared when looking at an exported report for the first time—you may not always get what you wanted.

Project 7-1: Exporting Your Report

Using an existing report file, we are going to export a report to Excel format and work with the report design to achieve the desired result. During this project, you should gain an understanding of how report features are translated into elements of an exported file (in this case, Microsoft Excel).

Note

The report file for use in this project (Region_Sales.rpt) can be found in the folder for this module, which can be downloaded from www.osborne.com.

Step-by-Step

1. From the Start | Programs menu, start Crystal Reports.

2. From the Welcome dialog box, select Open an Existing Report, select More Files, and click OK.

3. Locate and open the Region_Sales.rpt file.

4. To export your report, select File | Print | Export to open the Export Options dialog box.

5. Using the drop-down list of formats, locate and select the Excel 8.0 (XLS) (Extended) format.

6. For the destination, select Disk File and click OK.

7. In the Format Options dialog box, accept all of the default settings except for Format. For Format, select Tabular Format. Arrange all objects in one area into one row and click OK.

8. In the Choose Export File dialog box, enter the file name and location for your exported file. In this case, we will name the exported field **RegionReport.xls**. (Don't forget the location you specify; you will need it later.) Click OK to start the file export.

A progress dialog box will appear indicating the number of records exported. When the export is finished, you will be returned to your report preview.

9. Minimize Crystal Reports and open Microsoft Excel from the Start menu.

10. In Excel, select File | Open and locate and open the RegionReport.xls report you just exported from Crystal Reports. It should appear similar to the Excel spreadsheet shown in Figure 7-16.

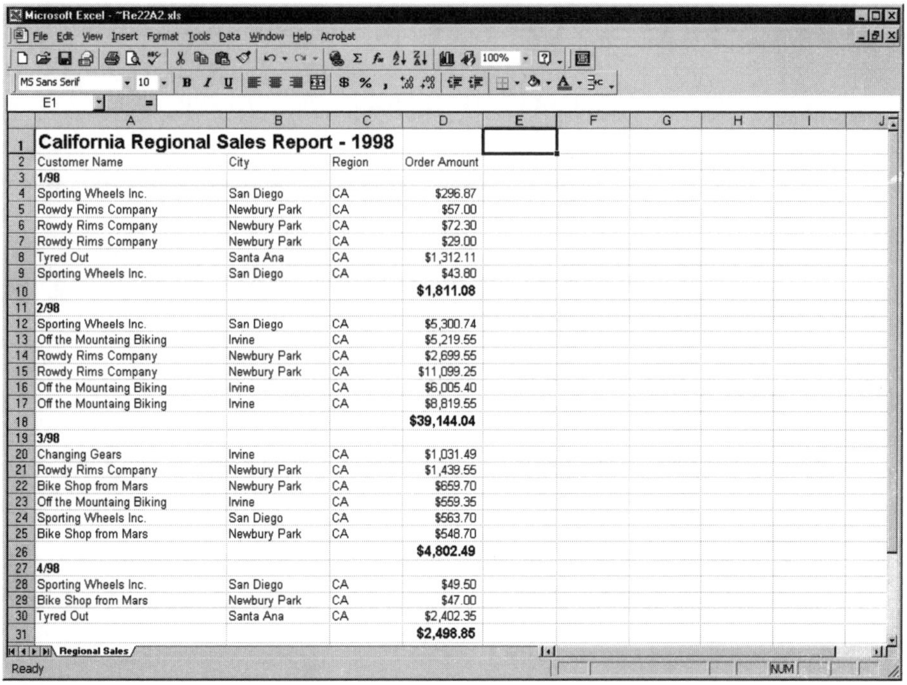

	A	B	C	D
1	California Regional Sales Report - 1998			
2	Customer Name	City	Region	Order Amount
3	1/98			
4	Sporting Wheels Inc.	San Diego	CA	$296.87
5	Rowdy Rims Company	Newbury Park	CA	$57.00
6	Rowdy Rims Company	Newbury Park	CA	$72.30
7	Rowdy Rims Company	Newbury Park	CA	$29.00
8	Tyred Out	Santa Ana	CA	$1,312.11
9	Sporting Wheels Inc.	San Diego	CA	$43.80
10				$1,811.08
11	2/98			
12	Sporting Wheels Inc.	San Diego	CA	$5,300.74
13	Off the Mountaing Biking	Irvine	CA	$5,219.55
14	Rowdy Rims Company	Newbury Park	CA	$2,699.55
15	Rowdy Rims Company	Newbury Park	CA	$11,099.25
16	Off the Mountaing Biking	Irvine	CA	$6,005.40
17	Off the Mountaing Biking	Irvine	CA	$8,819.55
18				$39,144.04
19	3/98			
20	Changing Gears	Irvine	CA	$1,031.49
21	Rowdy Rims Company	Newbury Park	CA	$1,439.55
22	Bike Shop from Mars	Newbury Park	CA	$659.70
23	Off the Mountaing Biking	Irvine	CA	$559.35
24	Sporting Wheels Inc.	San Diego	CA	$563.70
25	Bike Shop from Mars	Newbury Park	CA	$548.70
26				$4,802.49
27	4/98			
28	Sporting Wheels Inc.	San Diego	CA	$49.50
29	Bike Shop from Mars	Newbury Park	CA	$47.00
30	Tyred Out	Santa Ana	CA	$2,402.35
31				$2,498.85

Figure 7-16 California Regional Sales Report exported to Excel

Project Summary

Crystal Reports provides a number of export formats. In this project, we learned how to use the Excel extended format to export the contents of a report to an Excel spreadsheet.

✓ Mastery Check

1. Which of the Crystal Reports export formats provides a WYSIWYG view of your report?

_____

_____

2. Do you need to pay any additional licensing costs when distributing your report using Adobe Acrobat format?

_____

_____

3. What is the best format available for exporting to Microsoft Word when you want to retain the majority of the formatting features within your report?

A. Word for Windows

B. Rich Text Format (RTF)

C. Comma-Delimited Text (CSV)

D. Text (TXT)

4. What are the two options for exporting your report to Microsoft Excel?

_____

_____

5. Before you can export and e-mail a report from within Crystal Reports, what do you need to check first?

_____

_____

Module 8

Formulas and Functions

Goals

- Become familiar with the way that formulas are used
- Create formulas using the formula editor
- Use fields, functions, and operators within a formula
- Troubleshoot and debug formula text

The Crystal Reports formula language is a powerful tool for performing calculations, analysis, and summarization in your reports. In this chapter, you will learn how to use the formula language and create and debug your formulas, and you will gain an understanding of the behind-the-scenes processing that makes Crystal Reports tick. When you complete this chapter, you should be able to create formulas that add real value to your reports.

Formula Overview

By now, you are already somewhat familiar with the Crystal Reports formula language—it is used throughout the product in record selection, conditional formatting, and more. But the Crystal Reports formula language goes beyond those uses, giving you the ability to add complex calculations to your reports and manipulate report fields and elements.

If you have ever worked with a programming language or development tool, the Crystal Reports formula language will seem familiar. Likewise, if you can create formulas within Excel, you should easily be able to transfer your skills to Crystal Reports. (In fact, many of the functions work just like the ones you find in Excel.) But even if you are neither a crusty old software developer nor an Excel wizard, don't give up hope! Writing formulas within Crystal Reports is something that can easily be learned.

Formulas are written using the Crystal Reports formula editor, shown in Figure 8-1. A formula can consist of any number of database or other fields, operators, functions, text, numbers, and control structures such as If...Then statements. Before we can start our discussion of how formulas are put together, we need to look at the formula editor and see how it works.

Toolbar   **Functions**   **Operators**

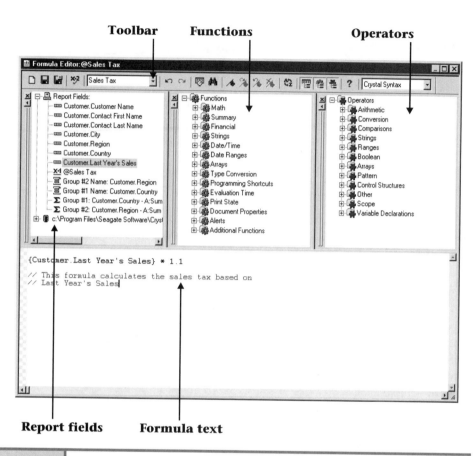

Report fields   **Formula text**

Figure 8-1   The Crystal Reports formula editor

8

Using the Formula Editor

To open the formula editor, choose Insert | Field Object, locate the Formula Fields section, right-click directly on top of the section header, and choose New. You will be prompted for a name for your formula. After you enter a name and click OK, the Crystal Reports formula editor opens.

The formula editor consists of five main areas:

- **Toolbar** The toolbar contains icons for creating a new formula, switching between formulas, finding and replacing, and more (see Figure 8-2).

- **Report Fields** The Report Fields section lists all fields present in your report, followed by your data source and all of the tables and fields contained within.

- **Operators** The Operators list contains a hierarchical view of all of the operators available within Crystal Reports: all of the arithmetic operators, variable declarations, comparison operators, and so on.

Note

Some of the operators, such as +, −, /, and *, you may find easier to just type, but you can double-click any operator in this list to add it to your report.

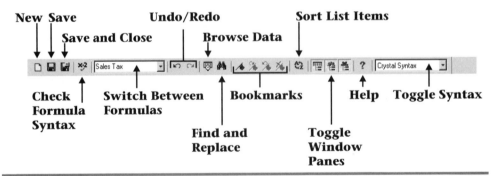

Figure 8-2 The formula editor toolbar

- **Functions**   The Functions section lists all of the functions that are available. These range from simple summaries (sum, average, and so on), to type conversion and field manipulation functions, to functions for complex statistical and financial analysis.

- **Formula Text**   The largest section in the formula editor is used for the formula text you enter. This area behaves similarly to other text editors (such as Notepad) or word processing applications you may have used in the past.

Tip

When working with formula text, you may notice that Crystal Reports uses different colors for words or phrases within your formula text. This color-coding is designed to identify reserved words, functions, and comments. You can control this and many other aspects of the formula editor's appearance by selecting File | Option | Editors.

Formula Syntax Overview

8

When creating a new formula, a good starting point is to write down exactly what you want the formula to do: for example "Calculate 10% sales tax on the Last Year's Sales field."

Once you have the English version of what you want to accomplish, you need to translate this into instructions in a language that Crystal Reports understands. Just as English has its own syntax that dictates how words and sentences are put together, so does Crystal Reports—in fact, it has two types of syntax: Crystal syntax and Basic syntax.

So now you need to translate the text version of your formula into a formula syntax that Crystal Reports understands. The first thing you need to learn is how to create a new formula in Crystal Reports.

Ask the Expert

Question: What is the difference between Crystal syntax and Basic syntax?

Answer: Crystal Reports 8.5 features two types of formula syntax: Crystal syntax and Basic syntax. Crystal syntax has been around the longest, and up until Version 8.0, it was the only choice for report developers. Crystal syntax has no direct relationship to any programming language (although it does resemble Pascal or dBase at times), so even experienced report and application developers needed to learn the syntax.

With the release of Crystal Reports 8.0 came a new formula syntax, Basic, with structures and functions that closely resemble those used in Visual Basic. For application developers, the Crystal Reports formula editor then became familiar territory, as they could apply the concepts and functions they knew from Visual Basic. New report developers who already know Visual Basic can immediately start to create Crystal Reports formulas using familiar functions, operators, and so on.

In Crystal Reports 8.5, both types of syntax can be used, side by side in different formulas in your report, according to your needs. When it comes to choosing a particular syntax, there is no clear winner—Crystal syntax is preferred by users who don't have a programming background, whereas Visual Basic programmers getting started with Crystal Reports will prefer Basic syntax. You will find most of the functions you need in both.

We will exclusively use Crystal syntax for the examples and projects in this chapter. Not only is it easier to learn, but also it will help you understand other areas where formulas are used, because all of the Crystal Reports features that are formula based (such as record selection and conditional formatting) rely on this syntax.

Working with Formulas

Before we look at the specific operators, functions, and text that make up formulas, we need to know some of procedures for working with formulas.

Creating a New Formula

Like most fields within Crystal Reports, formula fields can be created and inserted using the Field Explorer. To open the Field Explorer, select Insert | Field Object; you should see a section marked Formula Fields. To insert a new formula, right-click directly on top of the section marked Formula Fields and select New from the right-click menu, as shown in Figure 8-3.

The next dialog box that appears, shown in Figure 8-4, prompts you for a name for your formula. This name can be anything that makes sense to you and can include spaces, special characters, and so on. Enter a name for your formula field and click OK to proceed.

Tip

If you are going to create multiple formulas, you may want to consider a naming convention (for instance, SalesTax1, SalesTax2, and so on) for your formula names.

8

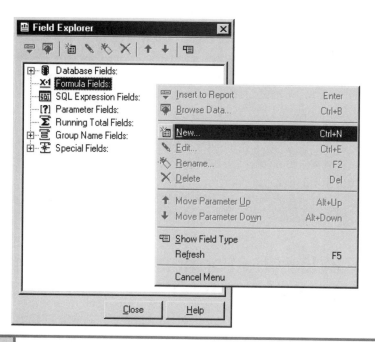

Figure 8-3   You create new formulas from the Field Explorer dialog box

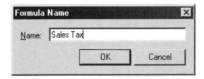

Figure 8-4 You will need to specify a name for your formula field

The formula editor will appear, and you can enter your formula text. At any time, you can check the syntax of your formula by clicking the X+2 button on the toolbar, but remember that Crystal Reports also performs a syntax check whenever you exit the formula editor.

When you are finished editing your new formula, just click the Save and Close icon located in the upper-left corner of the formula editor. You will then be returned to your report design or preview, where you will be able to insert your newly created formula onto your report.

Inserting a Formula into Your Report

Inserting your formula into your report may be easier from the Design tab of your report. Then you can see all of the sections clearly and understand where you are placing your formula field.

In the Field Explorer (which you opened by selecting Insert | Field Object), your formula should be listed under the section marked Formula Fields. From the Field Explorer, you can simply drag and drop your formula field onto your report. Alternatively, you can click to select the field and then press ENTER, which will attach the field to the tip of your mouse. When you have the field positioned on your report, simply click once to release the field and place it in your report. It's that easy!

Editing an Existing Formula

Crystal Reports identifies formula fields you insert into your report by placing the @ symbol in front of the name and curly braces around the name. For instance, the field name for the SalesTax1 formula would appear as {@SalesTax1}.

You can edit any existing formula that has been inserted into your report by locating the formula field you want to edit and right-clicking directly on top of that formula field. Then select Edit Field Object from the right-click menu, shown in Figure 8-5. This opens the Crystal Reports formula editor, where you can edit the formula field.

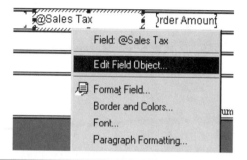

Figure 8-5 To edit an existing formula, right-click directly on top of the formula shown in your report

When you have finished editing your formula, click the Save and Close icon in the upper-left corner to close the formula editor and save your changes. You will be returned to your report's Design or Preview view, and your changes should be reflected in the formula results.

1-Minute Drill

● How do you create a new formula field?
● How can you tell whether a field is a formula field?

8

Renaming a Formula

Often you will want to revisit your report design and clean up the names of formulas, parameter fields, and running totals that appear in your report, to make it easier for other report designers or users to understand the logic behind your report design. To rename a formula, select Insert | Field Object to open the Field Explorer, locate the Formulas section, and find the formula you want to rename.

If you right-click directly on top of the formula name, you should see the Rename option in the right-click menu, shown in Figure 8-6. Select Rename to edit the formula name.

When you are finished editing the formula name, click anywhere outside of the formula name to accept your changes.

● To create a new formula field, select Insert | Field Object, locate the Formula section, right-click, and select New.
● Formula fields are prefixed with the @ symbol.

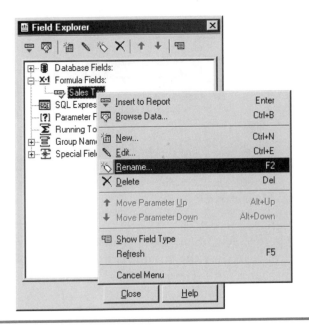

Figure 8-6 You can edit a formula name from the Field Explorer

─┤*Tip* ──

Even if the formula is used on your report multiple times or referenced in multiple
other formulas, the name change will be propagated everywhere it is used.

Creating Simple
Arithmetic Formulas

The most basic formulas use one of the simple arithmetic operators (+, −, *, /)
and perform a calculation. To see how arithmetic formulas are written, we are
going to write a Crystal Reports formula from the English version in the example
presented earlier that will calculate the sales tax on the Last Year's Sales field. We
know that there is a field in our database that contains the Last Year's Sales figure
and that the sales tax is 6 percent; the rest is up to Crystal Reports.

To create a simple arithmetic formula, you select Insert | Field Object and,
from the Field Explorer, right-click directly on top of the section marked
Formula Fields and select New from the right-click menu.

In the next dialog box, you enter a name for your formula field—in this case, Sales Tax—and click OK. The formula editor will appear and allow you to enter your formula text.

In this example, we need to locate the field Last Year's Sales. Look in the Fields pane of the formula editor, shown in Figure 8-7; you should be able to locate the Last Year's Sales field. All of the fields that appear in your report are located in the top section, marked Report Fields.

Tip

If you want to use a field that does not appear in your report, you can do so. All of the tables and fields in your data source are available in the list.

To place a reference to a particular field in your formula text, simply double-click directly on top of the field name, and the reference should immediately appear in the formula text below.

8

Figure 8-7   The Fields pane of the formula editor contains all of the fields that appear in your report, as well as all of the fields available from your report's data source

Tip

You'll notice that database fields are represented in the format of *TableName.FieldName*, with a set of curly braces around the entire lot. This format indicates that this is a database field.

All of the formula editor panes—Fields, Functions, and Operators—behave the same way; double-click any of the items listed, and it will be inserted into your formula text.

For this formula, not only do we need a reference to the Last Year's Sales field, we also need to do some simple arithmetic to multiply this field by 0.06 (6 percent). To do this, move to the Operators pane.

The Operators pane, shown in Figure 8-8, contains all of the operators that are available within Crystal Syntax. These operators are separated into categories: Arithmetic operators, Conversion operators, and so on.

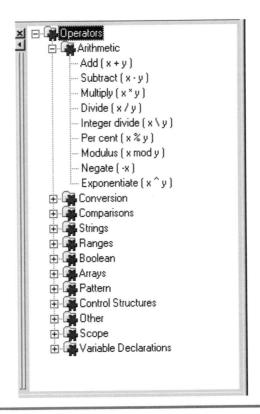

Figure 8-8   The Operators pane lists all of the operators available within Crystal Reports

In this instance, we know that multiplication is an arithmetic operator, so we can expand the Arithmetic section, locate the operator for multiplication (*), and then double-click it to insert it into our formula text.

Tip

It is also sometimes just as easy to type the operator yourself, once you are familiar with them all.

Now all we need to do is enter the 0.06 value. The formula should then look something like this:

```
{Customer.Last Year's Sales} * 0.06
```

Congratulations—you have just created your first arithmetic formula! If you were to place this formula in the Details section of your report, it would calculate the sales tax on the Last Year's Orders field for every customer in your report.

Project 8-1: Creating an Arithmetic Formula

Step-by-Step

1. From the Start | Programs menu, start Crystal Reports 8.5.

2. From the Welcome dialog box, select Create a New Crystal Report Document and the option Using the Report Expert.

3. From the Crystal Report Gallery, select the Standard report expert.

4. Click the Database button to open the Data Explorer and navigate to Xtreme Sample Database under the ODBC node.

5. From Xtreme Sample Database, select the Orders table and click the Add button. A green check mark should appear next to the table, and the Data tab should reflect your selection. When you are finished, click Close to close the Data Explorer and to return to the Report Expert.

6. On the Fields tab, select the fields that you want to see in your report. For this project, select the following fields:

- Orders.Order ID
- Orders.Order Date

8

- Orders.Ship Date
- Orders.Order Amount

To select a field, highlight it in the list on the left and click the right arrow button to move it to the list on the right.

7. Click the Finish button to preview your report.

8. Select Insert | Field Object.

9. From the Field Explorer, right-click directly on top of the section marked Formula Fields and select New from the right-click menu.

10. In the next dialog box, enter **Sales Tax** as the name for your formula field and click OK; the formula editor will appear, where you can enter your formula text.

11. In the Report Fields list in the upper-right of the dialog box shown in Figure 8-9, find the Orders.Order Amount field and double-click to add this field to your formula text.

12. In the Operators list on the right side of the formula editor, expand the Arithmetic node and double-click the Multiply (x * y) operator to insert it into your formula text.

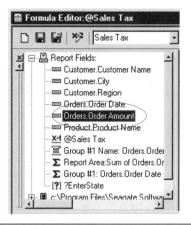

Figure 8-9   The Report Fields list contains all of the fields that are inserted onto your report, as well as any other fields that you can use

13. Click inside the box containing your formula text and add the number **0.06** at the end, so the formula reads:

```
{Orders.Order Amount} * 0.06
```

14. Click the Save and Close icon in the upper-left corner of the formula editor.

15. Insert the formula into your report into the Detail section, alongside the {Orders.Order Amount} field, as shown in Figure 8-10.

16. Preview your report to verify that the formula performs the correct calculation.

17. Save your report as **Order Listing Ch8-1.rpt**.

Project Summary

Using formulas in your report is a great way to add value to the information presented. Arithmetic formulas are the most common type of formula and can quickly be created using the Crystal Reports formula editor.

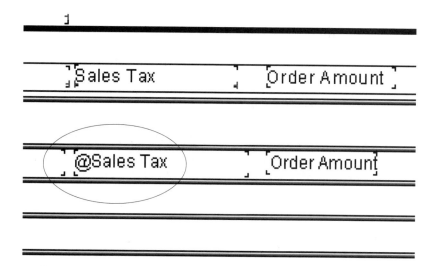

Figure 8-10   Place your new formula field beside the Order Amount field in the Details section

Using Crystal Reports Functions

Functions extend the Crystal Reports formula language and can be used to simplify complex calculations. If you expand the Functions pane of the Crystal Reports formula editor, you will see all of the functions available, arranged by function type. To insert a function into your formula text, simply locate the correct function and double-click directly on top of the function name.

Functions generally require one or more arguments, enclosed in parentheses and separated by commas. When you insert a function into your formula text, Crystal Reports automatically adds the parentheses and commas to indicate the arguments required, as shown here for the Round function:

```
Round ( , )
```

In this example, you would need to specify a number to be rounded and the number of decimal places to be used, like this:

```
Round ({Orders.Order Amount}, 2)
```

Crystal Reports includes over 200 functions, and keeping track of all of their names, parameters, and syntax can be tough. To find an explanation of a Crystal Reports function, go to Crystal Reports online help. First press the F1 key from within Crystal Reports (or select Help | Crystal Reports Help) to display the main Crystal Reports help screen, shown in Figure 8-11.

Select the Index tab, type **Functions** in the text entry box, and press ENTER. This should take you to the function listing by category. Click a category to see all of the functions of that type; click the link to go to the specific property page for a function. The help page lists the function's required and optional arguments, the information that is returned, and some examples of the function.

Tip

To copy a formula example from the help text, highlight the text you want and press CTRL-C to copy to the clipboard and then CTRL-V to paste the text into your formula.

Click the close button in the upper-right corner to close the Crystal Reports online help when you are finished.

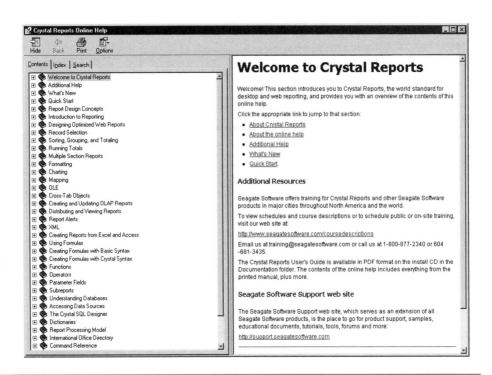

Figure 8-11   The standard help file; select Functions to see a description of all Crystal Reports functions and their parameters, plus examples

8

Summary Functions

You can use summary functions to summarize fields that appear in your report. The most common summaries are performed on numeric or currency fields, but you can also apply summary fields to other field types as well, to create a count of countries represented in a report, for example. There are a number of summary functions available within Crystal Reports, but the ones listed in Table 8-1 are the most popular.

Function	Purpose	Usage
Sum( )	Calculates the sum of a particular field.	Sum({Orders.Order Amount})
Avg( )	Calculates the average for a particular field.	Avg({Orders.Order Amount})

Table 8-1   Common Summary Functions

Function	Purpose	Usage
Min( )	Finds the minimum value.	Min({Orders.Order Amount})
Max( )	Finds the maximum value.	Min({Orders.Order Amount})
Count( )	Returns a count of all values	Count({Orders.OrderId})
Distinct Count( )	Returns a distinct count of all values, meaning that each item is counted once: for example, if you create a formula using DiscountCount({Orders.OrderId}), and if OrderId includes duplicates, each distinct record will nevertheless only be counted once.	DiscountCount({Orders.OrderId})

Table 8-1 Common Summary Functions (*continued*)

String Functions

The Crystal Reports formula language also includes a number of functions for manipulating string fields. String fields contain alphanumeric characters and are the most common field type; you can put just about anything in a string field.

One of the handiest tricks for working with strings is concatenation. Using special concatenation operators, you can combine two or more string fields for use in your report. For example, you may have separate First Name and Last Name fields in your data, but when this information is displayed on your report, you may want the information from the First Name field to appear, followed by a space and then the information from the Last Name field. Crystal Report's special concatenation operators make this possible.

There are two concatenation operators available within Crystal Reports: + and &. The plus sign (+) operator works just like the operator for adding two numbers together, but it applies to string fields. Using this operator, the formula for the example mentioned earlier would look like this:

```
{Customer.First Name} + " " + {Customer.Last Name}
```

Hint

The formula text in the middle—the space surrounded by double quotation marks—adds a space between the first and last names. Likewise, if you want to include any other specific text in the concatenation, you would enclose it in quotation marks, like this: "Mr" + {Customer.Last Name}).

The ampersand (&) concatenation operator can be used just like the plus sign:

```
{Customer.First Name} & " " & {Customer.Last Name}
```

The difference between the two operators is that the ampersand is a bit more flexible and can be used to concatenate numeric and other types of fields as well (without having to convert them to strings). Extending the earlier example, for instance, we can show the customer's first name, last name, and customer ID using the ampersand:

```
{Customer.First Name} & " " & {Customer.Last Name} & {Customer.CustomerID}
```

If you tried to create this same formula using the plus sign operator, Crystal Reports would return an error, as the Customer.ID field is numeric, and the + operator works only with strings.

Now that you know how to put strings together, what about ripping them apart? Crystal Reports includes a function called Subscript that numbers each position within a string, as shown in Figure 8-12.

Using the Subscript function, you can rip off a particular position of a string. For example, you can display the first initial of a customer's first name by using the following formula:

```
{Customer.First Name}[1]
```

Likewise, if you want to display both the first initial of a customer's first name followed by the customer's last name, you can combine the two types of string functions we have worked with so far, like this:

```
{Customer.First Name}[1] + " " + {Customer.Last Name}
```

JOHN
1 2 3 4

{Customer.First Name}[1] = J
{Customer.First Name}[3] = H
{Customer.First Name}[2 to 3] = OH

Figure 8-12 An example of how Crystal Reports works internally with string fields

In addition to ripping strings apart and putting them back together, Crystal Reports also includes functions for converting strings to all uppercase or lowercase characters, determining the length of a string, and trimming blanks from the start and end of a string. Table 8-2 lists some of the most commonly used string functions, along with an example of how each is used.

1-Minute Drill

● What operator is used to concatenate two strings?

● What is the difference between a count and a distinct count?

Type-Conversion Functions

In using Crystal Reports, you may run into problems related to the types of fields contained in a particular database. The field types may be set by the database or application developer, and you can't change them without changing the database or application itself. For example, you may find numeric information, such as an order amount, stored in a field that has been defined as a string field. With the information held as a string, you can't apply all of the handy summary functions within Crystal Reports.

If your organization has developed the database or application you are reporting from, you may be able to submit a change request to get the information stored in a more appropriate field type. But even if you are using a commercial application, or if your own database or application can't be

Function	Purpose	Usage
Uppercase( )	Converts strings to all uppercase.	Uppercase({Table.FieldName})
Lowercase( )	Converts strings to all lowercase.	Lowercase({Table.FieldName})
Length( )	Calculates the length of a string.	Length({Table.Fieldname})
Trim()	Deletes extra spaces at the start and end of a string.	Trim({Table.Fieldname})

Table 8-2   Common String Functions

● Either the plus (+) or ampersand (&) operator can be used to concatenate strings.
● A count counts every item; a distinct count counts only the unique items.

changed, don't give up! Instead of changing the type in the database, you can let Crystal Reports do the type conversion.

The Conversion section of the function list includes a number of functions that can convert field types. To find the appropriate function, first determine the target type (that is, what type do you want the field to be when you are done?). Then select a function from Table 8-3 and create a formula to perform the conversion.

With all of these functions, the formula text will look something like this:

```
ToText({Orders.Order Amount})
```

In this example, the values in the Order Amount field would be converted to text and displayed on your report.

Some of the functions listed in Table 8-3 may have additional, optional parameters that can be passed to control the output. For example, the ToText() function can be passed a number of decimal places to convert, as shown here:

```
ToText({Orders.Order Amount},0)
```

In this example, no decimal places will be displayed.

Remember that you can find a complete list of functions and their parameters by selecting Help | Crystal Reports Help | Search and searching on the function name.

8

Target Type	Function	Input
Text	ToText( )	Number, Currency, Date Time, Date, Time
Number	ToNumber( )	String, DateTime, Date, Time
Boolean	Cbool( )	Number, Currency
Currency	Ccur( )	Number, Currency or String
Date Time	CdateTime( )	Number, String, Date Time, Date, Time
Integer	CDbl( )	Number, Currency, String or Boolean
String	Cstr( )	Number, Currency, String, Date Time, Date or Boolean
Date	Cdate( )	Number, String, Date Time
Time	Ctime( )	Number, String, Date Time

Table 8-3   Type-Conversion Functions

Ask the Expert

Question: Why does my type-conversion formula fail with the message "The string is nonnumeric," even when I know that the field contains numeric information?

Answer: This error occurs when the values in the input and target fields cannot be resolved. For example, if you store Order Amount in a string field, database users can enter just about anything in that field (90.99, 100.00, N/A, and so on). If you create a formula to convert the Order Amount field from string to numeric, you will get the nonnumeric string error when the formula evaluates the value N/A.

Try to make sure that fields are used consistently; if you can't, you may need to use an If...Then statement to make sure that the field contains the correct values before you attempt to convert the field to another type. For the preceding example, the formula would look something like this:

```
If IsNumeric({Order.Order Amount) Then
     ToNumber({Order.Order Amount})
Else 0
```

You can apply similar logic to other errors as well. It is always a good idea to go back and check the source data to see if a rogue value is causing the error.

Tip

If the code here looks a bit scary, don't worry. If...Then formulas are discussed later in this module, in the section "Writing If...Then...Else Formulas."

Period Functions and Date Fields

Crystal Reports has a number of predefined periods for use with dates. Up until now, we have applied date periods only to record selection. However, you can use these same periods in the formula editor.

When you work with periods, Crystal Reports does all of the hard work for you. When you use the MonthToDate period, for example, Crystal Reports goes behind the scenes to check today's date and then builds a list of all of the dates that should be in MonthToDate—you don't ever need to lift a finger.

Periods within the formula editor are used most often in conjunction with an operator called *In* that determines whether a specific date is within that period. An example of the In operator is shown here. This snippet of formula text looks at the Order Date field, and if a date is in the period Over90Days, then it displays the words PAST DUE ACCOUNT! on the report.

```
If {Order.OrderDate} in Over90Days then "PAST DUE ACCOUNT!!"
```

You can also use this technique with the other date periods, listed here and found in the Date Ranges section of the Function list:

- WeekToDateFromSunday
- MonthToDate
- YearToDate
- Last7Days
- Last4WeeksToSun
- LastFullWeek
- LastFullMonth
- AllDatesToToday
- AllDatesToYesterday
- AllDatesFromToday
- AllDatesFromTomorrow
- Aged0to30Days
- Aged31to60Days
- Aged61to90Days
- Over90Days
- Next30Days
- Next31to60Days
- Next61to90Days
- Next91to365Days
- Calendar1stQtr
- Calendar2ndQtr
- Calendar3rdQtr
- Calendar4thQtr
- Calendar1stHalf
- Calendar2ndHalf

8

In addition to using these period functions with dates, Crystal Reports allows you to perform some simple arithmetic on date fields. For instance, Crystal Reports allows you to calculate the difference between two dates as well as add a number of days to a particular date, where the result is also a date field. Date arithmetic is especially handy when calculating aging or an invoice due date.

For example, suppose you want to look at the difference between when an order was placed and when it was actually shipped. Using the subtraction operator (–), you can find out how many days have passed:

```
{Orders.ShipDate} - {Orders.OrderDate}
```

Note

The value returned will be in days. If you want to determine how many years this represents (as when calculating age, for example), enclose the existing calculation in parentheses and divide by 365.25.

Likewise, if you want to calculate a due date, say in 30 days, you can add 30 days to the ship date, like this:

```
{Orders.ShipDate} + 30
```

Tip

You can add and subtract dates, but you cannot multiply or divide them.

Keep in mind that when performing calculations between dates, you may need to use parentheses to force the order of operation; Crystal Reports will display an error message when you try to combine calculations involving dates with calculations involving numbers.

Writing If...Then...Else Formulas

At this point, we have talked about simple arithmetic formulas, strings, date fields, and periods, but we really haven't gotten into adding any logic to your formulas. In a few examples earlier in this chapter, you might have noticed the use of If...Then statements. These statements work on the simple premise that if some condition is true, then something will happen (if A is true, then B will happen). Although Crystal Reports has a number of other structures available to perform this sort of logic, If...Then statements are by far the most popular.

To see how If...Then statements can be used, we are going to look at a common example. In the previous examples, we worked with an Order Amount field. If we want to flag all Order Amount values that are over $1,000, we can use an If...Then formula that looks something like this:

```
If {Orders.Order Amount} > 1000 then "Great Sale!"
```

If we place this formula right beside the Order Amount field on the detail line, this formula will be evaluated for every record in the table. Where the condition is true (for orders greater than $1,000), then the message "Great Sale!" will appear on the report, as shown in Figure 8-13.

With If…Then statements, we also have the option of adding an Else statement to the end. An If…Then formula states some condition and what will happen if the condition is true; an Else statement goes into effect when the If condition is *not* true.

Using the previous example, we can add an Else statement that prints "Good Sale" for all of the Order Amount values less than $1,000. That formula would look like this:

```
If {Orders.Order Amount} > 1000 then "Great Sale!" else "Good Sale"
```

In this case, if the condition is true (the Order Amount value is *greater* than $1,000), then the first condition will fire, printing "Great Sale!" on the report; otherwise, if the condition is false (the Order Amount value is *less* than $1,000), the "Good Sale" message will be printed.

8

Regional Sales

Customer Name	City	Region	Message	Order Amoun
January 1998				
Sporting Wheels Inc.	San Diego	CA		$296.87
Rowdy Rims Company	Newbury Park	CA		$57.00
Rowdy Rims Company	Newbury Park	CA		$72.30
Rowdy Rims Company	Newbury Park	CA		$29.00
Tyred Out	Santa Ana	CA	Great Sale!	$1,312.11
Sporting Wheels Inc.	San Diego	CA		$43.80
February 1998				
Sporting Wheels Inc.	San Diego	CA	Great Sale!	$5,300.74
Off the Mountaing Biking	Irvine	CA	Great Sale!	$5,219.55
Rowdy Rims Company	Newbury Park	CA	Great Sale!	$2,699.55
Rowdy Rims Company	Newbury Park	CA	Great Sale!	$11,099.25
Off the Mountaing Biking	Irvine	CA	Great Sale!	$6,005.40
Off the Mountaing Biking	Irvine	CA	Great Sale!	$8,819.55
March 1998				
Changing Gears	Irvine	CA	Great Sale!	$1,031.49
Rowdy Rims Company	Newbury Park	CA	Great Sale!	$1,439.55

Figure 8-13   An example of an If…Then formula in action

Regardless of whether you use the Else statement on the end, If…Then formulas can be combined with other functions and operators you have learned about in this chapter to create complex formulas to calculate the values you need.

Tip

Looking for more information on formulas and advanced topics? Check out *Crystal Reports 8.5: The Complete Reference* by George Peck, also from McGraw-Hill/Osborne.

Order of Operations

Crystal Reports follows the standard order of operations, reading formulas from left to right and following this order:

- Parentheses (any formula text enclosed in parentheses)

- Exponents (such as in X^2)

- Multiplication

- Division

- Addition

- Subtraction

When working with the order of operations, make sure that you use parentheses to force calculations that may not fall under the scope of normal algebraic equations.

For example, if you are attempting to calculate someone's age from a database field that holds the person's birthday, you could use a formula that looks like this:

```
Today - {Staff.BirthDate}
```

The only problem with this formula is that when you insert it onto your report, it shows the number of days, instead of years. An easy solution would be to divide by 365.25 (the 0.25 accounts for leap years), making your formula read like this:

```
Today - {Staff.BirthDate} / 365.25
```

When you attempt to save this formula or perform a syntax check, an error will occur, due to the order of operations. When Crystal Reports attempts to calculate the division part of the formula first, it doesn't understand how to divide a date field by 365.25, so an error results.

If you add parentheses to your formula, as shown in the following code, the formula will work correctly:

```
( Today - {Staff.BirthDate}) / 365.25
```

In these special cases, where a function or operator cannot be immediately used with the field you need, you will need to use parentheses to force a type conversion or other manipulation and then use the result in your formula.

As long as you keep the order of operations in mind and plan what calculations need to occur first, you should be all right.

Debugging Formulas

When you use formulas, you need to make sure that the syntax you have entered for your formulas is correct. As luck (or good design) would have it, Crystal Reports includes its own syntax checker, and it can be invoked in two ways.

When you save your formula by clicking the Save icon on the toolbar, Crystal Reports automatically performs a syntax check, just to make sure there are no missing parentheses, misspelled words, and so on. The second method of invoking the syntax checker is to click the X+2 icon, shown here.

You can click this icon at any time while working in the formula editor. If you are building a complex formula, you may want to check the syntax each time you add a major piece, to make sure that what you have entered is syntactically correct.

Regardless of which method you use, the syntax check Crystal Reports performs is very simple: it makes sure you have spelled all of the function and field names correctly, that you have used the correct function values, and so on. This is where debugging your formulas starts. The error messages returned by the syntax checker will eliminate a large number of your formula problems by making you use the correct syntax and notation.

Syntax error messages, such as the one shown in Figure 8-14, are returned to the formula editor, and the cursor will be moved to the area where the error occurred, to help you pinpoint and correct any problems.

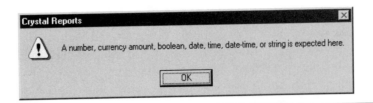

Figure 8-14 A typical Crystal Reports error message

A list of common errors and steps to resolve these errors is included here:

- **Unmatched Parentheses/Brackets** One of the most common errors in writing Crystal Reports formulas is leaving off a parenthesis or bracket. Make sure that for every opening parenthesis or bracket, there is a closing parenthesis or bracket to match it.

- **Function Parameters** Most Crystal Reports functions have required parameters. When you insert a function into your formula text, the function should display a set of parentheses, with or without commas; this will be your clue that parameters are required. Make sure that you not only provide the number of parameters required, but that you also use the correct data types.

Tip

If you are unsure of what parameters a function is asking for, use the F1 (help) key to locate the function in the Crystal Reports online help.

- **If...Then...Else** Unlike other programming languages, Crystal Reports does not require an EndIf or other statement to close a statement. With Crystal Reports, the end of an If...Then...Else statement is implied. However, for every If statement, you need a Then statement; the Else statement is optional.

Note

The same rules as for If...Then...Else statements also apply to any of the other control structures Crystal Reports uses, such as While...Do statements and For...Next loops.

Project 8-2: Using a Formula Function

If...Then...Else formulas provide an easy-to-use control structure for formulas and are used throughout Crystal Reports, not only for formulas to be inserted into your report, but also for conditional formatting and record selection as well. In this project, we are going to build on the report we created earlier in this chapter, this time using If...Then statements to print a message beside each order shown.

Step-by-Step

1. Open the Order Listing report (Order Listing Ch8-1.rpt) you created in Project 8-1.

2. Select Insert | Field Object.

3. In the Field Explorer, right-click directly on top of the section marked Formula Fields and select New from the right-click menu.

4. In the next dialog box, enter a name for your formula field—for this project, call it **Sales Message**. Then click OK.

5. In this example, you are creating a complex If...Then...Else formula to display a message depending on the Order Amount, as shown here:

Order Amount	Message To Be Displayed
>10,000	"Super Great Sale!"
>5,000	"Excellent Sale"
>1000	"Great Sale"
<=1000	"Good Sale"

Enter the following text in the formula editor:

```
If {Orders.Order Amount} > 10000 then "Super Great Sale!" else
  If {Orders.Order Amount} > 5000 then "Excellent Sale!" else
    If {Orders.Order Amount} > 1000 then "Great Sale" else
      "Good Sale"
```

Note

Make sure that when you are writing a compound If...Then...Else statement that your conditions appear in the correct order. When Crystal Report reaches a condition that is true, it will stop processing your If...Then...Else statement. In this example, we put the highest comparison value (> 10000) first, followed by the second highest, and so on. This ensures that if a sale is less than $1,000, it makes it all the way through the If...Then...Else statement and is properly evaluated.

8

6. When you are finished editing your If...Then...Else formula, click the Save and Close icon in the upper-left corner to close the formula editor and save your changes.

7. Drag the formula field onto your report, beside the formula field you created earlier for Sales Tax.

8. Preview your report to verify that the formula produces the correct messages, as shown in Figure 8-15.

9. Save your report as **Order Listing Ch8-2.rpt**.

Project Summary

If...Then statements can be used within your formulas to create complex calculations and add a logical control structure to your formula text.

Regional Sales

Customer Name	City	Region	Message	Order Amoun
January 1998				
Sporting Wheels Inc.	San Diego	CA	Good Sale	$296.87
Rowdy Rims Company	Newbury Park	CA	Good Sale	$57.00
Rowdy Rims Company	Newbury Park	CA	Good Sale	$72.30
Rowdy Rims Company	Newbury Park	CA	Good Sale	$29.00
Tyred Out	Santa Ana	CA	Great Sale	$1,312.11
Sporting Wheels Inc.	San Diego	CA	Good Sale	$43.80
February 1998				
Sporting Wheels Inc.	San Diego	CA	Excellent Sale	$5,300.74
Off the Mountaing Biking	Irvine	CA	Excellent Sale	$5,219.55
Rowdy Rims Company	Newbury Park	CA	Great Sale	$2,699.55
Rowdy Rims Company	Newbury Park	CA	Super Great Sale!	$11,099.25
Off the Mountaing Biking	Irvine	CA	Excellent Sale	$6,005.40
Off the Mountaing Biking	Irvine	CA	Excellent Sale	$8,819.55
March 1998				
Changing Gears	Irvine	CA	Great Sale	$1,031.49
Rowdy Rims Company	Newbury Park	CA	Great Sale	$1,439.55

Figure 8-15 The finished report showing the sales messages based on the Order Amount value

☑ *Mastery Check*

1. What are the two ways to check the syntax of your formula?

_____

_____

2. What is the difference between the two save options on the formula editor toolbar?

_____

_____

3. Where can you find a list of all Crystal Reports functions?

_____

_____

4. Which of the functions listed here can be used to convert numeric type fields to text?

   A. SendToText( )

   B. MakeText( )

   C. ToText( )

   D. Ctext( )

5. What operator can be used to concatenate string and numeric fields?

_____

_____

6. Where can you find the correct syntax for an If...Then statement?

_____

_____

8

Module 9

Advanced Record Selection

Goals

- Understand how advanced record selection can be used
- Use the formula editor to edit the record selection formula
- Select records based on lists and ranges of values
- Select records based on pattern matching
- Select distinct records

Record selection is key to good report design, narrowing the results of a report to extract only the information required. In Module 5, we had a first look at record selection and how it can be used with the Select Expert. In this module, we look at advanced record selection techniques, including a behind-the-scenes look at the record selection formula, how it is created, and how it can be used to create criteria to help narrow and focus report content.

Advanced Report Selection Overview

Up until now, you have used the Select Expert to select fields, specify operators, and add record selection to your reports. Behind the scenes, Crystal Reports has taken all of the options you have selected and created a record selection formula. The record selection formula, shown in Figure 9-1, can be viewed by clicking the Show Formula button, and directly corresponds to the fields, operators, and criteria you have entered using the Select Expert.

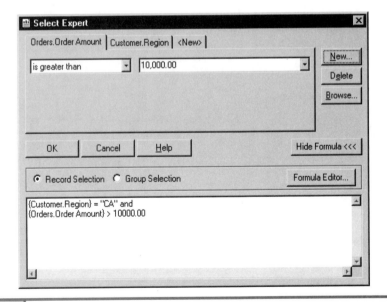

Figure 9-1 The Select Expert can be used to build record selection criteria

For the majority of your report designs, most of your record selection criteria can be created using the Select Expert. However, there will be times when you will want to use a different operator between the criteria in your record selection formula or use complex control structures to perform some decision making, branching, and so on.

For this type of advanced record selection, you need to edit the record selection formula directly. You can edit the formula within the Select Expert or by using the Crystal Reports Record Selection Formula Editor, shown in Figure 9-2.

The difference between using the formula editor here and, say, with a formula field you place on your report is that the formulas created for record selection must always return a Boolean (true or false) value. This Boolean value is applied to a record read from the database; if the value is true, then the database record is returned to Crystal Reports.

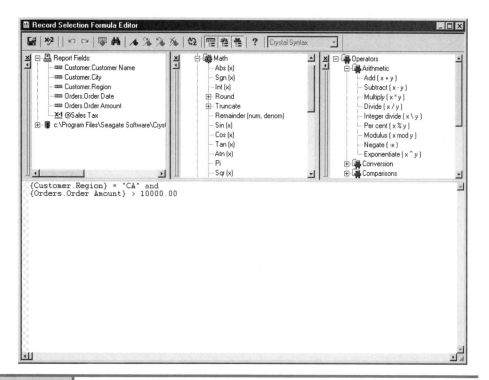

9

Figure 9-2 The Crystal Reports Record Selection Formula Editor can be used to edit the record selection formula directly

For example, suppose you are looking for records from a particular region, such as California. Your record selection formula might look something like this:

```
{Customer.Country} = "CA"
```

This record selection formula is evaluated for every record in the Customer table; where this condition is true, that record will be returned to the data set.

To make things more complicated, Crystal Reports puts no restriction on the formula text you enter for record selection, as long as the syntax is correct and the formula itself returns a Boolean value. Here is an example of a complex record selection formula in action:

```
If {Customer.Country}="CA" and {Customer.YTDSales}>10000 then
    If Length({Customer.PostCode}) > 5 then TRUE
Else If  {Customer.Country}="NC" and {Customer.YTDSales}>5000 then
    If Length({Customer.PostCode}) > 5 and
ToText({Customer.Phone})[1 to 3] <> "704" then TRUE
Else FALSE
```

This formula text is typical of that used for sending letters or marketing materials, checking the state of a particular customer, checking last year's sales figure, and finding valid postal codes. The point is that the formula can be as simple or as complex as you like, as long as the results are Boolean.

Editing the Record Selection Formula Using the Select Expert

We will start by looking at some of the most common scenarios in which you need to edit or create your own record selection formulas.

Tip

Remember that you can edit or create these formulas within the Select Expert by clicking Show Formula.

Using an OR Statement in Your Record Selection Formula

By default, Crystal Reports puts an AND statement between record selection criteria created using the Select Expert. That means if you use the Select Expert and specify two fields for record selection, the formula will look something like this:

```
{Customer.Region} = "CA" AND
{Customer.YTDSales} > 10000
```

When the report is run using these criteria, it will look for all customers in California who *also* have year-to-date (YTD) sales of greater than $10,000.

Changing the relationship between the two criteria is as simple as changing the word AND to OR by clicking the Show Formula button in the Select Expert and editing the text:

```
{Customer.Region} = "CA" OR
{Customer.YTDSales} > 10000
```

When your report is previewed now, it should bring back all records where *either* of the two conditions is met: the customer is in CA *or* has YTD sales of more than $10,000.

Note

If you go back to the Select Expert to edit the record selection formula, you may notice that the tabs are now dimmed, and the message "Composite Expression: Please Use Formula Editor to Do Editing" appears. Crystal Reports cannot translate this record selection formula back into a form that can be displayed using the tabs provided. From this point on, you will need to edit the record selection formula manually.

9

Using Comparison Operators

In Module 5, you had a first look at the simple record selection operators within the Select Expert. Whenever you select an operator in the Select Expert, it is translated into a record selection formula. As you become more familiar with creating and editing record selection formulas, you may want to enter the formula directly.

Table 9-1 lists the simple record selection operators and provides examples of their use.

Note

You can type these operators directly into your formula text or select them from the Operators list, in the Comparisons section.

If you get a bit confused when using these simple operators, remember that you are not looking for an outcome. If you were creating a formula to insert into your report, for example, you would want to have an outcome to display. With record selection formulas, your formulas should be written to return a true or false value: if the conditions you enter are met (are true), then the record will be returned from the database.

Retrieving Records Based on a List or Range of Values

Another handy function is the In operator, shown in Figure 9-3, which compares a field against a list of values that have been entered. We sometimes call lists of values an array, and the In operator will check to see if a particular value is within an array.

Tip

This corresponds to the record selection operator Is One Of

Name	Operator	Example
Is equal to	=	{Customer.Country} = "CA"
Is not equal to	<>	{Customer.Country} <> "CA"
Is less than	<	{Customer.YTDSales} < 10000
Is less than or equal to	<=	{Customer.YTDSales} <= 10000
Is greater than	>	{Customer.YTDSales} > 10000
Is greater than or equal to	>=	{Customer.YTDSales} >= 10000

Table 9-1   Record Selection Operators

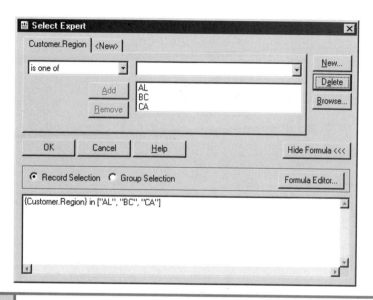

Figure 9-3   Using the In operator, you can build a list of values to be returned from the database

To use this operator to make a comparison against a list of values, you need to build that list or array yourself by entering each value between square brackets, separated by commas, as shown here:

```
{Customer.State} in ["KY", "NC", "SC"]
```

Tip

You can also use this formula to *not* select certain records, by putting parentheses around the entire statement and preceding it with the Boolean operator NOT: for example, NOT({Customer.State} in ["KY", "NC", "SC"]).

You are working with string fields here, so the values have to be enclosed within quotation marks. If you were comparing against a numeric field, such as Zip Code, the array would look like this:

```
{Customer.ZipCode} in [28720, 28009, 20092]
```

You can also use this operator to find parts of strings. From your work with formulas, you should remember that Crystal Reports can treat strings as an array (that's what enables you to rip off the first-position character, second-position

9

character, and so on). Applying that knowledge to record selection, you can easily search for a value within a particular string, such as the word *Bike* in the ProductName field:

```
"Bike" in {Products.ProductName}
```

This usage is case sensitive, so you may want to convert both the value you are searching for and the string itself into all uppercase or lowercase:

```
"BIKE" in UpperCase({Products.ProductName})
```

1-Minute Drill

● What type of value must the result of a record selection formula be?

● What operator is used when selecting from an array of values?

Retrieving Records Using Pattern Matching

Pattern matching is a powerful selection method; it allows you to build complex patterns to retrieve data using wildcards and single-character placeholders. You can use pattern matching in several ways; the two operators used most often are Starts With and Like.

Starts With looks at the first section of a string to determine whether there is an exact match. For example, you can use this function if you know the start of a particular company name. With the following formula, Crystal Reports will look at the first three letters of each customer name in your database and bring back only those records where there was a match for "MCA."

```
{Customer.Name} starts with "MCA"
```

Again, this type of formula is case sensitive, so you might want to change the case of the field to make things easier.

● The result of a record selection formula must be a Boolean value—that is, true or false.

● When selecting from an array of value, you use the In operator: for example, {Customer.State} in ["KY", "NC", "SC"].

The other pattern-matching operator is Like. Like uses wildcards (an asterisk for multiple characters and a question mark for a single character) to determine whether a string is located within another field. Using Like and the asterisk wildcard, for example, you can find all of the customers in your database with the word *David* in their name. The formula would look something like this:

```
{Customer.Name} like "*David*"
```

This formula would return results such as "David's Cycles" and "Mt. Davidson Bikes"—any records that contain the word *David* in the customer name.

Another way of using the Like operator is with a question mark, which indicates a single character. For example, assume that you are working with both U.S. and international customers and know part of a postal code stored in a string field, but you need to find all possible matches for the 287 prefix; you would enter a formula like this:

```
{Customer.PostCode} like "287??"
```

This formula would return the values 28720, 28721, and so.

The Like operator can be used with a combination of the asterisk and question mark wildcards, allowing you to create complex record selection formulas like the one shown here:

```
{Customer.Address3} like "*NC*287??"
```

This formula uses a combination of the two wildcards to find all customers that reside in North Carolina within the 287 range of area codes. This formula would return records containing text such as "Chimney Rock, NC 28720" and "Lake Lure, NC 28731."

Whether you use the wildcards alone or together, Like is powerful operator for use in record selection.

Retrieving Records That Are Not Null

Often, the data contained within your database and tables may include null values. A null value occurs in a database when no data has been entered into a particular field. Using a standard Crystal Reports function, you can retrieve only those records where a particular field is not null. You can use this function to return only valid records. For example, if you are creating a report that is grouped by state and some of the states in the database are null values (meaning that there is nothing entered for the state field), you can have a separate group just for those records with null values, as shown in Figure 9-4.

Tip

It is a good idea to point out any anomalies in your database to your database or application administrator—they should be able to fix any data entry errors that have occurred and make your reports more accurate.

Using the IsNull function in conjunction with the record selection formula allows you to find only those records that have a value entered. Like most of the other functions within Crystal Reports, IsNull requires a parameter to be passed:

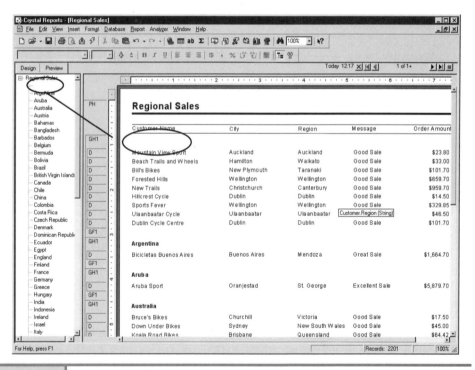

| **Figure 9-4** | An example of grouping with null records present |

in this case, it is the name of the field you want to check for null values. When this formula is evaluated, it will return True if the field is null and False if the field contains a value. To use this function with record selection and get rid of the null records, you need to apply the Not function to change the Boolean values around, as shown in Figure 9-5. So your record selection formula would look something like this:

```
Not (IsNull ({Customer.Country}))
```

Tip

Remember that any record selection formula you create should result in a Boolean value. True means that the record will be returned; False means that the record will be discarded.

Keep in mind that Crystal Reports also has another way of dealing with null values. Choose File | Report Options | Convert Null Field Value to Default; this will convert a null value to a space for strings or a zero for numeric fields in the report you are working with. This setting makes your record selection easier, as

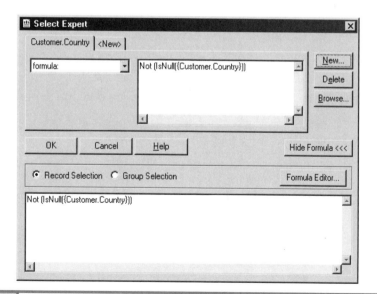

9

| **Figure 9-5** | The Crystal Reports formula language can be used to check for null values |

you don't need to use the IsNull function; you can simply compare the field to a blank or zero, as shown here:

```
{Customer.Country} <> " "
```

Tip

You can also use File I Options to set this option globally.

Which method you use is up to you. They both achieve the same results.

Project 9-1: Selecting Records Based on a List of Values

Using the Crystal Reports formula language, we can quickly create a selection formula to retrieve records based on a list of values we have entered. In this project, we are going to create a new Customer Listing report that will display only the customers from the regions we specify.

Step-by-Step

1. From the Start I Programs menu, start Crystal Reports 8.5.

2. From the Welcome dialog box, select Create a New Crystal Report Document, and from the same dialog box, select Using the Report Expert.

3. From the Crystal Report Gallery, select the Standard Report Expert.

4. Click the Database button to open the Data Explorer and navigate to the Xtreme Sample Database under the ODBC node.

5. From the Xtreme Sample Database, select the Customer table and click the Add button. A green check mark should appear next to the table, and the Data tab should reflect your selection. When you are finished, click Close to close the Data Explorer and to return to the report expert.

6. On the Fields tab, select the fields that you want to see in your report. For this project, select the following fields:

- Customer.Customer Name
- Customer.Phone
- Customer.Region
- Customer.Country

To select a field, highlight it in the list on the left and click the right arrow button to move it to the list on the right.

7. Click the Finish button to preview your report.

8. Select Report | Select Expert.

9. Select the field that contains the data you want to use to retrieve records; in this case, select {Customer.Region}. Then click OK to proceed.

10. Click the Show Formula button at the bottom to display the simple formula editor, shown in Figure 9-6.

11. Use the following syntax to build an array and use the In operator to select the records for only Kentucky, North Carolina, and South Carolina:

```
{Customer.Region} in ["KY", "NC", "SC"]
```

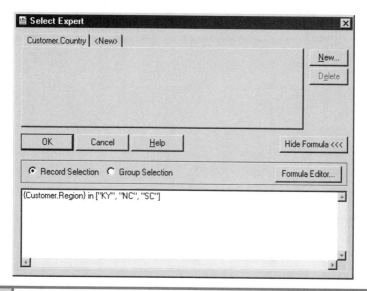

Figure 9-6   You can edit the record selection formula from directly within the Select Expert

Tip

To select everything except the records for this states, you can put parentheses around the entire statement and precede it with the Boolean operator NOT, like this: NOT({Customer.State} in ["KY", "NC", "SC"]).

12. With the record selection formula in place, click OK to accept your changes and return to the report design or preview.

When the report is previewed, it should now show only the customers in the three states specified, as shown in Figure 9-7.

13. Save your report as **Adv Record Selection Ch9-1.rpt**.

Project Summary

As you become more familiar with record selection and writing record selection formulas, you will be able to quickly create formulas to narrow the focus of your report to exactly the information you require.

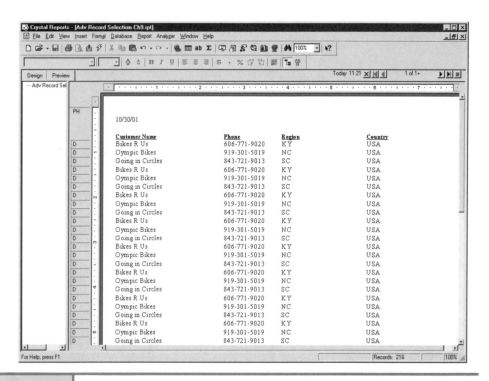

Figure 9-7   The finished report

Editing the Record Selection Formula Using the Formula Editor

Up until now, you have been editing the record selection formula from within the Select Expert. Although the Select Expert provides the quickest way to create or edit a record selection formula, you may have noticed that working with more complex formulas can be difficult. For instance, the Select Expert does not provide any way to check the syntax of your record selection formula, so you have to be careful to spell all of the field names, functions, operators, and so on correctly.

For more complex record selection formulas, you will probably want to use the formula editor. To invoke the Crystal Reports Record Selection Formula Editor, select Report | Edit Selection Formula | Record. The Record Selection Formula Editor, shown in Figure 9-8, is identical to the formula editor you use to create a formula to appear on your report, with one difference: the record selection

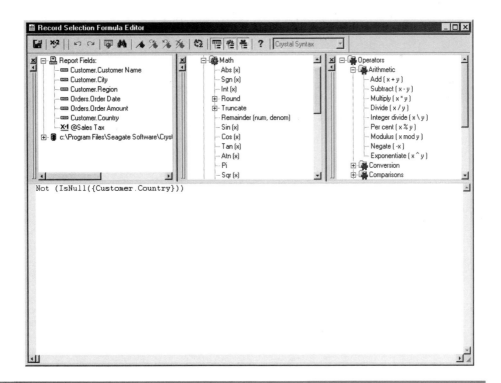

Figure 9-8   The Crystal Reports Record Selection Formula Editor

9

formula is used to retrieve records and cannot be inserted onto your report to display formula results.

Tip

You can also invoke the formula editor from the Select Expert by clicking the Formula Editor button.

Again, regardless of whether you use the simple text box within the Select Expert or the full formula editor, the results of your formula must be Boolean. When you are finished editing your record selection formula, click the Save and Close icon in the upper-left corner of the formula editor to return to your report design or preview.

Note

You may want to turn back to Module 8 for a review of the formula editor toolbars and other features.

Ask the Expert

Question: The data within my database is not very consistent. Some of the data is in uppercase letters, some is in lowercase letters, and some is in mixed-case style. Is there any way that I fix the problems I am having with record selection?

Answer: Record selection within Crystal Reports is case sensitive, which can cause problems if your database has values in different capitalization styles. One way of correcting these problems with case is to select File | Report Options and check the option for case-insensitive SQL data. (This option is also available globally when you select File | Options and choose the Database tab.) Another alternative is to use the Uppercase and Lowercase functions to make sure that the fields and values you are comparing use the same case: for example, Uppercase({Customer.Country}) = "USA").

Selecting Records Based on a Date

When working with date fields, you will find a couple of functions and constants very handy. The Month, Day, and Year functions can be used to strip out the month, day, or year from a date field; they are used whenever you need to isolate one element of a date field to make some calculation or comparison.

If you want to use the year component of a date field in record selection, you can create a record selection formula that looks something like this:

```
Year ({Invoice.InvoiceDate}) = 1997
```

Likewise, you can use the Month or Day function to strip the InvoiceDate field even further.

Tip

If you are working with a date/time field, you also have functions to strip out the hour, minute, and second components.

The second trick we have for working with dates involves constants that are generated by Crystal Reports. Knowing that it would be repetitive to have users enter the current date and/or time, Crystal Reports has a number of constants that are system generated to track these values:

- CurrentDate

- CurrentTime

- CurrentDateTime

9

Tip

If you have worked with Crystal Reports before, you may notice that the constant Today is no longer included in the function list within the formula editor. This value is still available for use, however, for backward compatibility.

You can use these functions just like you would any other values. For example, to select all of the invoices that were created up until today, you can enter this record selection formula:

```
{Invoice.InvoiceDate} < CurrentDate
```

And just as you can perform calculations using dates in formulas whose results you want displayed in your report, you can do the same in record selection formulas. If you want to change your record selection formula to return all of the invoices created within the last seven days, for instance, you can simply subtract the number of days from the current date, like this:

```
{Invoice.InvoiceDate} < (CurrentDate - 7)
```

Tip
Remember to use parentheses to force evaluation within your formula text.

With these tricks up your sleeve, record selection with dates should be a bit easier. If you frequently work with dates, keep reading: you are going to love working with periods!

Selecting Records Based on a Period

Crystal Reports has a number of built-in arrays of dates, called periods, for use in record selection. Periods provide a shortcut to some of the most commonly used types of record selection.

Tip
To use these period functions, you will need to make sure that your record selection formula is created using at least one true date field. If you do not have a date type field available in your database tables, but you do have a date contained within some other type of field (string, numeric, and so on) , you may need to perform type conversion before you can use the period functions.

In your record selection formula, you can check whether a value in your date field is within a particular period by using the In operator with the appropriate period name:

- WeekToDateFromSun
- MonthToDate
- YearToDate
- Last7Days
- Last4WeeksToSun
- LastFullWeek
- LastFullMonth
- AllDatesToToday
- AllDatesToYesterday
- AllDatesFromToday
- AllDatesFromTomorrow
- Aged0to30days
- Aged31to60days
- Aged61to90days
- Over90Days
- Next30days
- Next31to60days
- Next61to90days
- Next91to365days
- Calender1stQtr
- Calendar2ndQtr
- Calendar3rdQtr
- Calendar4thQtr
- Calendar1stHalf
- Calendar2ndHalf
- LastYearMtd
- LastYearYtd

If you want to bring back only records that are in the MonthToDate array, for example, your formula might look like this:

```
{Orders.OrderDate} in MonthToDate
```

Keep in mind that these date periods are calculated using the print date within Crystal Reports. By default, this print date is set to the system date on your computer, but you can change the print date by selecting Report | Set Print Date/Time and using the dialog box shown in Figure 9-9. This will trick

9

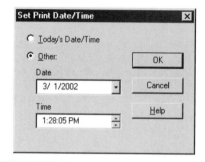

Figure 9-9 You can set the print date and time for your report

Crystal Reports into reporting that it is a different date and time. After you have changed the print date, all of the period operators will use that as their frame of reference when determining what dates should be in a particular period.

Tip

If you do change the print date and time, don't forget to change it back once you are finished; or if you are going to leave it set to that date, use a text object to make a note that this option has been changed.

Another handy approach when creating record selection formulas is to use the current date and time in calculations to provide a reference point to find dates and times that don't fit the periods listed earlier.

To use the current date or time in record selection, you can use the reference Today or CurrentDate—they are interchangeable. For example, you can use the current date and time to find all records updated in the last 48 hours, combining the current date and time with the simple arithmetic subtraction (–) and addition (+) operators.

Tip

You cannot use the multiplication (*) and division (/) operators with dates.

If you want to return all of the records that have been updated in the last two days, your formula would look something like this:

```
{Customer.UpdateDate} <= Today - 2
```

Today is a reserved word that returns today's date. When you subtract 2 from Today, the result is the date value from two days ago. Any records updated since then would be returned.

Tip

You can also substitute PrintDate for Today if you want to take advantage of the PrintDate functionality mentioned earlier.

Using Parameter Fields with Record Selection

In Module 6, we had a first look at parameter fields within Crystal Reports. Parameter fields provide an easy way to prompt users for required information to apply in your record selection formula. In its simplest form, this type of record selection formula looks like this:

```
{Customer.Region} = {?EnterRegion}
```

Here, {?EnterRegion}is the parameter field you have created, and {Customer.Region} is the field you are comparing against.

You can also use parameters within the record selection formula to create even more complex record selection, giving users the ability to select exactly what they want to see in the report. In the following example, users can be prompted to enter a particular region, or they can enter ALL to indicate they want the report to provide information on all regions:

```
If {?EnterRegion} = "ALL" then True else
{Customer.Region} = {?EnterRegion}
```

When you preview your report, you should be prompted for the parameter field you have created, and this value should be passed through to record selection. When the record selection formula is evaluated for the ALL value, a true value

9

will always be passed, and all records will be returned. Where another value is entered (for example, a specific region), Crystal Reports will use that value when evaluating the {Customer.Region} = {?EnterRegion} part of the formula, and where it is true, it will return that record to your report.

Tip

For more information on using parameters with complex record selection, check out *Crystal Reports 8.5: The Complete Reference* by George Peck (McGraw-Hill/Osborne, 2001).

Ask the Expert

Question: My report returns multiple records showing the same information. How can I prevent the display of duplicate records?

Answer: When using Crystal Reports with multiple tables, you may sometimes retrieve duplicate records due to the way the database tables are joined together. In SQL, you can use the SELECT DISTINCT command to return only distinct records in response to your query. Remember from earlier discussions that you cannot edit the SELECT portion of the SQL query that Crystal Reports generate, but you can ask Crystal Reports to select distinct records through the user interface by following these steps. First, choose Database | Select Distinct Records. Then select Database | Show SQL Query to verify that the first line of the generated SQL statement has been changed to read SELECT DISTINCT.

If you are working with a PC-type database (Dbase, Paradox, and so on) that does not support the DISTINCT clause, you may get an error and will need to remove this setting before your report can be used.

Performance Considerations

Crystal Reports 8.5 features improved report-processing performance: as much as ten times the processing performance of version 7.0. Nevertheless, databases continue to get larger, and queries continue to get more complex. There are a few performance considerations to keep in mind when creating record selection formulas for Crystal Reports:

- Try to use only database and parameter fields when creating record selection formulas. If you use a formula field in your record selection formula, Crystal Reports must evaluate this formula first before it can apply record selection, and this will drag down database performance.

- Spend a few minutes with your database or application administrator to learn which fields in your database are best used for record selection. Databases will often have indexed fields, and Crystal Reports can take advantage of the indexes.

- If you find you are applying the same record selection formula to multiple reports, you may want to ask your database administrator about creating a view or stored procedure to serve as the basis of your report. Some databases do not support views or stored procedures, but for databases that do, you can reduce the complexity of your record selection and your development time by reporting from a particular view of the data or letting a stored procedure do the record selection work for you.

9

✓ Mastery Check

1. What is the relationship between record selection criteria you create using the Select Expert?

_____

_____

2. Which operator is used to denote not equal to?

_____

_____

3. Where can you find the settings to control the formula editor's appearance and behavior?

_____

_____

4. Which of these record selection formulas is incorrect:

   A. {Customer.Country} in ["USA", "Canada", "Mexico"]

   B. {Customer.Country} in [USA, Canada, Mexico]

   C. {Customer.Country} in [USA and Canada and Mexico]

   D. {Customer.Country} in ("USA", "Canada", "Mexico")

5. Where would you find the setting to select only distinct records?

_____

_____

Module 10

Working with Sections

Goals

- Understand how sections are used within a report
- Learn how to insert, remove, and resize sections
- Format sections
- Create multicolumn reports

Sections Overview

A Crystal Report's design can be divided into several sections. In Module 2, we took a brief look at the basic sections that make up a Crystal Report. By default, each report you create has a report header and footer, a page header and footer, and a Details section. (It will also have a group header and footer if you have any groups inserted into your report.)

For basic reporting, chances are good that you won't need more than one occurrence of any of these sections, but Crystal Reports allows you to create multiple sections and set a number of section-specific properties to assist with tricky formatting problems you may encounter with complex reports.

For example, the multiple section concept could come into play if you were creating form letters for your company and wanted to show two different return addresses on the letter: one for your head office and one for a regional office, as appropriate. Using multiple sections, you could create two page headers, as shown in Figure 10-1, and use conditional formatting to show the correct header for each page, based on the customer's address.

To create this type of report, you need to insert two page headers—Page Header a and Page Header b—and apply a little *conditional formatting*. Conditional formatting may be something new to you, but your knowledge of formulas from previous modules will help you understand it. Conditional formatting allows you to create a formula that, if the results of the formula are true, causes something to happen. For example, when creating two page headers, you can create two formulas: where the state is equal to CA, you can display a header with a California return address, and where the state is any other value, you can display a North Carolina return address. If this sounds like a bit much, don't worry—we'll take it one step at a time!

This is just one example of how multiple sections can be used to solve common formatting problems. Before we get into the specifics of how sections can be used, though, let's see how to perform some basic operations, such as inserting, removing, and merging sections.

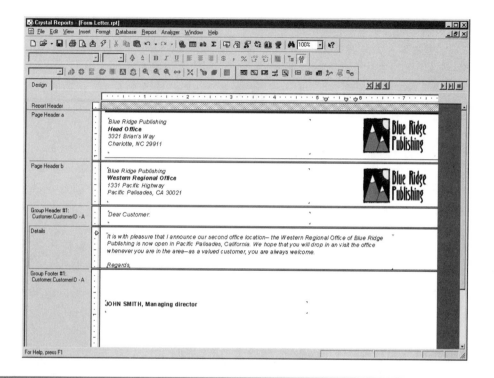

Figure 10-1   An example of multiple sections in a report

Working with Sections

10

When working on the Design tab of Crystal Reports, you will note that each section has its own area on the left side of the design environment. If you were to right-click on top of this area, a menu would appear, similar to the one shown in Figure 10-2.

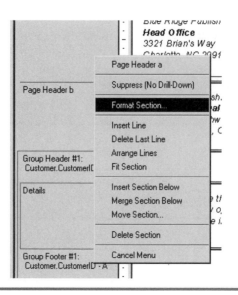

Figure 10-2 Each section can be edited from the Design tab

This menu provides a quick and easy means of working with the different sections in your report and is where you will find the basic section functions (insert, merge, and so on).

Inserting a New Section

The example at the beginning of this module described a situation in which you might want different page headers for your report to display two different return addresses for a form letter report. To insert a new Page Header section into your report, all you need to do is locate the Page Header section, right-click directly on top of it, and select Insert Section Below. Crystal Reports would then insert a section immediately below the page header, as shown in Figure 10-3.

You'll notice that Crystal Reports has named this section Page Header b, and your original page header has been named Page Header a. Crystal Reports follows this naming convention throughout the different sections, so if you were to create a section below Page Header b, it would be labeled Page Header c, and so on.

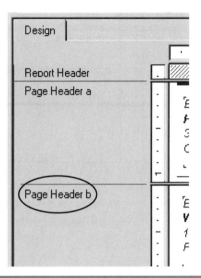

| **Figure 10-3** | Sections you have inserted appear below the original section |

Deleting a Section

When working with sections, you can also delete any unused sections you may have inserted by right-clicking the section and selecting Delete Section from the right-click menu. Any objects that you have placed within that section will also be deleted, so if you want to keep any of them, make sure that you move them out of the section before you delete it.

Note

You will be unable to remove the following sections from your report using this method: the report header and footer, the page header and footer, the group header and footer, and the Details section. You can delete the group header and footer, however, by deleting the group they relate to.

Resizing a Section

Another handy trick when working with sections is resizing. Sections can be resized to accommodate whatever information you need to insert, but they

10

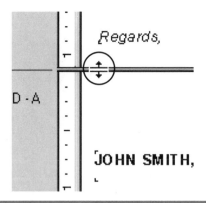

Figure 10-4 You can resize a section by dragging its bottom border

may not be larger than the page itself. The first step in resizing a section is to locate that section in the Design view of your report. At the bottom of each section is a divider line. Move the mouse pointer over the divider line until the pointer changes to a double-headed arrow with two horizontal lines, as shown in Figure 10-4 above.

Using the mouse, you can drag the bottom border of the section up or down to resize. It helps if you select an area that is free of objects; otherwise you may end up moving the object instead of the section border.

Tip

You can always use CTRL-Z to undo your action if you accidentally move an object instead of a border line.

Splitting a Section

Splitting a section separates that one section into two: for instance, the Details section becomes Details A and Details B. Splitting is tricky and takes a little practice, but it comes in handy when you don't want to move a lot of objects around to get two separate sections.

To split a section of your report, locate the section you want to split and move the mouse to the left along the bottom of the section until you reach the intersection of the ruler line and the section's divider line. The mouse pointer should turn into the split icon, shown in Figure 10-5, with a *single* horizontal line and an up-and-down arrow.

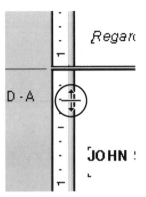

Figure 10-5	The split icon indicates that you can drag another section out of the one you are currently working with

Use the split icon at the intersection of the ruler line and bottom of a section, dragging the mouse down to split the section into two.

Note

This technique takes a little practice. Remember that a double line with an up-and-down arrow indicates that you can resize the section, whereas a single line with an up-and-down arrow indicates that you can split the section.

After spending a half hour trying to get the technique down, a lot of people find it is just easier to insert another section and drag all of the objects down from the original section. Either way, the results are the same; the choice of method is up to you.

10

Merging Report Sections

When working with multiple sections, you may occasionally need to merge sections together to clean up or simplify the report's design. To merge two sections together, right-click the section above the one you want to merge and select Merge Section Below from the right-click menu. When you merge two sections, all of the objects within those sections are retained. For example, in Figure 10-6, Page Header a and Page Header b have been merged into one section.

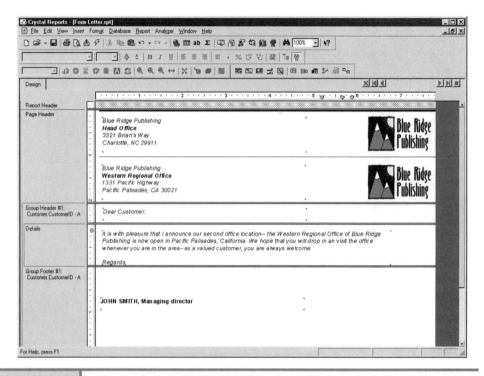

Figure 10-6   When you merge two sections, the objects within those sections are combined into one section

---

Tip

This can be especially handy if you are working with multiple sections and discover that you no longer need to split a section into two.

Note that you can merge only sections of the same type. For example, you can merge Page Header a and Page Header b, but you cannot merge Report Header a and Page Header a.

Changing the Order of Sections

You can also change the order of sections that appear in your report without having to delete and re-create them. To change the order of sections, simply drag and drop sections to their new locations. When you press the mouse button to drag, the cursor should change to the hand icon, shown in Figure 10-7.

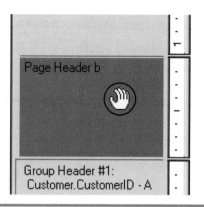

| **Figure 10-7** | When your cursor changes to the icon shown, you can drag and drop your section |

When you have positioned your section where you want it, release the mouse button to drop it into place. It's that simple.

1-Minute Drill

- When two sections are merged, what happens to the objects within the sections?

- What happens to the objects in a section when you delete the section?

Formatting Sections

10

The Section Expert (found by selecting Format | Section) is key to understanding how the different sections of a report work together. All of the sections of your report are listed, as shown in Figure 10-8, and all of their formatting options are available from this dialog box.

The Section Expert provides a number of options that deal specifically with creating, rearranging, and deleting sections of your report. Although some of these are also available from the right-click menu you used earlier, using the

---

- The objects are all placed together in one section.
- All of the objects within the section are deleted as well.

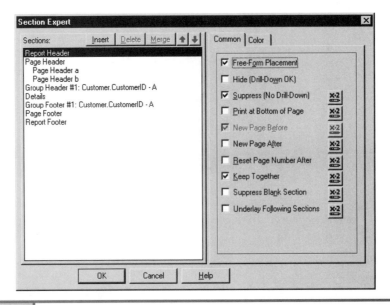

Figure 10-8 The Section Expert contains all of the formatting options for sections contained in your report

Section Expert can be better for showing you the big picture. These options can be found at the top of the Section Expert dialog box:

- **Insert**   Inserts a new section into your report.

- **Delete**   Deletes a section that you have inserted into your report.

- **Merge**   Takes all of the objects from two sections and merges them into one section.

- **Move Up/Move Down**   Changes the order of multiple sections you have inserted into your report.

Each section in your report also has a number of specific options associated with it that control the section's behavior and appearance. Here are the available options:

- **Free-Form Placement**   Allows you to place objects anywhere within a section, disregarding the underlying grid and/or guidelines.

- **Hide (Drill-Down OK)**   Hides a section of your report but still allows drill down, to show this section when required.

- **Suppress (No Drill-Down)**   Completely suppresses a section of your report. You will not be able to drill down to show this section.

- **Print at Bottom of Page**   Prints an entire section of your report at the bottom of the page.

- **New Page Before**   Creates a page break immediately preceding a section.

- **New Page After**   Creates a page break immediately following a section.

- **Reset Page Number After**   Resets the page number immediately following a section.

- **Keep Together**   Attempts to keep a particular section on one page to eliminate orphaning of sections split between multiple pages.

- **Suppress Blank Section**   Suppresses sections that do not contain any data, text fields, and so on.

- **Underlay Following Sections**   Makes a section transparent and places it underneath the section immediately following.

- **Format with Multiple Columns (Details section only)**   Creates multicolumn reports for mailing labels and so on.

- **Reserve a Minimum Page Footer (Page Footer section only)**   Maintains the minimum page footer required by your printer or report design.

- **Color**   Enables and sets the background color for a particular section.

10

Tip

We will be discussing the most commonly used options later in this module.

Ask the Expert

Question: When I am previewing my report, how can I tell which section is which?

Answer: When previewing your report, you will be unable to view the names of the different sections until you set a default option by following these steps. First, select File | Options. Click the Layout tab, which contains many user environment settings for Crystal Reports. Next, select the Show Section Names in Preview option, as shown here.

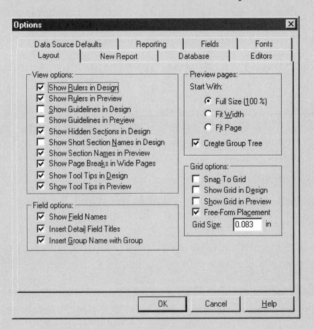

Finally, click OK to accept your changes and return to your report's design or preview.

Hiding or Suppressing a Section of Your Report

Earlier in this book, you learned how to create drill-down reports by hiding different sections of your report, and you learned how to create summary reports by suppressing the details of your report. The Section Expert provides the same functionality and provides a quicker method for hiding or suppressing multiple sections. From the Section Expert, you will need to click to highlight a particular section name and then select the Hide or Suppress property from the options shown on the right side of the page.

This has the same effect as right-clicking the section name in Design view and selecting Hide or Suppress from the right-click menu.

Showing Hidden Sections in Design View

When you return to your report's design, it is sometimes difficult to determine what sections are present or hidden, but you do have some options to help you. To show all of the hidden sections on the Design tab, select File | Options and click the Layout tab. Then select the Show Hidden Sections in Design option and click OK to accept your changes. When you return to your report's design, the hidden sections in your report will now appear on the Design tab, but will be dimmed, as shown in Figure 10-9.

Ask the Expert

Question: Is there any way to remove blank space in a section?

Answer: When you are working with multiple sections, your report design can sometimes get a bit crowded, with sections taking up more room than they should. One of the tricks for removing blank space in a section and generally tightening up the spacing is to use the Fit Section option, available when you right-click directly on top of a section. This should tighten up the section spacing, and the bottom bar of the section you are working with should move up to the bottom of the lowest object in the section.

10

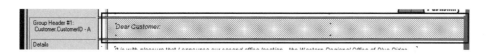

Figure 10-9   Hidden sections will appear dimmed on the Design tab

Printing a Section at the Bottom of the Page

Another handy feature is the ability to print a section at the bottom of the page. This technique can be used with invoices to print a remittance slip or with form letters to include a return comments form. To print a section of your report at the bottom of each page, first identify the section you want to print.

Note

This section will be shown above the bottom page margin when the report is previewed or printed, but it will appear on the Design tab in its correct place.

From the Section Expert, select the Print at Bottom of Page option, and this section will be printed at the bottom of the page, as shown in Figure 10-10.

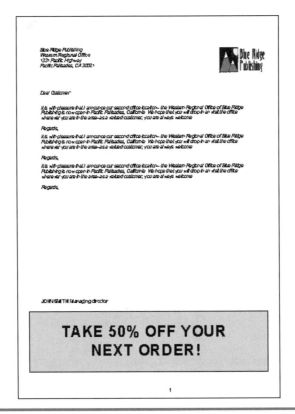

Figure 10-10   An example of Print at Bottom of Page in action

Where the section appears in your report depends on the section you select. If you select the Report Header section, for example, the section will be printed at the bottom of the very first page and nowhere else (and likewise, setting this option for the Report Footer section will print the section at the bottom of the very last page).

Creating a Page Break Before or After a Section

Often you will want to create a page break before or after a section. This technique can be used with invoices (to place a page break between invoice numbers) or form letters (to print a separate page for each letter) or anywhere else you need to add a break. To create a page break before or after a section, you can set the properties within the Section Expert, using New Page Before or New Page After. When your report is previewed or printed, a page break will occur in the location you specified.

Tip

If you use New Page Before, the first page of your report may be blank. This occurs because first the report header appears, and then a page break occurs. To eliminate this problem, suppress the Report Header section.

Resetting Page Numbering After a Section

When working with statements, invoices, form letters, or reports created for distribution to a number of different parties, you can reset the page numbering after a specific section, so that the pages in each section show the correct page numbers. To reset page numbering after a section, first make sure that you have a page number field inserted onto your report. If you don't, there won't be any way to tell whether this option actually worked.

Using the Design view of your report, select Insert | Field Object. Expand the Special Fields section of the Field Explorer and, from the list, select either the Page Number or Page N of M field and drag it onto your report.

Click to select the last section of the page. For example, in an invoice statement, where you might be grouping using a Customer Name field, this would be the group footer for the Customer Name group.

Using the properties on the right side of the Section Expert, select Reset Page Number After, as shown in Figure 10-11, and then click OK to return to

10

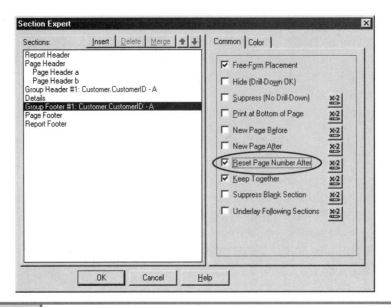

Figure 10-11 You can reset page numbering after a particular section using the Section Expert

your report's design or preview. When you preview your report, the Page Number or Page N of M field that you have inserted should be reset after the section you have specified.

Suppressing a Blank Section

You can suppress a blank section to tighten up your report's design and get rid of any unwanted white space. This technique is frequently used when working with addresses. For instance, you can create two different sections for the address lines (Address and Address2 in Figure 10-12) and enable the Suppress a Blank Section option whenever there is no Address2 field. Then, when your report is printed, it won't appear as if there is a line missing from the address.

To suppress a blank section, use the Section Expert, select a particular section, and from the properties on the right side of the page, select Suppress If Blank.

Group Header #1a: Customer.CustomerID - A		Customer_Name
Group Header #1b:		Address
Group Header #1c:		Address2 ←
Group Header #1d: Customer.CustomerID - A		City, State, Postal_Cod
		Dear Customer:

Suppress this section if there isn't a second line for the customer's address.

Figure 10-12   Using the Section Expert, you can suppress blank sections within your report

Creating a Multicolumn Report

So far, all of the report designs we have looked out have been single column—in other words, all of the fields and elements of the report were simply listed down the page. Through some special section formatting, reports can be created with multiple columns, allowing you to create flexible reports for phone lists, contact lists, and any other listing that includes a large amount of information within a set area.

To create a report with multiple columns, you create a report as you normally would, using the Standard Report Expert, inserting any fields you want to appear in your report, as well as any groups or summary fields. Once you have a preview of your report, it is time for some multicolumn magic.

In the Section Expert, you may have noticed that whenever you selected the Details section of your report, an additional option—Format with Multiple Columns—appears at the bottom of the list on the right side of the page. Click the check box next to this option to format your report with multiple columns for more complex report designs.

Once you have selected this option, a third tab will appear at the top of the list of options, marked Layout. Click this tab to open the options shown in Figure 10-13.

First you need to choose the width for your columns and the horizontal and vertical gaps between columns.

10

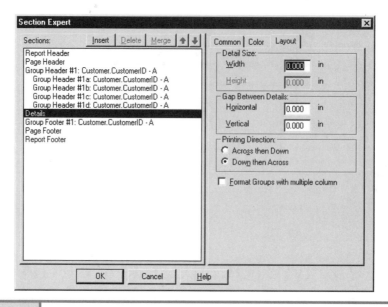

Figure 10-13 The Layout tab will not appear in the Section Expert unless you have specified you want the details section formatted with multiple columns

---

Tip

If you have a ruler, it will definitely come in handy for this section.

Using this dialog box, you also need to select a print direction using the radio buttons: either Across Then Down or Down Then Across (the default). If you also want to format any groups you have inserted with multiple columns, select the check box at the bottom of the dialog box.

Now click OK to accept your changes and return to your report's design or preview. The Design view of your report will display a gray box indicating the column size you have indicated, as shown in Figure 10-14. Use this box as a guide to rearrange your report fields to fit within the columns you have created.

Figure 10-14 The gray outline indicates your column size

If you need to resize the column or change the horizontal or vertical spacing or anything else, you will need to return to the Section Expert by selecting Format | Section and selecting the Details section.

Project 10-1: Creating a Form Letter Using Multiple Sections

One of the many uses of multiple sections is with reports for form letters or billing statements. In this project, we are going to use what we now know about sections and formatting to create a form letter that will go out to the customers of our fictional company. We will create a report that combines contact information from the Customer table with text we have created ourselves.

Step-by-Step

1. From the Start | Programs menu, launch Crystal Reports 8.5.

2. In the Welcome dialog box, select Create a New Crystal Report Document and, in the same dialog box, select Using the Report Expert.

3. From the Crystal Report Gallery, select the Standard Report Expert.

4. Click the Database button to open the Data Explorer and navigate to Xtreme Sample Database under the ODBC node.

5. From Xtreme Sample Database, select the Customer table and click the Add button. A green check mark should appear next to the table, and the Data tab should reflect your selection. When you have finished, click Close to close the Data Explorer and return to the report expert.

6. On the Fields tab, select the fields that you want to see in your report. For this project, select the following fields:

- Customer.Customer Name
- Customer.FirstName
- Customer.LastName
- Customer.Last Years Sales

To select a field, highlight it in the list on the left and click the right arrow button to move it to the list on the right.

7. On the Group tab, select the Customer ID field and click the right arrow button to move it to the list on the right. When your report is created, a group will be inserted using this field.

8. Click the Finish button to preview your report.

10

9. To create a form letter, you need to look at the different sections of your report and decide which section corresponds with what part of a standard letter. A list of sections has been included for you here. Resize each of these sections to accommodate the information shown by dragging the bottom line of each section downward.

- **Group Header #1**   The customer name and address
- **Details**   The salutation and body of the letter
- **Group Footer #1**   The closing of the letter and the signature

10. With the sections resized, you need to add the content of the letter. For each of these sections, select Insert | Text Object to insert a text object. Then place database fields inside the text object to create the content (that is, place the fields for the name and address inside a text object in the Group Header #1 section, place the salutation and letter contents in a text box in the Details section, and so on). When you are finished, your letter should look similar to the one shown in Figure 10-15.

Tip

Your letter may look different due to the different formatting, fields, and so on that you have selected for your letter.

11. Once you have created the text boxes in each section, you will need to insert a page break after each Group Footer #1 section. To do so, select Format | Section and click Group Footer #1 to select it.

12. From the section formatting options on the right side of the page, select New Page After.

Note

You also may want to suppress sections of your report that are not required for your form letter, including the Report Header/Footer and Page Header/Footer sections.

13. Click OK to accept your changes and return to your report's design or preview.

14. Preview your report. It should now show one page (or letter) per customer, depending on the length of the letter body you have created.

15. Save your report as **Form Letter Ch10-1.rpt**.

Project Summary

Crystal Reports are divided into a number of sections that can be shown and formatted independently to create complex reports.

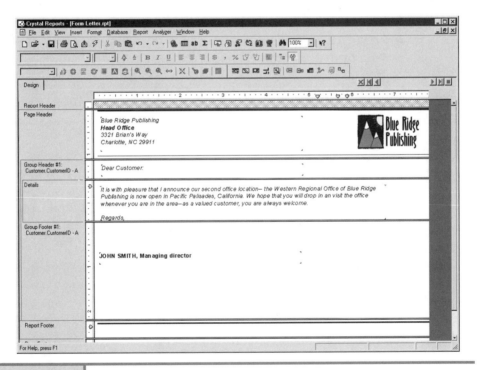

Figure 10-15   A typical section layout for a form letter

✓ Mastery Check

1. If you insert a section below the Page Header a section, what will that section be called?

   _____

   _____

2. What happens to the objects within a section when it is deleted? Merged?

   _____

   _____

3. When you change the order of a section, do you need to change the location of all of the objects within the section as well?

   _____

   _____

4. How do you invoke the Section Expert?

   _____

   _____

5. Which of these is not a formatting option within the Section Expert:

   A. Suppress

   B. Color

   C. Print at Top of Page

   D. New Page After

6. Which section supports multicolumn layout?

   _____

   _____

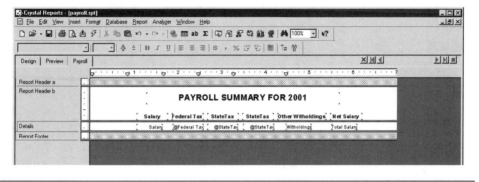

Figure 11-3   Each subreport has its own Design tab

—|—*Tip*————————————————————————

You may want to switch to the Design tab before inserting a subreport, so you can easily see the sections and their boundaries.

Use the radio buttons to indicate whether you will choose a subreport or create one. If you select Choose a Report, you can click the Browse button to locate a Crystal Report that you created earlier. If you select Create a Subreport,

11

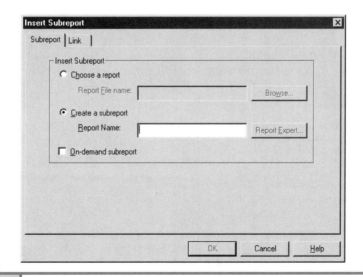

Figure 11-4   You can insert an existing report or create a new one

you will need to enter a name for your subreport and then you can click the Report Expert button to invoke an expert to create your report. When you are finished, click OK to return to the Insert Subreport dialog box.

Tip

For a refresher on working with the report expert, check out Module 2.

When you are finished with the Insert Subreport dialog box, click OK, and your subreport will be attached to the tip of your mouse pointer. You can then position the subreport on your main report and click to place it.

You should choose the location of your subreport carefully. Where you position it determines how many times it is processed. If you place your subreport in the *report* header or footer, for example, the subreport will be processed only once for each report. If you place the subreport in the *page* header or footer, the subreport will be processed for every page, which can cause significant performance problems when your report is run or refreshed.

Inserting a Linked Subreport

Working with linked subreports is just as easy as working with their unlinked counterparts. The only difference is that you will need to specify a field in both the main report and subreport that will determine the relationship between the two. In the Insert Subreport dialog box, there is an additional tab for Link, shown in Figure 11-5.

The first step in linking the two reports is to decide which field in your main report to use. From the list of available fields on the left side of the dialog box, select a field and use the right arrow to move the field from this list to the one on the right.

Once you have selected a field, additional options at the bottom of the dialog box will appear, as shown in Figure 11-6, to allow you to select a field within your subreport. You'll notice that a parameter field is automatically created for you; all you need to do is select a field in use in your subreport.

Tip

If you don't want the value in the parameter field to be used for record selection, you can remove the check mark from the Select Data in Subreport Based on Field box, and the subreport will be linked and the parameter field value will be passed, but the parameter will not be used in record selection.

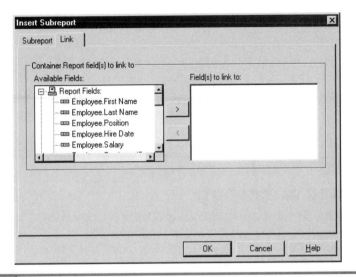

Figure 11-5 You can specify the links between your main report and subreport

You can select multiple fields within your main report for linking in the same manner. You will need to specify a field within the subreport for each.

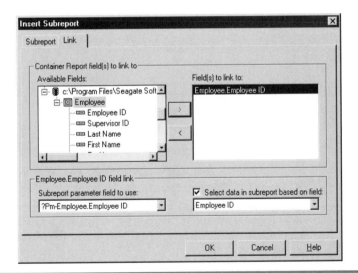

11

Figure 11-6 You will need to select a parameter field and a field from your subreport

When you are finished, click OK to accept your changes and place the subreport in your main, or container, report.

Again, it is important where you place a linked subreport. A subreport will be processed once every time the section appears. If you have a report with 500 detail records and place the subreport in the Detail section, it will be processed 500 times, adding to the total report processing time.

Project 11-1: Inserting an Unlinked Subreport

Unlinked subreports provide an easy means of showing two sets of unrelated data in one report. In this project, we are going to prepare a management report for our fictitious company, Xtreme Bike, showing information about orders our customers have placed, as well as orders Xtreme has placed with its suppliers. To help us get a jump-start on development, we are going to use the Order Listing report created in Module 8 as our main report.

Step-by-Step

1. From the Start | Programs menu, launch Crystal Reports.

2. In the Welcome dialog box, select Open an Existing Report, select More Files, and click OK.

3. Locate and open the Order Listing report from Module 8 (Order Listing Ch8-2.rpt).

Tip

If you are unable to locate a copy of the report, it is also available in the supporting downloads for this module, available at www.osborne.com.

4. Switch to the Design tab and verify that your Report Footer section is visible and not hidden or suppressed.

5. Select Insert | Subreport.

6. Choose the Create a Subreport option, enter the name **Product Listing**, and click the Report Expert button.

Tip

You could also select Choose a Report to insert an existing Crystal Report file as a subreport.

---

7. In the report expert, click the Database button to open the Data Explorer and navigate to Xtreme Sample Database under the ODBC node.

8. From Xtreme Sample Database, select the Product table and click the Add button. A green check mark should appear next to the table, and the Data tab should reflect your selection. Use the same procedure to select the Purchases table. When you are finished, click Close to close the Data Explorer and to return to the report expert.

9. On the Fields tab, select the fields that you want to see in your report. For this project, select the following fields:

- Product.Product Name
- Purchases.Units on Order

To select a field, highlight it in the list on the left and click the right arrow button to move it to the list on the right.

10. On the Group tab, select the Product.Product Name field and click the right arrow button to move it to the list on the right. When your report is created, a group will be inserted using this field.

11. On the Total tab, Crystal Reports will automatically select any numeric fields for summarization. If no fields appear, select the Units on Order field and click the right arrow button to move it to the list on the right. Verify that the Summary operator is set to Sum. When your report is created, a summary field will appear at the bottom of each product group, showing you the sum of all the units ordered within that group.

12. On the TopN tab, select a sort of TopN, based on Sum of Purchases.Units on Order, and enter 10 as the value of N, as shown in Figure 11-7.

13. Use the check box to turn off the Include Other Groups with the Label option.

14. Click OK to return to the Insert Subreport dialog box.

15. Click OK again; your subreport will be attached to the tip of your mouse pointer.

11

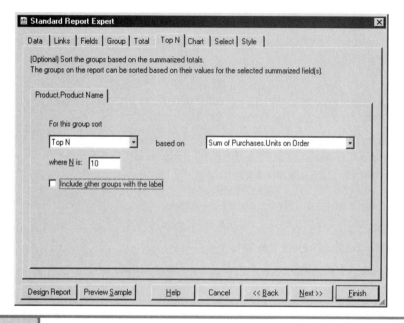

Figure 11-7 For this report, you will be using TopN analysis

16. Click to place your report in the report footer of your main report. When the report is previewed and printed, the Order Listing report will be printed, followed by the Top 10 Products Ordered subreport you just created.

17. Save your report as **Unlinked Subreport Ch11-1.rpt**.

Project Summary

Unlinked subreports provide a handy means of putting disparate pieces of information together in the same report and can add value to the information presented within the main report.

Formatting Subreports

Once you have inserted a subreport into your report, you can apply a number of formatting options and techniques to integrate the main report and subreport into one seamless presentation.

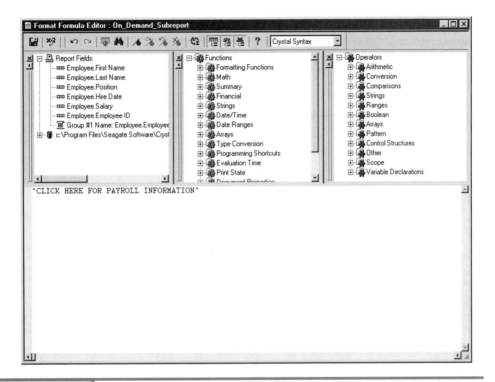

Figure 11-12 You will need to enclose your on-demand subreport caption in
quotation marks

that appears when the subreport is processed and previewed. Again, click the
X+2 button to open the formula editor and enter a caption, enclosed in quotation
marks, for this tab. Click Save and Close in the upper-left corner to exit the
formula editor. In Figure 11-13, the tab has been given a caption of "PAYROLL
INFORMATION."

11

1-Minute Drill

● What are the two options for inserting either a linked or unlinked subreport?

● What is an on-demand subreport?

● You can either insert an existing report as a subreport or create a new one.
● An on-demand subreport is a subreport that is not processed until the user so requests.

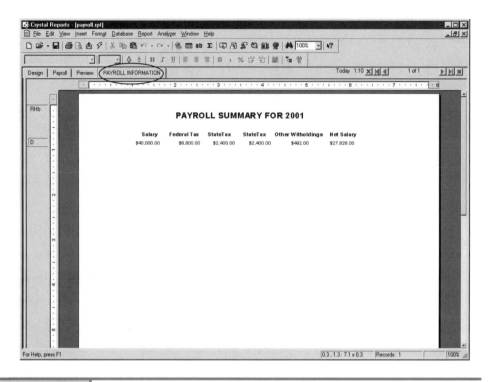

Figure 11-13 You also can set the preview tab text for an on-demand subreport

Saving and Reimporting Subreports

Subreports can be saved to a separate, independent report file and can also be reimported when the main report is opened.

Saving subreports to an external file allows you to break up main reports and subreports, so users can print the subreport independently or use it in other reports. To save a subreport, right-click directly on top of the subreport object in your main report and select Save Subreport As. Specify a file name and click OK, and your subreport will be saved to a separate file.

Reimporting subreports provides a creative way of using subreports. You can create a number of reports that can serve both as subreports and as reports in their own right. This setting is available for linked or unlinked subreports that have been inserted from an existing report file. To enable this setting, locate a subreport that has been inserted from an existing file, right-click directly on top of the subreport object, and select Format Subreport from the right-click menu.

The Subreport property page contains a Re-import When Opening check box. Enable this option, and Crystal Reports will look in the last file location and attempt to reimport the report file you originally used. If the report file name or location has changed, Crystal Reports will display the error message shown in Figure 11-14 and allow you to select the correct file name or location for the subreport you want to import.

Tip

You can also force reimport at any time by right-clicking the subreport object and selecting Re-import Subreport from the right-click menu.

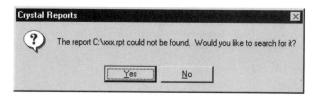

| **Figure 11-14** | If your subreport file has changed names or moved, you will need to search for the new file name or location |

11

Project 11-2: Inserting a Linked Subreport

Linked subreports provide a flexible method of displaying related data from disparate data sources in one report. In this example, our fictional company, Xtreme Bikes, wants to investigate the feasibility of shipping products directly from its suppliers to its customers, to eliminate the cost of holding stock, maintaining a warehouse, and so on. To help with this investigation, we are going to create a report listing all of the company's suppliers, the regions where they are located, and so on. Then, using a subreport, we are going to show a list of all of the customers within the same region.

Step-by-Step

1. From the Start | Programs menu, launch Crystal Reports 8.5.

2. In the Welcome dialog box, select Create a New Crystal Report Document, and in the same dialog box, select Using the Report Expert.

3. From the Crystal Report Gallery, select the Standard Report Expert.

4. Click the Database button to open the Data Explorer and navigate to Xtreme Sample Database under the ODBC node.

5. From Xtreme Sample Database, select the Supplier table and click the Add button. A green check mark should appear next to the table, and the Data tab should reflect your selection. When you are finished, click Close to close the Data Explorer and return to the report expert.

6. On the Fields tab, select the fields that you want to see in your report. For this project, select the following fields:

- Supplier.Supplier Name
- Supplier.City
- Supplier.Region
- Supplier.Phone

To select a field, highlight it in the list on the left and click the right arrow button to move it to the list on the right.

7. On the Group tab, select the Supplier.Supplier Name field and click the right arrow button to move it to the list on the right. When your report is created, a group will be inserted using this field.

8. Click the Finish button to preview your report.

9. Verify that a group field has been inserted into your report.

10. Stretch the group header for the Supplier Name group to about five times its current size, as shown in Figure 11-15. (To resize a section, drag its bottom border.) This is where we are going to insert the subreport.

11. Select Insert | Subreport.

12. Choose the Create a Subreport option, enter the name **Customers**, and click the Report Expert button.

13. In the report expert, click the Database button to open the Data Explorer and navigate to Xtreme Sample Database under the ODBC node.

14. From Xtreme Sample Database, select the Customer table and click the Add button. A green check mark should appear next to the table, and the Data tab should reflect your selection. When you are finished, click Close to close the Data Explorer and return to the report expert.

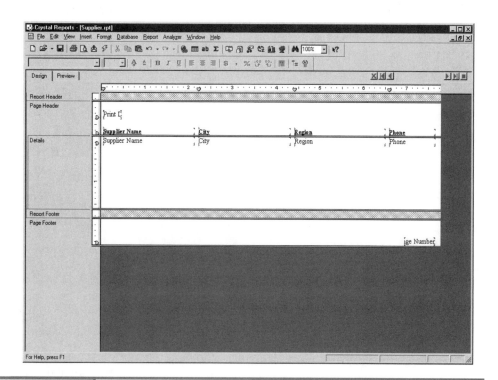

11

Figure 11-15   Make room in the group header to insert a subreport

15. On the Fields tab, select the fields that you want to see in your report. For this project, select the following fields:

   ● Customer.Customer Name

   ● Customer.Contact First Name

   ● Customer.Contact Last Name

   ● Customer.Phone

   ● Customer.E-mail

   To select a field, highlight it in the list on the left and click the right arrow button to move it to the list on the right.

16. Once you have selected the fields for your subreport, click OK to return to the Insert Subreport dialog box; click the Link tab to proceed.

17. Locate and select the Supplier.Region field and then click the right arrow button to move it from the list of available fields on the left to the Field(s) to Link To box on the right. This will open a second set of drop-down boxes.

18. In the drop-down box below Select Data in Subreport Based on Field (which is selected by default), select the Customer.Region field from your subreport.

19. When you are finished, click OK to accept your changes. Your subreport is now attached to the tip of your mouse.

20. Click to place your subreport in the group header you expanded earlier. Your report should look something like the one shown in Figure 11-16.

21. Preview your report to verify that for each supplier, a list of customers is produced.

Tip

You can also change the formatting of the subreport, including its borders and shading, to suit your main report's design.

22. Save your report as **Linked Subreport Ch11-2.rpt**.

Project Summary

Linked subreports provide a flexible means of joining different data sets and displaying related information. Using a combination of linked and unlinked subreports, you should be able to show just about anything you want in your reports.

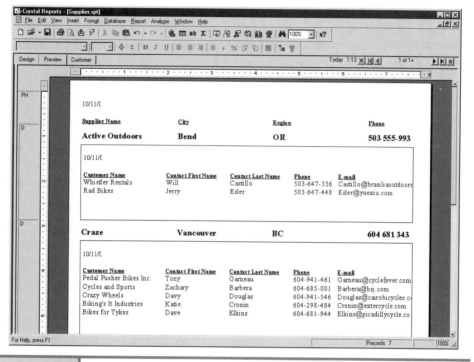

Figure 11-16 An example of a finished report

☑ Mastery Check

1. What is the difference between linked and unlinked subreports?

   _____

   _____

2. Can you insert an existing report as a subreport?

   _____

   _____

3. Which of the following is a benefit of on-demand subreports:

   A. Delays processing to a report server.

   B. Shows the subreport first and then the main report.

   C. Delays processing of the subreport until it is needed.

   D. Reduces the number of formulas required.

4. What type of field is used to link subreports with a main report?

   _____

   _____

Module 12

Cross-Tab Analysis

Goals

- Understand how cross-tabs are used
- Create cross-tab reports
- Format cross-tabs using predefined and custom styles
- Understand cross-tab uses and limitations

Cross-tabs provide an easy way to add complex data summarization and analysis to your report. As the main feature of a report, or as a supporting object within an existing report, they provide an at-a-glance view of information in your database. In this module, you will learn how to create, format, and manipulate cross-tabs, adding instant analysis and summarization to your reports.

Cross-Tab Overview

Cross-tabs are special objects that can be placed in your report to offer a summarized view of your report data. Cross-tabs, like the one shown in Figure 12-1, are composed of rows and columns of summarized data and can be placed within the structure of existing reports or can be the main focus and content of their own reports.

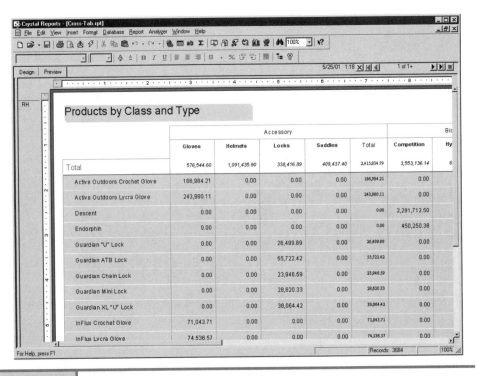

| **Figure 12-1** | A typical cross-tab inserted into a report |

Cross-tabs look similar to a spreadsheet, but it is important to remember that cross-tabs are database driven. In the Design view of your report, a cross-tab presents a simple row-and-column display. When viewed in the preview of your report, these rows and columns are filled with the data you have requested. The size of the cross-tab varies based on the number of records returned.

Inserting a Cross-Tab

To facilitate creation of reports specifically for use with cross-tabs, Crystal Reports includes a Cross-Tab Expert that walks you through the process of creating a cross-tab report. In addition, you can insert cross-tabs as an element of an existing report.

From the Insert menu, select Insert | Cross-Tab; the Format Cross-Tab dialog box should appear, as shown in Figure 12-2.

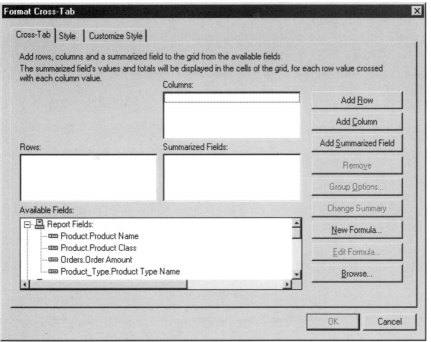

12

| **Figure 12-2** | The Cross-Tab Expert |

To create a cross tab, you need three elements: rows, columns, and summarized fields. For a basic cross-tab, you need only one of each. To create new rows, columns, or summarized fields, you can drag a field from the Available Fields box to the corresponding box for rows, columns, or summarized fields. The mouse pointer will change to the one shown in Figure 12-3 to indicate that you are adding a field to your cross-tab.

Tip

You can view the contents of a particular field by highlighting the field and clicking the Browse button at the lower right of the dialog box.

You can also highlight a field in the Available Fields box and click the Add Row, Add Column, or Add Summarized Field button. To remove a field from a cross-tab, highlight the field and click the Remove button.

With cross-tabs, you can add as many fields for the columns, rows, and summarized fields as required. When your cross-tab is printed, the fields you specified for the columns and rows will be used to create the cross-tab, and the summarized field you specified will be calculated at the intersection of the columns and rows. For example, in the cross-tab shown in Figure 12-4, the fields for Product Name and Region have been used to create the rows and columns, and the Sales value appears in the summarized field.

The value highlighted in Figure 12-4 is the summarized sales for Mozzie bikes in the California region. By default, the summary operator used for numeric fields

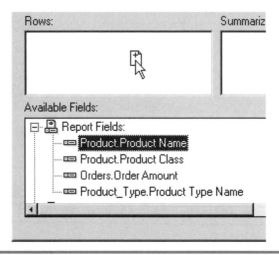

Figure 12-3   This cursor indicates that you can release the mouse to add the field

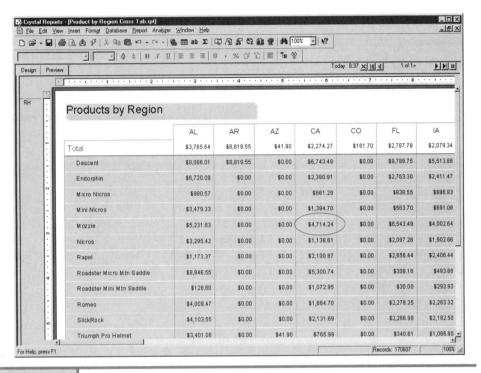

Figure 12-4   A typical cross-tab

is Sum. A little later, you'll learn how to change the summary operator for summarized fields, but for now it is important to remember that the summarized field is calculated by Crystal Reports at the intersection of rows and columns.

Once you have selected the elements that will make up your cross-tab, you can click OK to add the cross-tab to your report. Crystal Reports will attach your cross-tab to the mouse pointer, and you can click to place it in your report.

Tip

You may want to switch to the Design view of your report before inserting a cross-tab to make your work a little easier.

When determining where to insert your cross-tab, notice that Crystal Reports allows you to insert a cross-tab into only a report or group header or footer. If you insert your cross-tab into the report header or footer, the cross-tab will display the entire data set you have requested, showing all records. If you place a cross-tab in a group header or footer, your cross-tab will display only the records that relate to that one particular group.

Ask the Expert

Question: Is it possible to create a cross-tab that just shows my data in rows and columns, without a summarized field? Also, can I edit the information within cross-tabs?

Answer: A cross-tab cannot be created without a summarized field. Cross-tabs within Crystal Reports are a powerful summarization feature and can crunch tens of thousands of rows of data to produce a concise summary. Also, like all Crystal Reports and report elements, cross-tabs are read-only. You can create a report that displays information in rows and columns using grouping and formulas. An example of this type of report is the Year-to-Date Sales Analysis sample report included with the downloadable module for this module. Another alternative if you need a report that just displays information in rows and columns is to create a report within Crystal Reports and export it to Microsoft Excel for further data entry or manipulation.

On the Design tab, Crystal Reports displays your cross-tab as a small representative grid, as shown in Figure 12-5.

This grid lists the rows, columns, and summarized fields; when your report is previewed, this grid is expanded to include the information from your database tables, fields, and so on, as shown in Figure 12-6.

Tip

To revisit your cross-tab design or change any options, right-click directly on top of the cross-tab and select Format Cross-Tab from the right-click menu.

1-Minute Drill

● What three elements are required to create a cross-tab?

● How can you determine what values are in a field before you add it to your cross-tab?

● All cross-tabs require at least one row, column, and summarized field.
● Highlight the field and use the Browse button to view the field's contents.

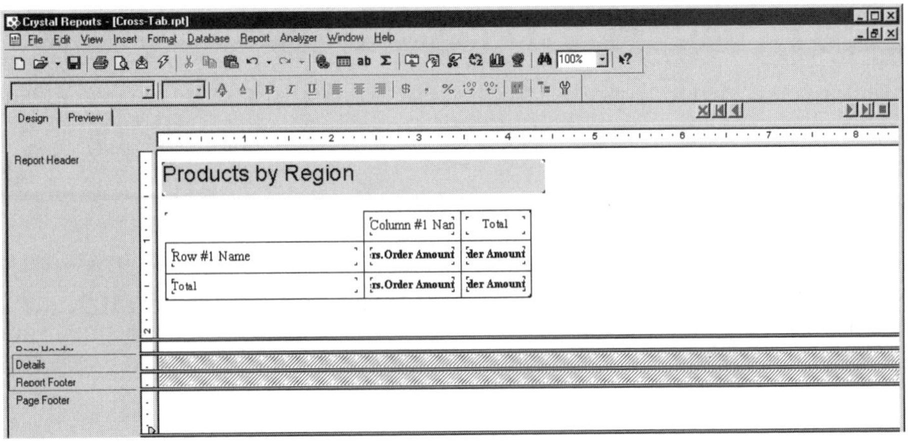

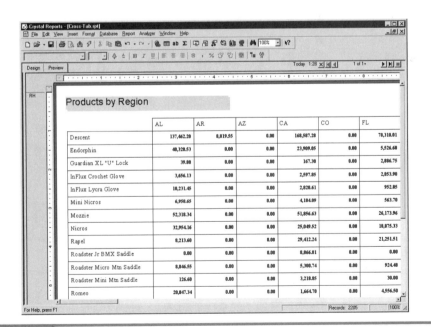

Figure 12-5 How a cross-tab appears in the Design view of your report

Figure 12-6 The same cross-tab in the report preview

Working with Cross-Tabs

Now that you understand the basics of creating cross-tabs, it's time to look at some of the options for organizing them.

Using Grouping Options

As with reports, you can control the way information is displayed within a cross-tab through the use of grouping. You can apply the same grouping concepts to your cross-tab by highlighting a row or column field, right-clicking, and selecting Format Cross-Tab. The Cross-Tab Group Options dialog box, shown in Figure 12-7, opens. Here, you can select a sort order from the following options:

● Ascending

● Descending

● Specified Order

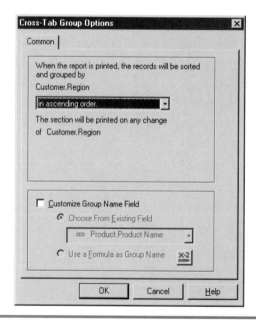

Figure 12-7   A number of grouping options are available for use with cross-tabs

Specified Order with cross-tab groups works just as it does for other specified groupings you insert onto your report. You need to name each group and then specify the criteria for each. You might use specified grouping with a cross-tab if you have a particular product grouping not represented in the database. You could use a specified grouping to create separate groups and to establish your own criteria (for example, in our fictional bike company, all the gloves, helmets, and so on could be grouped as Personal Accessories, and saddles and other items could be grouped together as Spare Parts).

Once you have selected Specified Order, a second tab should appear in the Cross-Tab Group Options dialog box, as shown in Figure 12-8. (If you selected one of the other sort orders, no additional information is required.)

The next step is to define a group name, and then you need to specify the group criteria. Start by typing all of the group names you want to create first, pressing ENTER after each. This will build a list of group names.

Once you have all of the group names defined, you can highlight each and click the Edit button to specify the criteria. To establish the criteria for records to be added to your group, use the drop-down menu to select an operator and values.

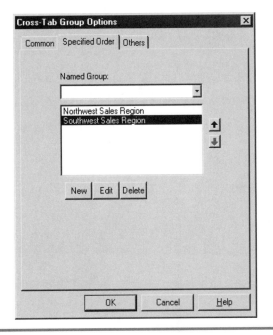

Figure 12-8 The Specified Order tab

12

Note

These are the same operators as used with record selection.

You can add criteria by clicking the New tab and using the operators to specify additional selection criteria, which are evaluated with an Or operator between the criteria that you have specified.

Tip

Make sure that you delete any groups you may have added by accident. Even if the criterion is set to Any Value, it can still have an effect on report performance.

After you have entered a single group, another tab appears with options for records that fall outside of the criteria that you specify. By default, all of the leftover records are placed in their own group, labeled Others. You can change the name of this group by simply editing the name on the Others tab, shown in Figure 12-9. You also can choose to discard all of the other records or to leave them in their own groups.

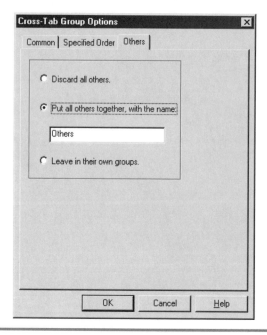

Figure 12-9 Options for handling other records

Products by Region

	Northwest Sales Region	Southwest Sales Region	Total
Descent	$ 738,462.07 $ 44,307.72	$ 900,170.46 $ 54,010.23	$1,638,632.53 $98,317.95
Endorphin	$ 121,026.12 $ 7,261.57	$ 153,789.68 $ 9,227.38	$274,815.80 $16,488.95
Guardian XL "U" Lock	$ 5,082.12 $ 304.93	$ 17,562.94 $ 1,053.78	$22,645.06 $1,358.70
InFlux Crochet Glove	$ 30,210.43 $ 1,812.63	$ 24,121.67 $ 1,447.30	$54,332.10 $3,259.93
InFlux Lycra Glove	$ 30,391.29 $ 1,823.48	$ 24,139.77 $ 1,448.39	$54,531.06 $3,271.86
Mini Nicros	$ 43,431.75 $ 2,605.91	$ 67,629.62 $ 4,057.78	$111,061.37 $6,663.68
Mozzie	$ 297,148.64 $ 17,828.92	$ 301,527.75 $ 18,091.66	$598,676.39 $35,920.58
Nicros	$ 177,863.26 $ 10,671.80	$ 229,942.75 $ 13,796.57	$407,806.01 $24,468.36
Rapel	$ 189,797.43 $ 11 207 05	$ 176,353.50 $ 10 501 21	$366,150.93 $21 060 06

Figure 12-13   An example of a cross-tab with a formula field inserted

Project 12-1: Inserting a Cross-Tab into Your Report

In this project, we are going to create a new report to analyze the sales of our fictional company's products across the regions where the products are sold. We are going to first create a report using the Standard Report Expert and then insert our cross-tab into it.

Step-by-Step

1. From the Start | Programs menu, launch Crystal Reports 8.5.

2. In the Welcome dialog box, select Create a New Crystal Report Document, and in the same dialog box, select Using the Report Expert.

3. From the Crystal Report Gallery, select the Standard Report Expert.

4. Click the Database button to open the Data Explorer and navigate to Xtreme Sample Database under the ODBC node.

5. From Xtreme Sample Database, select the Customer table and click the Add button. A green check mark should appear next to the table, and the Data tab should reflect your selection. Repeat this process for the Orders, Order Details, and Product tables. When you are finished, click Close to close the Data Explorer and return to the report expert.

Tip

Crystal Reports should automatically perform smart-linking to add the links between these tables.

6. On the Fields tab, select the fields that you want to see in your report. For this project, select the following fields:

- Customer.Region
- Product.Product Name
- Product.Product Type
- Orders.Order Date
- Orders_Detail.Quantity
- Orders_Detail.UnitPrice

To select a field, highlight it in the list on the left and click the right arrow button to move it to the list on the right.

7. Click the Finish button to preview your report.

8. Confirm that the report header is not suppressed or hidden. This is where you will place your cross-tab.

9. Select Insert | Cross-Tab to open the dialog box shown in Figure 12-14.

10. From the list of available fields, drag the fields that you want to use as your cross-tabs rows, columns, and summarized fields to the appropriate boxes.

Tip

Alternatively, you could highlight each field and click Add Row, Add Column, or Add Summarized Field.

11. For the columns, select the Product.Product Name field.

12. For the rows, select Customer.Region field.

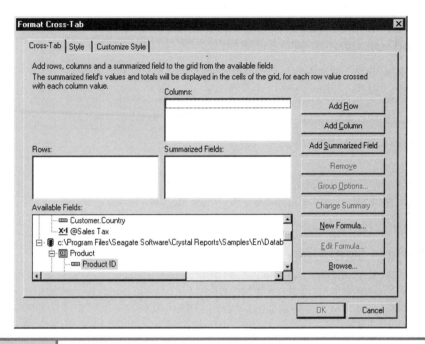

Figure 12-14 The Format Cross-Tab dialog box

13. For the summarized field, you are going to use a formula to multiply the quantity purchased by the unit price. To insert this formula field, click the New Formula button and enter the formula name Extended; this will invoke the Crystal Reports Formula Editor.

14. Enter the following formula:

```
{Orders_Detail.Quantity} * {Orders_Detail.Unit Price}
```

15. Click Save and Close. The formula should now appear in the list of available fields. Drag this field to the Summarized Field box.

Tip

The default summary operator for this field is Sum. You can change the summary operator if you want to show an average, count, or some other calculation.

12

16. Click OK when you are finished. You will be returned to your report's design, and your cross-tab will be attached to the tip of the mouse pointer.

17. Using the mouse to position the cross-tab, click to place the cross-tab on your report in the Report Header section.

Tip

Be sure that the report header is not suppressed!

18. Preview your report to verify that the cross-tab is working. It should appear similar to the cross-tab shown in Figure 12-15.

19. Save your report as **Product Analysis Ch12-1.rpt**.

Project Summary

Cross-tabs are a powerful analysis and summary feature that can be used to quickly summarize and show information within a report. In this project, we have summarized thousands of rows of data into a clear, concise format using cross-tab analysis.

	Descent	Endorph	Guardia	InFlux C	InFlux L	Mini Ni	Mozzie	Nicros	Rapel	Roadster
AL	120,533.85	9,718.39	39.80	135.00	229.40	1,409.25	39,494.61	5,211.64	7,461.69	0.00
AR	8,819.55	0.00	0.00	0.00	0.00	0.00	0.00	0.00	0.00	0.00
AZ	0.00	0.00	0.00	0.00	0.00	0.00	0.00	0.00	0.00	0.00
CA	147,727.50	17,727.06	99.50	118.80	124.00	1,691.10	43,496.25	15,189.64	13,723.73	60.00
CO	0.00	0.00	0.00	0.00	0.00	0.00	0.00	0.00	0.00	0.00
FL	52,623.32	5,399.10	119.40	27.00	62.00	563.70	15,571.66	4,766.36	7,101.79	0.00
IA	40,863.92	15,297.45	19.90	132.30	310.00	1,691.10	34,536.03	8,477.16	11,852.31	12.00
ID	85,843.66	10,528.26	39.80	182.94	75.95	1,944.77	20,704.22	5,574.47	12,812.01	24.00
IL	175,362.07	15,297.45	135.32	253.82	167.40	3,889.54	72,464.77	24,211.02	36,636.58	0.00
KS	0.00	0.00	0.00	0.00	0.00	0.00	0.00	0.00	0.00	12.00
KY	0.00	0.00	0.00	0.00	0.00	0.00	0.00	313.36	0.00	0.00
MA	54,975.21	10,618.24	35.82	0.00	0.00	845.55	12,178.95	5,557.98	8,973.21	34.20
ME	0.00	0.00	0.00	0.00	0.00	0.00	0.00	0.00	0.00	0.00
MI	56,886.13	6,298.95	0.00	213.99	217.00	1,648.83	22,618.05	7,174.25	6,238.05	36.00
MN	115,242.16	22,406.27	39.80	25.66	31.00	1,677.01	5,219.55	12,385.89	8,997.20	0.00
MO	0.00	0.00	0.00	0.00	0.00	0.00	0.00	0.00	0.00	0.00
MS	0.00	0.00	0.00	0.00	0.00	0.00	0.00	0.00	0.00	0.00

Figure 12-15 The finished report with the cross-tab

Formatting Cross-Tabs

Now that you understand how to insert a cross-tab into your report and control its structure, it's time to take a look at formatting your cross-tab.

Changing Field, Column, and Row Size

Controlling the column and column sizes within a cross-tab is a little tricky—instead of changing the columns themselves, we change the field widths and heights of the objects within the columns. To change the field sizes within your cross-tab, locate the field you want to change and click to select it. This should put a single handle on each side of the field object, as shown in Figure 12-16.

You can resize the field by dragging these blue handles. As you resize one field in a column or row, the entire column or row is resized.

Tip

When you are finished resizing your fields, columns, or rows, click anywhere outside of the cross-tab to deselect the object you were working with.

Applying a Preformatted Style

Crystal Reports includes a number of preformatted styles that affect the formatting, font size, color, and so on. You can use these to give your cross-tab a standard look and feel. Even if you don't care for any of the styles available, they are often a good starting point for creating your own custom formatting. To apply a preformatted style to your cross-tab object, insert or edit an existing cross-tab and, in the Format Cross-Tab dialog box, click the Style tab (shown in Figure 12-17).

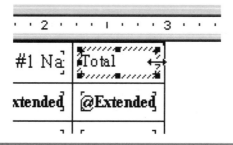

12

| Figure 12-16 | You can resize cross-tabs using the handles |

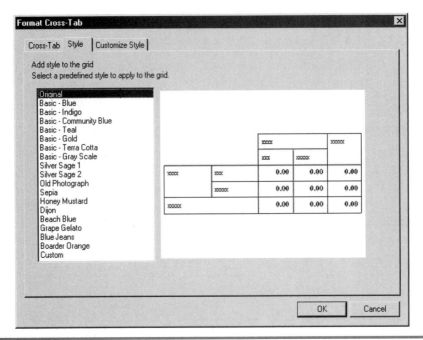

Figure 12-17 You can apply a preformatted style to your cross-tab

You can click to select a predefined style to apply to your cross-tab. As you click a style, the preview window on the right will display a sample of that style. When you are finished selecting your style, click OK to accept your changes and return to your report's design.

Customizing a Style

Cross-tab styles can be the starting point for creating your own cross-tab format. To modify a cross-tab style, click the Customize Style tab (shown in Figure 12-18).

Keep in mind that the changes you make here are for a specific cross-tab and do not change the underlying style within Crystal Reports.

The options for customizing a particular style are divided into two categories: Group Options and Grid Options.

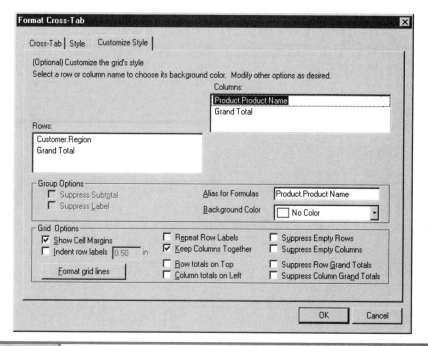

Figure 12-18   You can further customize a preformatted style using this dialog box

Changing Group Options

Group options include the ability to suppress a subtotal or label and change the background color of a particular row or column by highlighting the field and using the drop-down list to select a color. Another group option is the ability to set an alias for formula fields by highlighting a field and entering a new name in the Alias for Formulas text box.

Changing Grid Options

In addition to applying and modifying styles to your cross-tab, you also have complete control over the grid options and grid lines that appear in and around your cross-tab. Figure 12-19 shows an example of what you can do with a customized gridline style.

12

	Descent	Endorph	Guardia	InFlux C	InFlux L	Mini Ni	Mozzie	Nicros	Rapel	Roadster
AL	120,533.85	9,718.39	39.80	135.00	229.40	1,409.25	39,494.61	5,211.64	7,461.69	0.00
AR	8,819.55	0.00	0.00	0.00	0.00	0.00	0.00	0.00	0.00	0.00
AZ	0.00	0.00	0.00	0.00	0.00	0.00	0.00	0.00	0.00	0.00
CA	147,727.50	17,727.06	99.50	118.80	124.00	1,691.10	43,496.25	15,189.64	13,723.73	60.00
CO	0.00	0.00	0.00	0.00	0.00	0.00	0.00	0.00	0.00	0.00
FL	52,623.32	5,399.10	119.40	27.00	62.00	563.70	15,571.66	4,766.36	7,101.79	0.00
IA	40,863.92	15,297.45	19.90	132.30	310.00	1,691.10	34,536.03	8,477.16	11,852.31	12.00
ID	85,843.66	10,528.26	39.80	182.94	75.95	1,944.77	20,704.22	5,574.47	12,812.01	24.00
IL	175,362.07	15,297.45	135.32	253.82	167.40	3,889.54	72,464.77	24,211.02	36,636.58	0.00
KS	0.00	0.00	0.00	0.00	0.00	0.00	0.00	0.00	0.00	12.00
KY	0.00	0.00	0.00	0.00	0.00	0.00	0.00	313.36	0.00	0.00
MA	54,975.21	10,618.24	35.82	0.00	0.00	845.55	12,178.95	5,557.98	8,973.21	34.20
ME	0.00	0.00	0.00	0.00	0.00	0.00	0.00	0.00	0.00	0.00
MI	56,886.13	6,298.95	0.00	213.99	217.00	1,648.83	22,618.05	7,174.25	6,238.05	36.00

Figure 12-19 You can control gridlines by customizing a style

Table 12-2 summarizes the gridline options available on the Customize Style tab.

Option	Description
Show Cell Margins	Displays the internal cell margins within your cross-tab.
Indent Row Labels	For each row, indents the labels that appear on the left side of the cross-tab.
Repeat Row Labels	Repeats row labels on any new pages.
Keep Columns Together	Attempts to keep all columns together on the same page.
Row Totals on Top	Moves the row totals from their default location at the bottom of the cross-tab to the top.
Column Totals on Left	Moves the column totals from their default location on the right side of the cross-tab to the left.
Suppress Empty Rows	Suppresses any empty rows in the cross-tab.
Suppress Empty Columns	Suppresses any empty columns in the cross-tab.
Suppress Row Grand Totals	Suppresses the grand totals that would appear by default at the bottom of the cross-tab.
Suppress Column Grand Totals	Suppresses the grand totals that would appear by default on the right side of the cross-tab.

Table 12-2 Grid Options

You also can control the grid lines that appear in your cross-tab by clicking the Format Grid Lines button to open the dialog box shown in Figure 12-20.

Using this dialog box, select the part of your cross-tab that you want to format and choose the line color, style, and width. The following grid lines are available:

- Row Labels Vertical Lines
- Column Labels Top Border
- Row Labels Horizontal Lines
- Column Labels Bottom Border
- Row Labels Top Border
- Column Labels Left Border
- Row Labels Bottom Border
- Column Labels Right Border
- Row Labels Left Border
- Cells Vertical Lines
- Row Labels Right Border
- Cells Horizontal Lines
- Column Labels Vertical Lines
- Cells Bottom Border
- Column Labels Horizontal Lines
- Cells Right Border

When you are finished setting the grid lines for your cross-tab, click OK to return to your report design, and the changes you have made should be reflected in your cross-tab.

Using the Highlighting Expert

The Highlighting Expert can be used to quickly highlight exceptions or abnormal values within a cross-tab. To use the Highlighting Expert, right-click on top of the field in your cross-tab that you want to highlight. From the right-click menu, select the Highlighting Expert option to open the dialog box shown in Figure 12-21.

In the Item Editor section on the right side of the dialog box, select an operator from the pull-down Value Is list. In the box immediately below the operator, enter the criterion to specify when the highlighting should occur.

Now select the font color, background, and border that will be triggered when this criterion is met. If you want to enter multiple criteria, click New Item in the Item List on the left.

12

Tip

To change the order of precedence for highlighting criteria, use the up and down arrows.

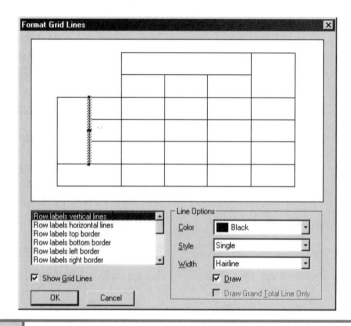

Figure 12-20   You can format individual grid lines as well

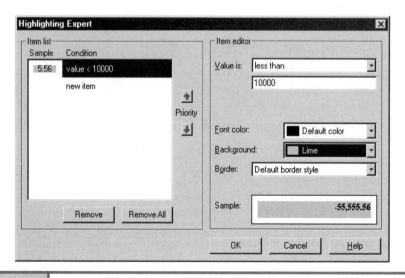

Figure 12-21   The cross-tab Highlighting Expert

After you have entered the criteria and formatting options, click OK to exit the Highlighting Expert. When you preview your report, the field you originally selected in your cross-tab should reflect the options set in the Highlighting Expert, as shown in Figure 12-22.

Cross-Tab Uses and Limitations

Traditionally, Crystal Reports developers have either loved or hated cross-tabs. One of the main reasons that report designers are sometimes unhappy with cross-tabs is that they look at a cross-tab and see rows and columns, similar to a those in a Microsoft Excel spreadsheet, for example, and they expect the same functionality. However, a cross-tab and a spreadsheet are not the same.

For starters, a cross-tab's rows and columns all share the same height and width. You can't show 10 columns of data, for example, and have one column wider than the rest. Another key point is that any formatting you apply to a field within a cross-tab will be applied to every field in the cross-tab grid.

	Descent	Endorphin	Guardian XL	InFlux Croche	InFlux Lycra (	Mini Nicros	Mozzie	Nicros	Rapel
AL	8,678,437.20	699,724.08	2,865.60	9,720.00	16,516.80	101,466.00	2,843,611.92	375,238.08	537,241.68
AR	635,007.60	0.00	0.00	0.00	0.00	0.00	0.00	0.00	0.00
AZ	0.00	0.00	0.00	0.00	0.00	0.00	0.00	0.00	0.00
CA	10,636,380.00	1,276,348.32	7,164.00	8,553.60	8,928.00	121,759.20	3,131,730.00	1,093,654.08	988,108.56
CO	0.00	0.00	0.00	0.00	0.00	0.00	0.00	0.00	0.00
FL	3,788,879.04	388,735.20	8,596.80	1,944.00	4,464.00	40,586.40	1,121,159.52	343,177.92	511,328.88
IA	2,942,202.24	1,101,416.40	1,432.80	9,525.60	22,320.00	121,759.20	2,486,594.16	610,555.52	853,366.32
ID	6,180,743.52	758,034.72	2,865.60	13,171.68	5,468.40	140,023.44	1,490,703.84	401,361.84	922,464.72
IL	19,505,318.04	1,311,981.30	9,743.04	30,911.04	12,052.80	662,576.04	6,031,713.24	2,900,566.94	3,985,252.56
KS	0.00	0.00	0.00	0.00	0.00	0.00	0.00	0.00	0.00
KY	0.00	0.00	0.00	0.00	0.00	0.00	0.00	22,561.92	0.00
MA	3,958,215.12	764,513.28	2,579.04	0.00	0.00	60,879.60	876,884.40	400,174.56	646,071.12
ME	0.00	0.00	0.00	0.00	0.00	0.00	0.00	0.00	0.00
MI	7,517,786.76	1,239,093.45	0.00	26,997.81	33,666.00	352,470.24	4,159,981.35	996,477.75	868,048.65
MN	8,297,435.52	1,613,251.44	2,865.60	1,847.52	2,232.00	120,744.72	375,807.60	891,784.08	647,798.40
MO	0.00	0.00	0.00	0.00	0.00	0.00	0.00	0.00	0.00
MS	0.00	0.00	0.00	0.00	0.00	0.00	0.00	0.00	0.00

12

Figure 12-22   An example of a cross-tab with highlighting

Ask the Expert

Question: Is there an easy way to swap the rows and columns within a cross-tab?

Answer: Cross-tabs within Crystal Reports can easily be pivoted, swapping all of the rows and columns that appear within them. To pivot a cross-tab, right-click directly on top of a blank area within the cross-tab and select Pivot Cross-Tab from the right-click menu that appears.

Over the different versions of Crystal Reports, improvements have been made to fix problems with page breaks, formatting, gridlines, row and column suppression, and so on that really do make cross-tabs a viable analysis and presentation option, but you must understand and work within the framework presented.

If you do need some of the specialized formatting features found in Microsoft Excel and other spreadsheet programs, Crystal Reports does include a number of export formats that allow you to export to a spreadsheet file. What you do with the data at that point is up to you. The advantage of using a cross-tab is that even though it may not have all of the formatting functions of a spreadsheet, the information presented is data driven and does not require manual updating as a spreadsheet would.

Project 12-2: Formatting Cross-Tabs

Using our understanding of cross-tab formatting, we are going to take the report we created in the first project in this module and create a presentation-quality report by applying a customized style to the cross-tab and suppressing the details.

Step-by-Step

1. Open the Product Analysis report (Product Analysis Ch12-1.rpt) you created in Project 12-1.

2. Locate the cross-tab you placed in the report header, right-click on top of it, and select Format cross-tab from the right-click menu.

3. Click the Style tab and select the Basic-Indigo style as the basis for your formatting.

4. Click the Customize Style tab to proceed.

5. Using the dialog box that appears, customize the cross-tab style and format with the following attributes:

- Show Cell Margins
- Indent Row Labels (0.5)
- Row Totals on Top

6. Click OK to accept your changes and return to your report.

7. On the Design tab of your report, right-click on each section except the report header and select Suppress from the right-click menu.

8. Preview your report. It should look similar to the report shown in Figure 12-23.

9. Save your report as **Product Analysis Ch12-2.rpt**.

Project Summary

Cross-tabs provide a concise view of the data within your report and can be formatted to provide presentation-quality reporting to users.

		Descent	Endorphin	Guardian X	InFlux Croc	InFlux Lycr	Mini Nicro	Mozzie	Nicros
Total		1,334,692.20	170,431.67	1,064.66	1,753.06	2,187.10	27,071.74	457,841.67	141,819
	USA	1,334,692.20	170,431.67	1,064.66	1,753.06	2,187.10	27,071.74	457,841.67	141,819
	AL	120,533.85	9,718.39	39.80	135.00	229.40	1,409.25	39,494.61	5,211
	AR	8,819.55	0.00	0.00	0.00	0.00	0.00	0.00	0
	AZ	0.00	0.00	0.00	0.00	0.00	0.00	0.00	0
	CA	147,727.50	11,727.06	99.50	118.80	124.00	1,691.10	43,496.25	15,189
	CO	0.00	0.00	0.00	0.00	0.00	0.00	0.00	0
	FL	52,623.32	5,399.10	119.40	27.00	62.00	563.70	15,571.66	4,766
	IA	40,863.92	15,297.45	19.90	132.30	310.00	1,691.10	34,538.03	8,477
	ID	85,843.66	10,528.26	39.80	782.94	75.95	1,944.77	20,704.22	5,574
	IL	175,362.07	15,297.45	135.32	253.82	167.40	3,889.54	72,464.77	24,211
	KS	0.00	0.00	0.00	0.00	0.00	0.00	0.00	0
	KY	0.00	0.00	0.00	0.00	0.00	0.00	0.00	313
	MA	54,975.21	10,618.24	35.82	0.00	0.00	845.55	12,178.95	5,557
	ME	0.00	0.00	0.00	0.00	0.00	0.00	0.00	0
	MI	56,886.13	6,298.95	0.00	213.99	217.00	1,648.83	22,618.05	7,174
	MN	115,242.16	22,408.27	39.80	25.60	31.00	1,677.01	5,219.55	12,389

Figure 12-23   The finished report.

12

✓ Mastery Check

1. What are the four grouping options for cross-tabs?

_____

_____

2. How do you change the size of a column within a cross-tab?

_____

_____

3. How do you display the option for pivoting a cross-tab?

_____

_____

4. Which of the following options cannot be used within a cross-tab:

    A. Suppress the summarized field

    B. Resize rows and columns

    C. Change background colors

    D. Highlight exceptions

5. Can you drag and drop columns within a cross-tab?

_____

_____

Module 13

Charting and Graphing

Goals

- Understand the different types of chart layouts
- Recognize the different chart types
- Create charts using the Chart Expert
- Format charts using the Chart Analyzer

If a picture is worth a thousand words, than a graph or chart must be worth double that. At a glance, charts and graphs provide a concise summary of the information represented in your report. Crystal Reports has always prided itself on its graphics capabilities, and this release is no different. In this module, you will learn about the different layouts and types of graphs as well as how to insert and edit them in your report.

Graphing Overview

Crystal Reports features a powerful graphing and charting engine that allows you to create graphs and charts using one of 36 different types of standard graphing templates, or you can create your own using the custom chart editor.

Note

Rather than reinvent the wheel, Crystal Reports 8.5 graphing technology is provided through a long-standing partnership with ThreeD Graphics (www.threedgraphics.com).

To make things a bit easier for users, Crystal Reports has hidden the complexity of its graphing and charting engine behind a number of experts and other easy-to-use interfaces. A little later in the module, we'll use the Chart Expert to create various types of graphs and charts, but for now we will take a look at the various chart layouts available within Crystal Reports.

Graph Layouts

While there can be many different templates applied to graphs (line, bar, pie, and so on), graphs in Crystal Reports generally fall into four distinct types or layouts: advanced, group, cross-tab, and OLAP grid.

Advanced Graphs

Advanced graphs work like the graphs you may remember from high-school algebra: you plot a chart or graph based on X and Y values. Crystal Reports' implementation of this type of graphing is a little more sophisticated: you can specify summary fields to be generated, perform TopN/Sort analysis, and control how the information is grouped when displayed on your graph.

Group Graphs

A group graph can be used where there is a group inserted into your report and some summary field has been created based on that group (Sum, Average, and so on). A group graph can appear once, representing the data in the entire report, or it can appear on the group level, showing one graph for each group.

Group graphs are probably the most common type of graph used with Crystal Reports. Group graphs can be used to create a drill-through effect, in which you start with a graph of the highest level of data (the whole report) and then drill down through the different groups, with a graph showing for each group, all the way down to the details.

Tip

An example of this type of drill-through graph can be found in the sample reports that ship with Crystal Reports. Look for World Sales Report.rpt. If you search the drive where you have installed Crystal Reports, you should be able to find this file under c:\program files\Seagate software\crystal reports\en\samples\reports\ general business.

A lot of people get confused at this point about the difference between advanced graphs and group graphs. Simply put, advanced graphs don't require a group or summary field to be inserted into your report. Frequently, advanced graphs are used with formula fields and can be used to create complex graphs that would not normally have been possible with just a group graph.

Cross-Tab Graphs

If you have a cross-tab inserted into your report, a graph or chart can be created based on the data contained within that cross-tab, adding an extra dimension to the data presented, as shown in Figure 13-1.

The information shown in a cross-tab graph will always directly correspond with the information shown in the corresponding cross-tab.

OLAP Grid Graphs

Like cross-tabs, OLAP grids can also be used as a data source for graphs or charts. In addition to showing dimensions that appear in your OLAP grid, you can also use other dimensions present in your OLAP data source to filter the results of a graph or chart.

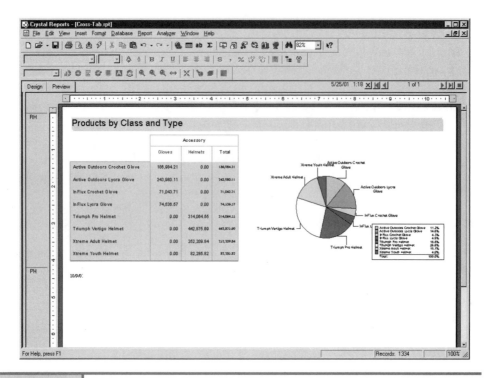

Figure 13-1 Information from cross-tab objects can be displayed on a graph or chart

Tip

Reporting and creating graphs from OLAP data is a bit beyond the scope of this book. If you are looking for information on working with Crystal Reports and OLAP data sources, check out *Crystal Reports 8.5: The Complete Reference*, also from McGraw-Hill/Osborne.

Graph Types

Different sets of data are particularly suited to different chart types. The following is an overview of the main chart types and their most common uses.

Bar

Bar charts represent data using bars, with the data plotted on the Y axis and broken out by values on the X axis. Using Crystal Reports, you can insert many different types of bar charts, including side-by-side bar (where each data item is given its own bar), stacked (where the items are stacked on top of each other), and percent (where the values are placed within a scale of 100 percent). A report showing a typical bar chart is shown in Figure 13-2.

Line

Line charts are frequently used to show trends, as they can show a greater level of detail than bar charts. For example, such a chart would be useful to show

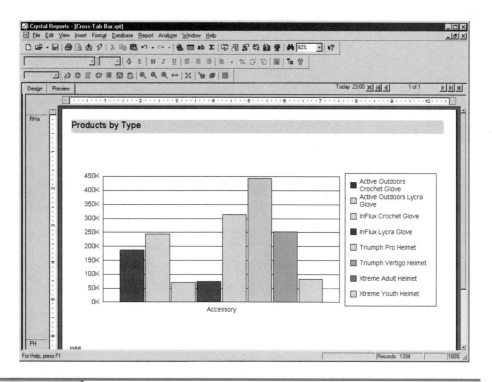

Figure 13-2   A typical bar chart

company share price; if the share price is updated every 15 minutes, it would be much easier to read a line graph of this data than, say, a bar chart.

A line chart shares some of the same options as a bar chart in that it can be presented in a side-by-side format, stacked, or using a percentage scale. Figure 13-3 shows a stacked line chart with two separate lines for two values within a single report.

Area

Area charts closely resemble line charts, except that underneath the line that indicates the trend, the area is solid to indicate the area the values represent. Area graphs can be inserted as stacked or percentage graphs and are an alternative to line charts. An example of a stacked area chart is shown in Figure 13-4.

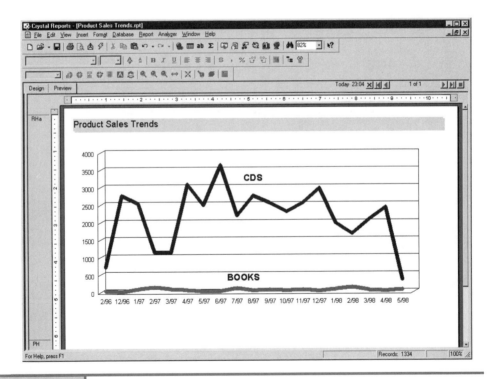

| **Figure 13-3** | A stacked line chart |

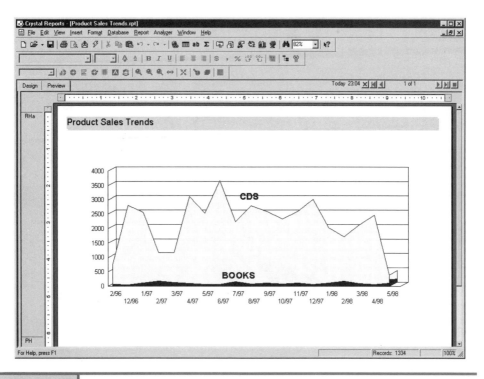

Figure 13-4 A stacked area chart

Pie

Pie charts are an old favorite, and Crystal Reports features a range of single, multiple, and proportional charts. You can explode pie pieces, rotate them, and set the depth and tilt of the pie, providing a flexible data presentation method for smaller data sets such as the one shown in Figure 13-5.

Doughnut

A doughnut chart can be thought of as a pie chart with a hole missing in the middle. Doughnut charts can easily represent small- to medium-sized data sets (1 to 20 items) and serve as an alternative to pie charts.

13

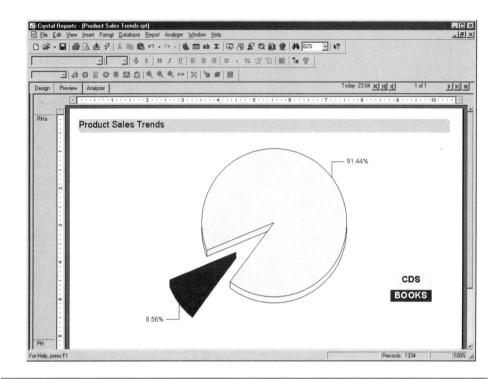

Figure 13-5   A typical pie chart showing an exploded slice

3D Riser and Surface

The 3D family of graph types place traditional graph types (bar, line, area, and so on) in a three-dimensional format, as shown in Figure 13-6. The information represented and graph types available in the 3D graphing family are identical to what you would find in their 2D counterparts, but they add a more sophisticated look to your report.

Note

Crystal Reports also includes a number of other graph types, including XY scatter, radar, bubble, and stock. You can preview these graph types from the Chart Expert.

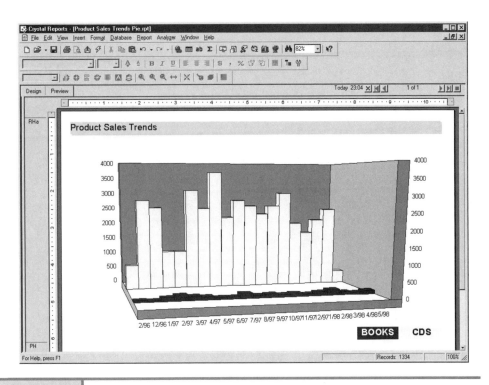

Figure 13-6 An example of a three-dimensional graph

Ask the Expert

Question: When I pick a particular graph type, I sometimes get an error message saying that the data does not fit the graph type. How can I avoid this problem?

Answer: Crystal Reports has many different types of graphs to choose from, but your data sets may not always match the graph type you choose to use. For example, to create an XY scatter chart, you need to have one X value and two or more Y values to plot. Crystal Reports

13

does a good job of managing the relationship between graph and data types by issuing warning messages like the one shown here.

If you have selected a graph type that does not match the data or configuration you have selected and attempt to exit the Report Expert by clicking OK, you are presented with three options:

- Continue with selected data and chart type

- Change data or chart type selection (return to chart expert)

- Let the expert choose the most appropriate chart for data Selected

The first option, using the selected data and chart type, will produce mixed results. In some cases, the chart that is presented may look like an accurate representation of the data, but there may be elements missing from the graph. The most common result of selecting this option is a completely blank report.

The second option, returning to the Chart Expert, gives you a chance to select another chart type and try again. Or if you feel like the Chart Expert can make a better choice than you can, you can have the expert select a chart type based on its internal logic.

Inserting a Group Graph

Now that you understand the different types of chart types and layouts, it's time to create one! To get started, we are going to take a look at the most common type of graph: the group graph. To be able to use a group graph, you will need to have two things in your report. The first is a group; this group can be created from a database field, formula field, and so on. The second requirement for a group graph is that you have some sort of summary field inserted onto your report. While this field is most frequently a summary on a numeric field, it can also be a summary on another type of field, such as a count of customers.

With these two elements in your report, you should be able to select Insert | Chart and start creating your first group chart. To begin, Crystal Reports will open the Chart Expert, shown in Figure 13-7. To help you quickly create a graph, Crystal Reports offers an option at the top of the dialog box, Automatically Set Chart Options, that is checked by default. If you were to uncheck this option, Crystal Reports would display a number of other property pages with other charting options. For this first chart, we will let Crystal Reports set the charting options for us.

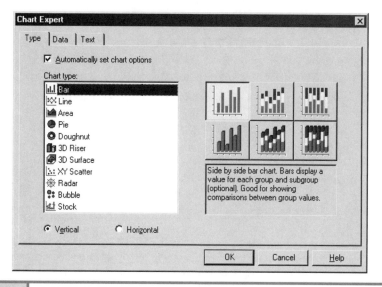

Figure 13-7   The Chart Expert

13

The first step in creating a group graph is selecting the type of graph you want to create. Referring to the descriptions of the different types of graphs, select a chart type from the list on the left, and then click an image of the specific type of graph you want to create.

The next step is selecting where the data will come from. Click the Data tab, shown in Figure 13-8. From the layouts on the left side of the page, select Group.

Tip

If you don't have a group inserted onto your report, this option will be dimmed.

You will need to specify where you want your new group chart placed. If you have only one group and summary inserted onto your report, your only options will be to place the graph in either the Report Header or Report Footer section. If you have multiple groups and summaries, you can place the graph in the group headers.

In the middle of the page, you will need to select On Change Of and Show values. These two options correspond directly to the groups and summaries

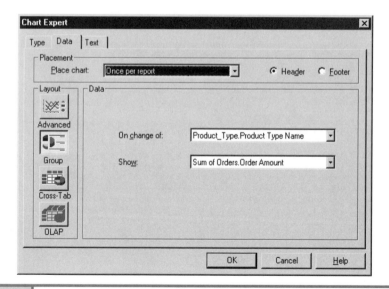

Figure 13-8   You will need to select where your graph data will come from

you have inserted onto your report. You should see all of the groups you have inserted in the On Change Of drop-down list, and all of the summaries should appear in the Show drop-down list.

The last step in creating a group graph is setting the text that will appear on your graph. Click the Text tab, shown in Figure 13-9.

By default, Crystal Reports will create text labels for your graph. To override these values, remove the check from the Auto-Text check box and enter the text you want to see on your graph. To change the formatting attributes associated with this text, select an item from the list at the bottom right of the dialog box and click the Font button, shown in Figure 13-10, to change the attributes.

Now click OK, and your newly created graph will be created and placed in the section you specified. Congratulations; you have just created your first group graph! We will look at some of the formatting options for charts a little later in this module, but now it is time to get some practice.

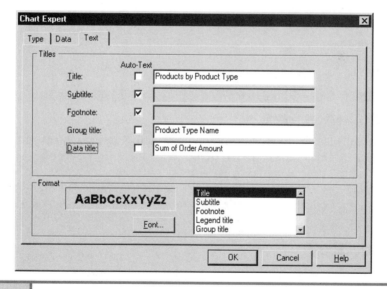

Figure 13-9   You can enter or edit the text for your graph

13

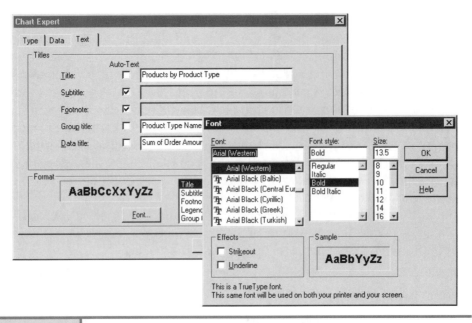

Figure 13-10
You can also change the font, size, color, and other attributes of your chart text

Project 13-1: Inserting a Graph Based on a Group

Group graphs are the most common type of graph and can be created in just a few steps. In this project, we are going to create a simple Product Mix report, listing all of the products sold by Xtreme, our fictional company, broken out by product type. From that point, we are going to create a pie chart based on the number of products within each product type and display the results in our report.

Step-by-Step

1. From the Start | Programs menu, launch Crystal Reports 8.5.

2. From the Welcome dialog box, select Create a New Crystal Report Document, and from the same dialog box, select Using the Report Expert.

3. From the Crystal Report Gallery, select the Standard Report Expert.

4. Click the Database button to open the Data Explorer and navigate to Xtreme Sample Database under the ODBC node.

5. From Xtreme Sample Database, select the Product table and click the Add button. A green check mark should appear next to the table, and the Data tab should reflect your selection. Use the same procedure to select the Product Type table as well. When you are finished, click Close to close the Data Explorer and return to the report expert.

6. On the Fields tab, select the fields that you want to see in your report. For this project, select the following fields:

● Product_Type.Product Type Name

● Product.Product Name

● Product.Product Class

To select a field, highlight it in the list on the left and click the right arrow button to move it to the list on the right.

7. On the Group tab, select the Product Type Name field and click the right arrow button to move this field to the list on the right. When your report is created, a group will be inserted in this field.

8. On the Total tab, select the Product ID field and click the right arrow button to move it to the list on the right. Change the Summary Type operator to Count. When your report is created, a summary field will appear at the bottom of each Product Type group, showing you the count of all the products in that group.

9. Click the Finish button to preview your report.

10. Verify that both a group and summary field have been inserted into your report.

11. Select Insert | Chart.

12. From the Chart Expert, shown in Figure 13-11, click the list of chart types on the left to select the type of chart you want to insert (in this case, Pie) and choose the exact layout by clicking the first sample graph on the right.

13. Click the Data tab to move to the next section of the Chart Expert.

14. Select Group from the Layout section on the left, as shown in Figure 13-12.

Tip

If the Group option is dimmed, double-check that you have both a group and a summary field inserted into your report.

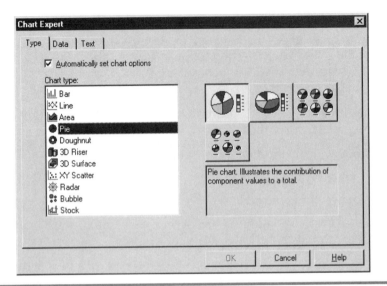

Figure 13-11 Crystal Reports includes a number of chart types; to preview, click the chart category on the left

15. Decide where you want to place your chart and use the pull-down box and radio buttons at the top of the dialog box to choose the section and specify whether the chart will appear in the header or footer of that section.

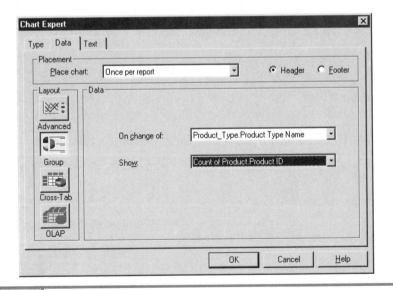

Figure 13-12 Options for group graphs

16. Using the pull-down boxes located in the Data section, specify how you want the graph broken out by selecting a group from the On Change Of pull-down list. Then select the summary field you want to drive the graph's content from the Show pull-down list. In this case, the selection is easy to make, as we only have one group and summary field inserted.

17. Click OK to accept your changes. Your new graph will be inserted into the section you have specified.

18. Save your report as **Product Type Chart Ch13-1.rpt**.

Project Summary

For reports that include both a group and a summary field in their structure, group graphing can be a quick and simple way to add extra value to the information presented.

Creating an Advanced Graph

Crystal Reports calls graphs that are based on X and Y values *advanced graphs* and allows you to specify multiple X and Y field values. To insert an advanced graph based on X and Y values, select Insert | Chart, which will open the Chart Expert.

After selecting the type of graph you want to create, click the Data tab and select the icon for an advanced graph, as shown in Figure 13-13.

There are two items that are required. The first is the field that will serve as the X axis in your graph. To select a field, highlight a field from the list on the left side of the dialog box and use the arrow to move it across to the right, below the drop-down box marked On Change Of. When working with this X-axis value, you have three options for how this field will be used:

- **On Change Of**   When the value contained within the field changes, a new bar, pie piece, and so on will be generated.

- **For Each Record**   A new bar, pie piece, and so on will be created for each record in the database.

- **For All Records**   One bar, pie piece, and so on will be created for all of the records in the database.

13

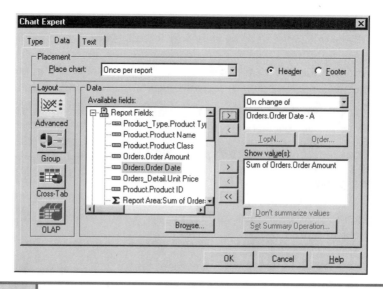

Figure 13-13 Advanced graphing options

Tip

You'll notice that you can have multiple X-axis values within an advanced graph. This allows you the flexibility you need to create complex graphs that require multiple X-axis values. Be warned that not all of the different graph types support multiple X axes.

With an X-axis value set, it is time to select the values that will be displayed in the Y axis of your graph, also called show values. Just as with the values for the X axis, select the field you want from the list on the left and use the arrow at the bottom of the page to move it to the list on the right.

Just as with the other graph types, by default Crystal Reports creates text labels for your graph. To override these values, remove the check from the Auto-Text box and enter the text you want to see on your graph. To change the formatting attributes associated with this text, select an item from the list at the bottom right of the dialog box and click the Font button to change the attributes.

From this point, you can click OK, and your advanced graph will be inserted into your report.

Now we will take a look at some of the formatting and other options that are specific to advanced graphs.

Changing the Sort Order

Often you will want to change the sort order of your advanced graph or use specified grouping to reorder the data represented.

On the Data tab of the Chart Expert, you may have noticed a button for Order, shown in Figure 13-14. This button is dimmed until you actually select one of the X-axis fields. Locate the field that controls sort order in the text box below the drop-down box labeled On Change Of and click to select it.

Note

If you have specified that the graph be printed for each record or for all records, you will not able to change the sort order.

With the field highlighted, the Order button should be enabled. Click to open the Sort Order dialog box. Four options are available:

- **Ascending**   A to Z, 0 to 9

- **Descending**   Z to A, 9 to 0

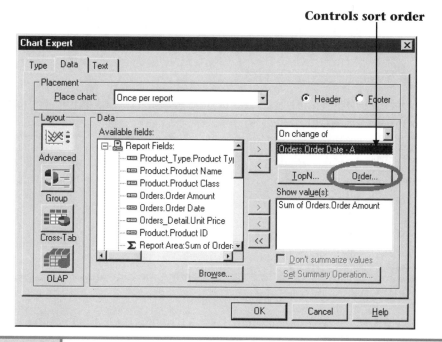

Figure 13-14 You can change the sort order of your chart without changing the underlying sort order of your report

- **Specified**   Similar to the specified grouping option available for groups inserted into your report—for naming a group and specifying the criteria for the values that should be included in that group.

- **Original**   The original order of the data as held in the database.

Tip

If you select Specified order, a second tab will appear in this dialog box for you to enter the names of the groups and the criteria for each.

When you are finished setting group options, click OK to accept your changes. When you return to your report preview, the sort order you specified should be reflected in your graph.

Applying TopN/Sort All Analysis

TopN/Sort All is a powerful analysis tool that can be applied to charts to zero in on important trends. To apply TopN/Sort All analysis to an advanced chart, locate the chart on your report and right-click directly on top of the chart. From the right-click menu, select Chart Expert. Then, in the Chart Expert dialog box, click the Data tab. Locate the field that controls sort order in the text box below the pull-down box labeled On Change Of and click to select it.

Note

If you have specified that the graph be printed for each record or for all records, you will not able to apply TopN/Sort All.

With the field highlighted, the TopN button should be enabled. Click to open the TopN/Sort dialog box. Three types of analysis are available using this feature, and each has its own parameters, as listed here:

- **TopN**   Enter a value for N to determine the TopN values based on the Y field you have selected.

- **BottomN**   Enter a value for N to determine the Bottom N values based on the Y field you have selected.

- **Sort All**   Choose this option to sort all data items in either ascending or descending order based on the Y value.

With TopN and BottomN, select the options for what to do with the other values not included in your N sample. Just as with TopN/BottomN analysis on a report, you can discard the other values, keep them in a group called Other, or simply leave them in their own groups—it's up to you.

When you are finished setting the TopN/Sorting options, click OK to accept your changes and return to your report design or preview. Your graph should now reflect the analysis options you have selected.

1-Minute Drill

- What two elements are required to create an advanced graph?
- What are the four sort orders available for advanced graphs?

Changing the Summary Operation

Locate the chart on your report and right-click directly on top of the chart. From the right-click menu, select Chart Expert. In the Chart Expert dialog box, click the Data tab. Locate the summarized field you want to work with in the Show Values dialog box at the lower right of the dialog box. Click to select it.

With the field highlighted, the Set Summary Operation button should be enabled. A number of summary operators are available depending on the field type; the most popular are listed here:

- **Sum**   Provides a sum of the contents of a numeric or currency field.

- **Average**   Provides a simple average of a numeric or currency field (that is, the values in the field are all added together and divided by the total number of values).

- **Minimum**   Determines the smallest value present in a database field; for use with number, currency, string, and date fields.

- **Maximum**   Determines the largest value present in a database field; for use with number, currency, string, and date fields.

- **Count**   Provides a count of the values present in a database field; for use with all types of fields.

- **Distinct Count**   Similar to Count, except any duplicate values are counted only once.

13

- Fields for the X and Y axes are required for an advanced graph.
- The four sort orders are ascending, descending, original, and specified.

Click OK to accept your summary type change and return to the Chart Expert. When you are finished, click OK to accept your changes and return to the report design or preview.

Inserting a Cross-Tab Graph

Cross-tabs are special objects that can be inserted into your report to provide complex summary and analysis features. To take those capabilities even further, you can insert a graph based on the data within a cross-tab.

Before you get started, you need to verify that a cross-tab has been added to your report's design and that it is working correctly. Preview the cross-tab and make sure the data appears in the rows, columns, and summarized fields. Then select Insert | Chart and select a chart type from the Chart Expert dialog box.

Tip

By default, the option Automatically Set Chart Options is enabled, reducing the number of formatting options required. If you want more control over your report, you can turn off this setting, and additional tabs will appear in the Chart Expert dialog box.

Click the Data tab to progress to the next step of the Chart Expert. In the dialog box that appears, click the Cross Tab layout type and select the placement for your chart.

Note

The options here are set by the cross-tabs you have inserted into your report and their locations. If you only have one cross-tab inserted in your report, you will be able to place the graph only in the report header or footer. If you have placed a cross-tab in the group header or footer, you can place a chart alongside it.

Using the combo boxes in the middle of the Data page (Figure 13-15), specify how the Chart will be printed, including how the chart components will be broken out (On Change Of), how they will be split within those breakouts (Subdivided By), and what values will be shown (Show).

Click the Text tab to advance to the final step of the Chart Expert and choose the text that will appear on your chart and the format of each text object.

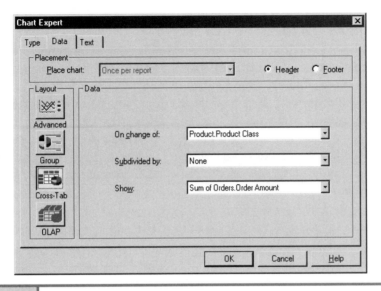

Figure 13-15   Options for a cross-tab graph

By default, the option for Auto-Text is enabled, allowing Crystal Reports to choose the text, but you can override this by removing the check from the Auto-Text box and typing your own text in the box provided.

When you are finished editing your chart's text, click OK to finish. Your cross-tab chart will now be attached to the tip of your mouse pointer. Click to place it in your report.

Tip

Crystal Reports will show a placeholder graph on the Design tab, so your data may not immediately appear. To see your own data, preview your report.

Formatting Graphs and Charts

Regardless of what type of graph or chart you have created, there are some common formatting options that can be applied to all. Most of the formatting options are available through menus that appear when you right-click directly on top of your graph or chart.

13

Changing Chart Placement

Charts can be placed almost anywhere on your report, depending on the type of chart you have created. To change a chart's position within a section, just click the graph and drag and drop the chart to its new position.

If you want to move a chart between sections (say, between the page header and a group header), you will need to use the Chart Expert. To start, right-click directly on top of the chart, select Format Chart, and then click the Data tab. Using the pull-down box at the top of the page, select a new section for your chart and use the radio buttons to specify whether the chart should be included in the heater or footer of that section.

Note

The options available at this point depend on what type of graph, groups, and so on you have inserted. All of your available options will be shown.

Click OK to accept your changes. Your chart should now be in the section you have specified.

Controlling Basic Chart Options

Basic chart options include the color scheme, marker size and shape, legend, and data points and can be controlled by clicking the graph you want to work with and selecting Format | Chart Expert. On the Type tab of the Chart Expert, turn off Automatically Set Chart Options. Two additional tabs marked Axes and Options should appear. Click the Options tab, shown in Figure 13-16.

Using this dialog box, choose the basic chart options:

- **Chart Color** Specify whether you want the elements (bars, slices, and so on) to be in color or black and white (gray scale).

- **Data Points** Specify whether you will show the label, the value, or no point at all on the bars or lines of your chart.

- **Customize Settings** Use to set the transparency of the chart object, as well as the marker size and shape.

- **Legend** Use to turn the legend display on or off and choose its placement (right, left, or bottom).

When you are finished setting your basic chart options, click OK to accept your changes.

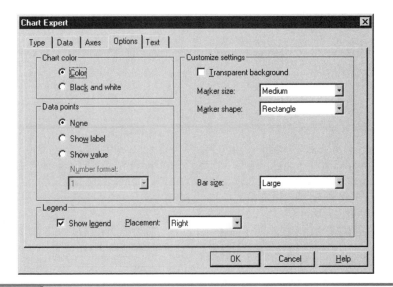

Figure 13-16 | A number of basic chart options are available to control the formatting and functionality of your graph or chart

Showing a Graph Legend

Crystal Reports automatically generates a legend for the charts and graphs you install. To work with legend options, click the graph you want to work with and select Format | Chart Expert. On the Type tab of the Chart Expert, turn off Automatically Set Chart Options. Two additional tabs should appear. Click the Options tab. Locate the section marked Legend and select the check box to enable the legend. Use the pull-down list beside this setting to choose the placement of the legend (right, left, or bottom).

When you are finished setting your basic chart options, click OK to accept your changes.

Changing a Graph from Color to Black and White

By default, Crystal Reports graphs and charts are shown in full color. You can change your chart or graph to use shading and patterns for better visibility when printing on a normal monotone printer. To change your graph from color to black and white, right-click directly on top of the graph you have inserted and select Chart Expert. On the Type tab, turn off Automatically Set Chart Options.

13

Two additional tabs should appear, marked Axes and Options. Click the Options tab, select the radio button marked Black and White, and then click OK to accept your changes. Your graph will now be recolored using only black and grayscale solids and patterns.

Tip

If you want to further customize the black-and-white formatting, you can use the Chart Analyzer to do so. To open the Chart Analyzer, right-click the graph and select this option from the right-click menu. You can then recolor or shade the different sections of your graph.

Controlling Chart Gridlines and Scale for Bar and Area Graphs

Gridlines are an easy way to add value to your chart or graph and provide an instant reference to the grid's dimensions and values. To control the gridlines and scale within your graph, right-click directly on top of your graph and select Format Chart | Grid. This will open a dialog box marked Numeric Axis Grids and Scales, shown in Figure 13-17, which has two tabs on the left side, for Group Axis and Data Axis. Click either of these tabs to select it.

On the horizontal tabs, click to select the tab marked Grids and set the gridline options for this axis, including the following:

- Show Gridlines

- Grid Style (regular, grids and ticks, inner ticks, outer ticks, spanning ticks)

- Draw Custom Line As

Click the Scales tab to set the options for scaling, including the following:

- Use Logarithmic Scale

- Always Include Zero

- Use Manual Settings for Minimum Value

- User Manual Settings for Maximum Value

When you are finished setting grid and scale options, click the vertical tab to select the other axis and repeat the process. Then click OK to accept your changes.

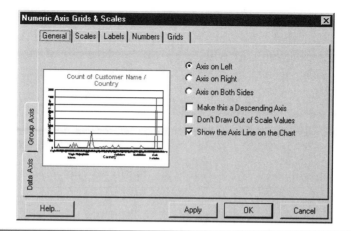

Figure 13-17 You can set the grid and scale options for the two axes
independently using this dialog box

1-Minute Drill

● How can you turn off the automatic settings for graphs?

● Where can you find the option to convert color graphs to black and white?

Changing the Graph Type

You can apply a number of different graph and chart types to your report data.
In addition to the standard types of bar, pie, and so on, there are chart types that
suit statistical data, radar and bubble graphs, three-dimensional graphs, and more.
To change the graph type, right-click directly on top of the chart you want to
change and select Format Chart | Template. From the Gallery tab, select a new
chart type by clicking an item on the list.

⊣Note

The preview image and options on the right side of the page will change according to
the graph type you choose.

13

● To turn off the automatic settings for graphs, remove the check from the box on the Type tab of the
Chart Expert.
● The option to convert color graphs to black and white is on the Options tab of the Chart Expert.

For custom chart types or any templates you may have saved, click the Custom tab. In this dialog box, click to select a category, and a preview of all of the charts within that category will appear on the right side of the page. Click a chart preview image to select it.

Tip

Any templates you have saved are in the category User Defined.

When you are finished selecting a new graph type, click OK to accept your change and return to your report's design or preview.

Setting Chart Titles and Text

Chart titles and text are set by default by Crystal Reports. To create your own chart titles and text for your graph, right-click your graph or chart and select Format Chart | Titles. Enter the text you want to appear for the title, subtitle, and so on.

Note

Changing the text that appears in this dialog box is the equivalent of unchecking the Auto-Text option in the Chart Expert and entering text.

When you are finished entering your text, click OK to accept your changes and return to your report design or preview.

Project 13-2: Formatting Your Graph or Chart

Using the report and graph we created earlier in this module, we are going to set some of the most common formatting options; we will edit the text that appears on our graph and change the graph color scheme (black and white) and legend options.

Step-by-Step

1. From the Start | Programs menu, launch Crystal Reports 8.5.

2. In the Welcome dialog box, select Open an Existing Report and then select More Files; click OK.

3. In the next dialog box, open the report created earlier in this module (Product Type Chart Ch13-1.rpt).

4. Right-click directly on top of the graph and select Chart Expert.

5. Turn off Automatically Set Chart Options. Two additional tabs should appear.

6. Click the Options tab and change the chart color from Color to Black and White.

7. Using the drop-down box located at the bottom of the dialog box, change the legend placement from Right to Bottom; the tab should look like Figure 13-18.

8. Click the Text tab and turn off Auto-Text beside the Title field. Enter a title for your graph (such as **Product by Product Type**) and click OK.

9. Click OK to accept your changes and return to your report's design or preview.

10. Save your report as **Product Type Chart Ch13-2.rpt**.

Project Summary

As a report developer, you have complete control over a graph or chart's appearance and attributes. Using the options presented in the Chart Expert, you can control most of these features without having to open another set of dialog boxes.

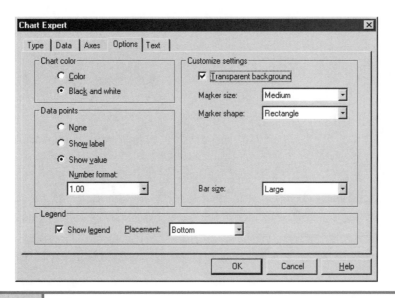

Figure 13-18   Advanced chart options

13

Creating Custom Graphs Using the Chart Analyzer

Crystal Reports includes a powerful analysis and formatting tool called the Analyzer that can be used with graphs, charts, and geographic maps. The Analyzer, shown in Figure 13-19, allows you to control the graph's or chart's appearance and formatting without having to enter a custom graphing editor (as you had to do in previous versions of the product).

In the Analyzer view of your chart, all of the chart objects are available. You can click the heading, for example, to change the font or color. Context-sensitive menus are available for most objects, detailing the formatting options available.

Once you have finished using the Analyzer to format your chart or graph, you can apply these changes to all graphs that appear in your report or discard

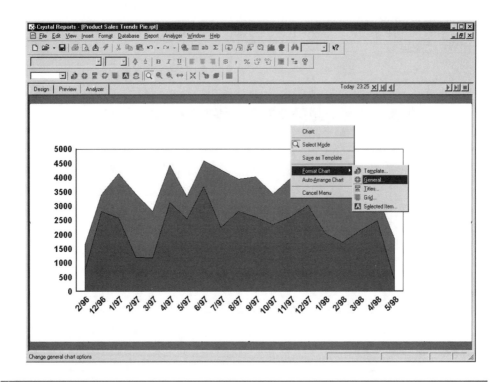

Figure 13-19   The Crystal Reports Analyzer can be used to format your graph or chart

them if you need to. If you have numerous reports that will need to have the same chart format, you can also save your settings to a template file that can be applied to any graph.

Right-click directly on top of the chart you want to work with and select Chart Analyzer from the right-click menu. A separate tab will open beside the Design and Preview tabs marked Analyzer. Using the formatting tools found within the Analyzer, set the general appearance and settings for your graph. When you are finished, click the red X on the toolbar at the upper right to close the Analyzer tab, or simply click the Design or Preview tab to return to your report.

Controlling Font Size and Color

One of the most commonly performed formatting tasks is changing the font size and color. To do so, right-click the chart you want to work with and select Chart Analyzer from the right-click menu. On the Analyzer tab that opens, locate the element of your graph that you want to change and click to select it. On the Analyzer toolbar, locate the text formatting icon, represented by the letter A, and click to open the Formatting dialog box.

Tip
You can also select the object and select Analyzer | Format Chart | Selected Item.

Using the dialog box shown in Figure 13-20, select the font, size, style, and color for the object you selected. When you are finished, click OK to return to the Analyzer. To return to the report design or preview, click the corresponding tab at the upper left of the report design interface.

Auto-Arranging Your Chart Contents

If you need a hand getting your graph or chart organized, you can have Crystal Reports do the arrangement for you with the Auto Arrange feature. To auto-arrange your chart contents, you will need to open the Chart Analyzer. Right-click on top of the graph you want to rearrange and select Chart Analyzer from the right-click menu. A separate tab will open beside the design and preview tabs, labeled Analyzer, showing only your graph. Right-click anywhere on the graph and select Auto-Arrange Chart from the right-click menu, as shown in Figure 13-21.

13

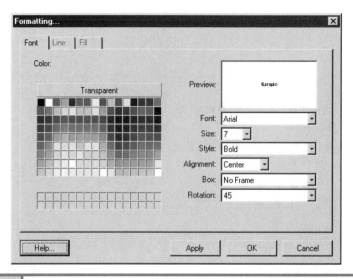

Figure 13-20 You can control the attributes of a specific element of your graph or chart

Your graph contents will be rearranged. To return to your report design or preview, use the red X to close the Analyzer tab, or click the Design or Preview tab. The changes you have made to your graph should be reflected in the graph in your report.

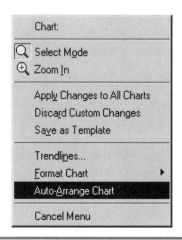

Figure 13-21 Crystal Reports can automatically arrange the contents of your chart or graph

Resizing a Chart

Charts and graphs may be just one element of a Crystal Report, and trying to get all of the elements to fit in the space allotted can be tricky. You can use the Chart Analyzer to resize your chart or graph so it fits within your report. To resize a chart, just click to select the chart you want to resize. A blue handle should appear on each side of your chart. Drag the blue handles to resize your chart.

Tip

Alternatively, right-click the graph and select Object Size and Position from the right-click menu. This will allow you to precisely control the size and position of your graph or chart within the Design or Preview tab.

Discarding Changes Made Using the Chart Analyzer

There will be times when you want to discard any custom changes you have made to your report and get back to basics. To discard changes made while using the Chart Analyzer, first verify that the graph you want to work with does not appear multiple times (for instance, that it is not repeated once for each group header). Remember that any formatting you discard from one instance of the graph will be lost from all instances.

Next, click the Preview tab to obtain a print preview of your report. Right-click directly on top of your graph and select Discard Custom Changes. The changes you have made using the Analyzer will be discarded, and your report should return to its original look and feel.

Note

When you right-click a graph, in addition to discarding changes, you also have the option of applying these changes to all graphs within your report.

Saving Chart Settings as a Template

Giving your graphs and charts a standard look and feel is a snap through the use of templates. Templates are graph or chart settings that can be saved to a file and reapplied to different graphs, even in different report files. To save your chart or graph settings as a template, right-click on top of the graph or chart you want to work with and select Chart Analyzer from the right-click menu.

13

Using the features and functionality of the Chart Analyzer, format your graph's fonts, colors, layout, and so on. When you are finished working with the formatting of your graph or chart, right-click on top of the chart in the Analyzer tab and select Save as Template from the right-click menu. A message will appear telling you that these formatting options have been saved in a template file.

Tip

To copy template files between computers, locate c:\Program Files\Seagate Software\Sschart\Templates\User Defined\1.3tf (which is incremented with each custom template you save) and copy this file to the same location on another machine.

To verify that your template has been saved, right-click the graph in the Analyzer view and select Format Chart | Template from the right-click menu. Click the Custom tab and then locate the category User Defined. If you click this category, a sample of the graph types should appear at the right, and your graph or chart template should be listed.

Project 13-3: Creating an Advanced (X, Y) Chart

An advanced chart offers more flexibility than a simple group graph and allows us to plot multiple X- and Y-axis values. In this project, we are going to create a new report that displays sales data from our fictional company's Orders table. We will create an advanced graph that will display these orders as a line graph, showing a sales trend across time, and then we will hide the details so that only the graph is displayed in our report.

Step-by-Step

1. From the Start | Programs menu, launch Crystal Reports 8.5.

2. From the Welcome dialog box, select Create a New Crystal Report Document, and from the same dialog box, select Using the Report Expert.

3. From the Crystal Report Gallery, select the Standard Report Expert.

4. Click the Database button to open the Data Explorer and navigate to Xtreme Sample Database under the ODBC node.

5. From Xtreme Sample Database, select the Orders table and click the Add button. A green check mark should appear next to the table, and the Data

tab should reflect your selection. When you are finished, click Close to close the Data Explorer and to return to the report expert.

6. On the Fields tab, select the fields that you want to see in your report. For this project, select the following fields:

● Orders.Order Date

● Orders.Order Amount

To select a field, highlight it in the list on the left and click the right arrow button to move it to the list on the right.

7. With the Data and Fields tabs completed, click the Finish button to preview your report.

8. Select Insert | Chart.

9. From the Chart Expert, click the list of chart types on the left to select the type of chart you want to insert, and choose the exact layout by clicking the sample graph on the right.

10. Click the Data tab to move on to the next step of the Chart Expert.

11. Select the Advanced layout, as shown in Figure 13-22.

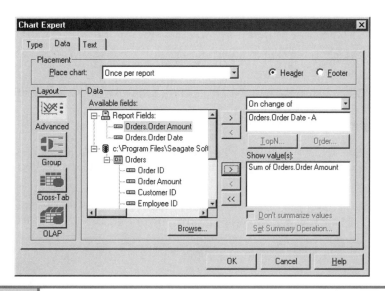

Figure 13-22 Advanced graphing options

13

12. Decide where you want to place your chart and use the options at the top of the dialog box to choose the section and specify whether the chart will appear in the header or footer of that section. In this case, we want our chart to appear in the Report Header section.

13. Locate the Orders.Order Date field in the Available Fields list. This represents the X values for our graph.

14. Highlight the Orders.Order Date field and click the right arrow (>) beside the box marked On Change Of. This should add this field to the list immediately underneath On Change Of.

15. Locate the Orders.Order Amount fields in the Available Fields list. This represents the Y values for our graph.

16. Highlight the Orders.Order Amount field and click the right arrow (>) beside the box marked Show Values. This should add field to the list below the Show Values label.

17. Click the Text tab to advance to the next step of the Chart Expert.

18. Review the autotext that will be added to your report, shown in Figure 13-23. To turn off autotext and enter your own title information, turn off the Auto-Text option and type the text in the box provided.

Tip

You can also control the format (font, size, and so on) of the text using the Format section at the bottom of the dialog box.

19. Click OK to exit the Chart Expert. Your graph will now be automatically inserted into the section you selected, and that section will be resized to accommodate it.

20. Switch to the Design tab of your report, and for each of the sections except the Report Header, right-click the gray area to the left of the section and select Hide Section or Suppress Section.

21. When you are finished, preview your report. Your chart should now appear on page 1 of 1, showing a sales trend across time.

22. Save your report as **Product Type Chart Ch13-3.rpt**.

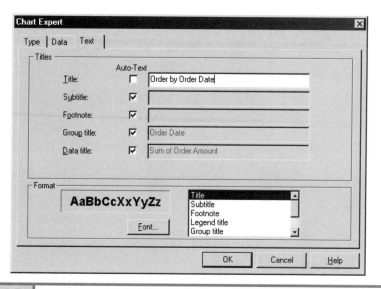

Figure 13-23 You can let Crystal Reports label your graph using autotext, or you can specify the text yourself

Project Summary

Using an advanced chart or graph, you have complete control over how the data elements are plotted and can specify multiple X- and Y-axis fields.

13

☑ Mastery Check

1. What are the four types of chart layouts available?

_____

_____

2. What must be inserted in your report before you can create a group graph?

_____

_____

3. What values are required to create an advanced graph?

_____

_____

4. How can you change a chart from full color to black and white?

_____

_____

5. Where would you find the option to change the size of a chart element:

   A. File | Options

   B. Chart Expert

   C. Chart Analyzer

   D. Section Expert

6. What types of graph allow drill down?

_____

_____

Module 14

Geographic Mapping

Goals

- Understand the uses of geographic mapping
- Use mapping in a report
- Format geographic maps
- Analyze maps to create presentation-quality reports
- Resolve common mapping problems

Geographic mapping provides report designers with a quick and easy method for displaying geographic data. Users can quickly check sales in the United States, statistical information on Europe, or population growth in Asia, with drill-down capabilities to display the underlying data as well. In this module, you will learn about the Crystal Reports mapping technology, how to insert and work with geographic maps, and some tricks and tips to make your maps more meaningful.

Geographic Mapping Overview

Crystal Reports offers report developers a number of powerful summary methods. One of the most popular is geographic mapping. Using technology from MapInfo, Crystal Reports now has an integrated mapping facility that allows you to create reports from your data and display it in a map in a variety of formats.

Map Layouts

There are many different map types (ranges, dot density, pie, and others), but maps in Crystal Reports can be categorized into four types, or layouts: advanced, group, cross-tab, and OLAP grid.

Advanced Maps

Advanced maps rely on a geographic field in your database to plot information on a map. They are similar in concept to advanced graphs. To create an advanced map, you need to specify a field to be plotted and a field containing a value to be shown. Optionally, you can also specify a geographic field to subdivide by (for instance, your main geographic field could be Country, and it could be subdivided by Region). With an advanced map, you can control the summary that is generated from these values or specify that no summary be generated.

Group Maps

A group map relies on a group you have inserted into your report for the points to plot, and a summary field you have created for the values to show. By inserting a group map into a drill-down or summary report, you provide users with a comprehensive view of the data in your report. When they view a particular region and want to see the details that make up that region's total value, for instance, they can drill down into the map to display the data they need, as shown in Figure 14-1.

Cross-Tab Maps

If you have a cross-tab inserted into your report, you can create a geographic map from the cross-tab data, provided that your cross-tab has some geographic fields inserted. As the information in the cross-tab changes, so should your report.

OLAP Grid Maps

Maps can be created from OLAP grids, which are used to display data from OLAP data structures.

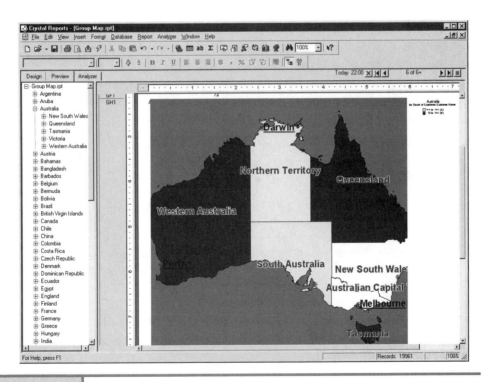

Figure 14-1 An example of a group map

14

Tip

For more information on working with OLAP grids and mapping, consult *Crystal Reports 8.5: The Complete Reference* by George Peck (McGraw-Hill/Osborne, 2001).

Map Types

Different sets of data are particularly suited to different map types. This section provides an overview of the main chart types and their most common uses.

Ranges

A ranges map separates values from your report into separate bands and assigns a color code to each. When a ranges map is generated, the map components are color coded according to the associated range. In the ranges map shown in Figure 14-2, the data on the number of customers in each country is separated into bands (or ranges) and shown in colors from white (for the highest infection rate) to black (the lowest).

There are actually a number of ways to break out the different bands, or ranges:

- **Equal Count**   Evenly splits data based on the number of items. For example, if you have 50 states and 5 ranges, each range would include 10 states.

- **Equal Ranges**   Evenly splits data based on the value of the items represented. A particular range could have 5 states or 20, depending on where the values for the states fell.

- **Natural Break**   Splits the data based on a combination of the values and count using the statistical formula of the same name.

- **Standard Deviation**   Calculates the standard deviation of the items you have selected and splits the data into equal bands centered around the mean.

With a ranges map, you can set the color for the starting and ending range, and Crystal Reports will adjust the colors accordingly, moving from one color to the next.

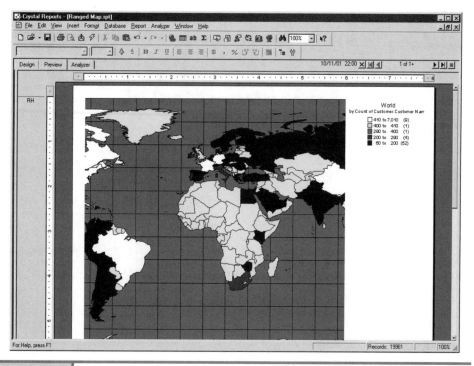

Figure 14-2 A typical ranges map

Dot Density

A dot-density map created with Crystal Reports, such as the one shown in Figure 14-3, closely resembles a paper map you might hang on the wall with push-pins used to mark locations. Each value in your map is plotted on a dot-density map. Areas with a higher number of corresponding values show a higher density of dots.

Graduated

A graduated map, like the one shown in Figure 14-4, uses a symbol whose size is based on a summary value in your report. You can control the symbol's appearance, font, rotation, color, and so on. Graduated map reports are best

14

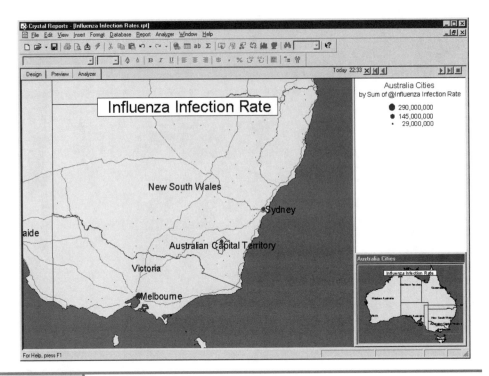

Figure 14-3 A dot-density map shows one point for each data item

used to display information where the values are not too close together; in Figure 14-4, for example, it would be hard to discern between a symbol for 10,000 and a symbol for 20,000.

Pie Chart

Pie charts can be displayed on your map, to show values for a particular country or region. This type of geographic map, such as the one shown in Figure 14-5, requires both a field to plot and a subfield. For example, if you tried to create a map based on just the Country field in your database, this

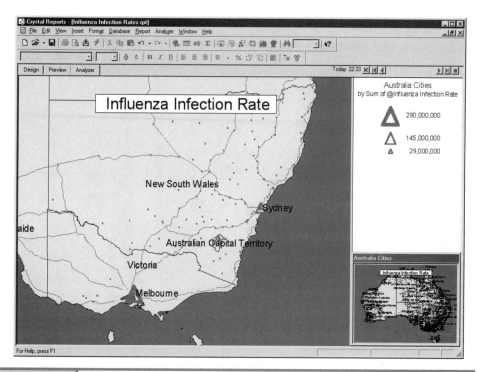

Figure 14-4   In a graduated map, the size of the symbol is based on the value of a summary field

option would not be available. To draw a pie chart and divide the pie pieces correctly, you need to also specify a subfield.

Bar Chart

Bar charts can also be displayed on your map, with a bar chart for each country or region. As with pie charts, this type of chart requires both a geographic field to plot and a subfield to determine how to break up the bars on the chart.

14

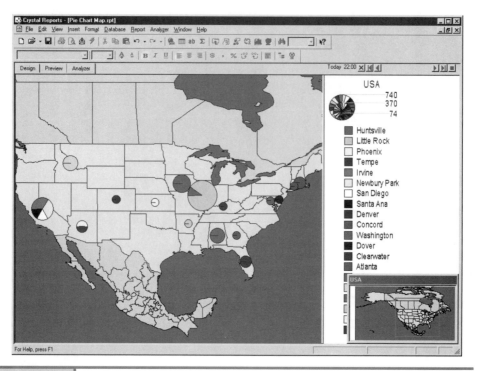

Figure 14-5 Pie charts can be displayed on your map to show values related to a particular geographic area

Inserting a Group Map

Probably the most popular layout for geographic maps involves groups that are inserted in your report and summary fields on report values. In addition to providing geographic analysis, these types of reports make it easy to locate the detailed data that has been plotted. To insert a map based on a group and summary field, you will need to verify that you have both a group and some summary field inserted in your report. Then select Insert | Map to open the Map Expert dialog box shown in Figure 14-6.

If it is not already selected, click the Group Layout option and select the values that are to appear on your geographic map from the drop-down menu

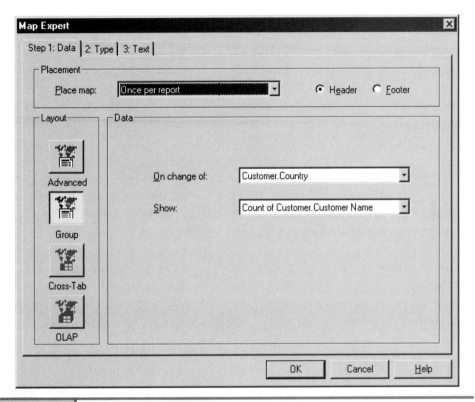

Figure 14-6 You need to have both a group and a summary field inserted in your report to use a group map.

of summarized fields that appear in your report. The On Change Of drop-down menu will display the groups that are inserted in your report and the Show drop-down menu displays all of the summaries that are available for that particular group. Choose the section where you want your map placed from the drop-down menu and select Header or Footer.

You will also need to click on the Type tab, select a map type, and set any options related to the map type you choose. Your options are listed in Table 14-1.

Note

Only ranges, dot-density, and graduated maps can be used with group maps.

Map Type	Options
Ranges	Number of Intervals, Distribution Method, Color of Intervals, Allow Empty
Dot Density	Number of Intervals, Distribution Method, Color of Intervals, Allow Empty
Graduated	Symbol Style

Table 14-1   Group Map Type Options

Next, you will need to click the Text tab and set the options for the text that will appear on your map. Enter a map title and set the options for the legend, choosing one of the following:

- Full Legend

- Compact Legend

- No Legend

Click OK to accept your changes and return to your report design or preview. Your map should be inserted into the section you specified. Just as with graphs, Crystal Reports will show a sample map on the Design tab. When your report is previewed, the information will be read from the database, and the correct map will be displayed.

Creating an Advanced Map

Advanced maps are similar to the advanced graphs you worked with in Module 13. Instead of specifying an X and Y value, you need to specify a geographic field from your database, a field to determine how this field should be divided, and a value to appear on your map.

Choose Insert | Map and select Advanced from the list of layouts. You will see the options shown in Figure 14-7.

Your first step is to set the geographic field. This can be any field in your database or tables that contains geographic information (for instance, Country,

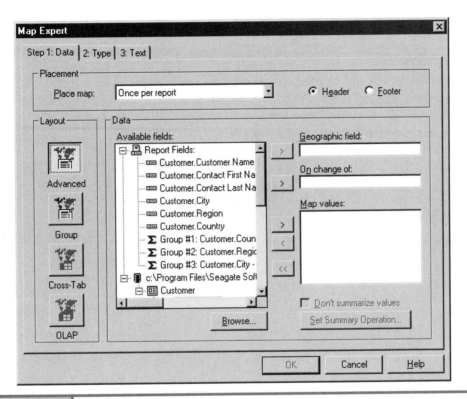

Figure 14-7   Options for creating an advanced map

Region, State, and so on) and should be a string field, as Crystal Reports will match the values contained within its own geographic data to identify that location on the map.

You also need to select a field for On Change Of. This field will be used to divide your geographic field even further. By default, this is set to the same value as the geographic field. If you were to use the Country field as both the geographic and On Change Of fields, your map values would be broken out by country. If you were to use Country as the geographic field and State as the On Change Of field, your map values would be broken down by country and then the individual states within those countries.

14

Finally, you need to specify the values that will be shown on the geographic map. You can specify multiple values and select a different summary operator for each. By default, Crystal Reports inserts Sum for the numeric values you specify for a map and Count for string and other fields, but you can use other summary operators as well. To do so, highlight the field you want to change in the Map Values text box. Then click the Set Summary Operation button to open the Change Summary dialog box, shown in Figure 14-8. Select a new summary type for your map value from the following options:

- Sum
- Minimum
- Count
- Correlation
- Weighted Average
- Pth Percentile
- Nth Smallest
- Nth Most Frequent
- Sample Standard Deviation
- Population Standard Deviation

- Average
- Maximum
- Distinct Count
- Covariance
- Median
- Nth Largest
- Mode
- Sample Variance
- Population Variance

When you are finished editing the summary field, click OK to return to the Map Expert.

You now need to select a map type. Just as for group maps, there are only three types of maps available: ranges, dot density, and graduated.

Tip

For more information on the options for each map type, see Table 14-1.

You also can select the text that appears on your map using the Text tab. You will find the options for displaying a legend there as well.

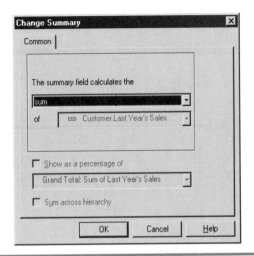

Figure 14-8 You can change the summary type of the field that drives your map values

With the text set, click OK and place your map in your report. When you preview the report, the map should look at the geographic and On Change Of fields you have specified and show the values you selected, as appropriate.

Inserting a Map Based on a Cross-Tab

Cross-tabs provide a summarized view of your data and can be used as the data source for a geographic map. To insert a map based on cross-tab data, you first need to verify that a cross-tab has been added to your report's design and that it is working correctly. You should be able to preview the cross-tab and have data appear in the rows, columns, and summarized fields. To create a map, click in your report to select the cross-tab that the map is to be based on; then select Insert | Map.

14

Tip

You can also right-click a cross-tab and select Insert Map from the right-click menu.

From the dialog box shown in Figure 14-9, select the geographic field from your cross-tab using the drop-down menu provided.

If you want your map to be subdivided by another field, use the second drop-down menu to select the appropriate field. Select the values that are to appear on your geographic map from the drop-down menu of summarized fields that appear on your cross-tab.

Note

The fields and summaries available for mapping are sourced directly from the underlying cross-tab. To add a field or summary or to change a summary field type, you need to change the content of the cross-tab itself.

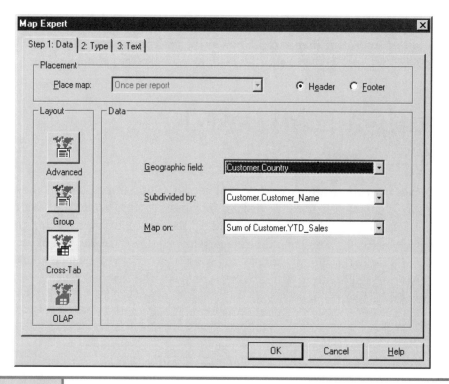

Figure 14-9   Your cross-tab will need to include a geographic field

Click the Type tab to continue. Choose the section you want your map placed in from the drop-down menu provided and select either Header or Footer. Then select a map type and set any options required for that particular type (Table 14-1 lists the map types and options).

Click the Text tab to continue. Then enter a map title and set the options for the legend, choosing one of the following:

- Full Legend

- Compact Legend

- No Legend

Click OK to accept your changes and return to your report design or preview. Your map should be inserted into the section you specified.

1-Minute Drill

- What is the difference between a group map and an advanced map?
- What are the three map types available for group maps?

Formatting Maps

With your basic map created, it's time to look at some basic formatting and navigation techniques that will help the users find what they are looking for on your report.

Changing Map Placement

Maps can complement most areas of your report and are most effective when placed as a focal point. To change your map placement for the optimum effect, you have two options.

To move maps within a section, you can simply click the map and drag and drop the map object to its new position. To move a map between sections,

- A group map is based on a group field and summary; an advanced map is based on any fields from your database.
- The three available map types are ranges, dot density, and graduated.

right-click directly on top of the map, select Map Expert, and then click the Data tab. Using the drop-down menu at the top of the page, select a new section for your map and use the radio buttons to specify whether the chart should be included in the header or footer of that section.

Note

The options that are available at this point depend on the type of map you have inserted. All of your available options will be shown.

Click OK to accept your changes and return to your report's design or preview.

Navigating Through a Map

The world is a big place, and Crystal Reports provides a number of methods to navigate through your geographic maps to find the information you need. To use the navigation tools within Crystal Reports, switch to the preview of your report, right-click directly on top of the map, and select one of the following navigation methods:

- Center Map
- Select Mode
- Zoom In
- Zoom Out
- Pan

When you are finished working with the navigation tools, click anywhere outside of the map boundaries to return your mouse pointer to normal.

Tip

The same navigation tools are available when you are working with your map in the Analyzer view.

Creating Custom Maps Using the Map Analyzer

Crystal Reports includes a powerful analysis and formatting tool called the Analyzer, which can be used with graphs, charts, and geographic maps. The Analyzer gives you control over the map's focus and formatting and can be used to tweak maps for better display and formatting in your report.

Using the Map Navigator

The map navigator provides a viewfinder window that you can quickly position to zero on a particular map location. To use the map navigator, click your map and select Analyzer | Map Analyzer. Locate the map navigator in the lower-right corner of the Analyzer, as shown in Figure 14-10.

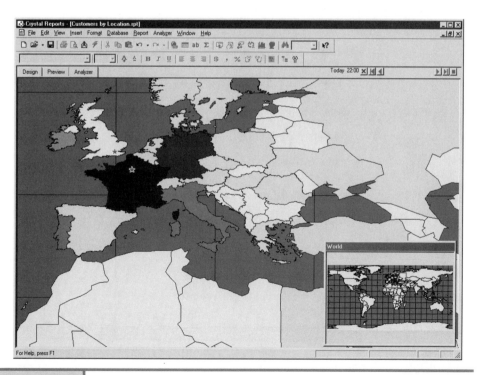

| **Figure 14-10** | The map navigator provides a quick method for moving around in your map |

Resize or drag and drop the outline box that appears within the map navigator to narrow the focus of the Analyzer. To close the map navigator, right-click the body of the map and select Map Navigator | Hide. When you are finished, you can return to your report by clicking the Design or Preview tab.

Changing the Map Type

There are a number of map types available, such as dot density, graduated, and pie chart, and you may not know which one to use. Luckily, Crystal Reports has provided a way to quickly switch between the different map types. To change the map type, click to select the map you are working with and select Analyzer | Map Analyzer. This will open a separate Analyzer tab to the right of the Preview tab. Right-click directly on top of your map in the Analyzer view and select Format Map | Type from the right-click menu. Using the dialog box shown in Figure 14-11, select a new map type and set the options relating to your selection.

When you are finished, click OK to return to the Analyzer. To return to your report, click the Design or Preview tab.

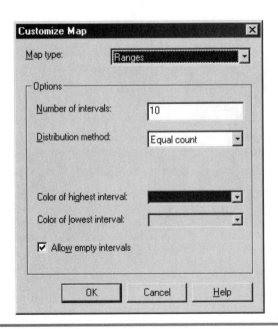

Figure 14-11 | The map types available depend on your report data and the content you want to see

Setting Map Titles

You can add a map title to your report by clicking to select the map you are working with and selecting Analyzer | Map Analyzer. This will open a separate Analyzer tab to the right of the Preview tab. Right-click directly on top of your map in the Analyzer view and select Format Map | Title from the right-click menu. In the dialog box that appears, type the text for the map title and click OK. To return to your report, click the Design or Preview tab.

Adding Map Layers (Data Sets)

When Crystal Reports creates a geographic map from your data, it uses the default layers or data sets. You can add layers to your geographic map to provide more detail and meaning to your map. Click to select the map you are working with and select Analyzer | Map Analyzer. This will open a separate Analyzer tab to the right of the Preview tab. Right-click directly on top of your map in the Analyzer view and select Format Map | Layers. In the dialog box that appears, click the Add button to open a file browser window.

Navigate to the directory c:\Program Files\Mapinfo MapX\Maps\. This is where Crystal Reports stores the data that drives the maps that are created within a report. From the list of available layers (*.tab), select the layers you want to add by holding down the CTRL key and clicking. When you are finished, click the Open button.

Using the Up and Down buttons in the Layer Control dialog box, shown in Figure 14-12, set the order in which the layers should be shown. Use the Visible check box to show or hide a particular layer, and select the Automatic Labels option if you want Crystal Reports to label the items on your map.

Tip

You can also click the Display button to set how far a particular map has to be zoomed in or out before the layer will appear.

When you are finished working with the layers of your map, click OK to return to the Analyzer. To return to your report design, click the Design or Preview tab.

14

Figure 14-12 You can control how layers are placed on top of each other

Resolving Mismatched Data

In the Analyzer view of your map, you can navigate through your map and change map options and settings, but without a doubt the most important feature of the Analyzer is the ability to correct mismatched data. In Crystal Reports, using the mapping technology, some underlying data structures associate a geographic location with a value in your report. If the report finds London, for example, it looks in its geographic data and makes the association to the correct location on the map for London.

But what happens when the location can't be found or is spelled differently? It is in these situations that you need to use the mismatch utility of the Analyzer. Using a simple interface, the Analyzer presents a list of unmatched values and a list of available locations. By manually making the match between these two lists, you can correct for any possible errors (for example, if London was entered into the database as LondoninEngland, you could correctly match this value back to the correct map value).

To resolve mismatched values, you'll need to be in the Map Analyzer within Crystal Reports. Once you are in the Map Analyzer, right-click directly on top of your map in the Analyzer view and select Resolve Mismatched Data from the right-click menu.

Note

If this menu item does not appear, Crystal Reports has been able to successfully match all values in your report to a location on the map.

From the dialog box shown in Figure 14-13, select the values that need to be matched in the list on the left and scroll through the keywords on the right. When you find a value that matches, click the Assign button to match the two fields.

Tip

To remove a mismatched field, highlight the match in the text box in the bottom half of the screen and click Remove.

When you have matched all of the listed fields, click OK to return to the Analyzer. The values you matched should now appear on your map.

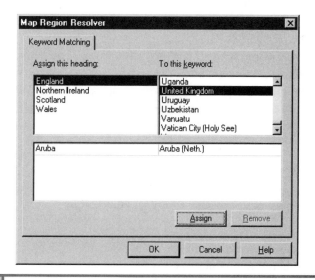

Figure 14-13 The mismatched data utility can help resolve database integrity issues in your geographic maps

14

Mapping Limitations

Just as with graphing, when you are working with geographic mapping, your data must match the type of map you have inserted. Pie and bar charts, for example, require subfields; without a subfield, you cannot create this type of chart.

Another consideration is the quality of the data that resides in your database. Crystal Reports will attempt to match values in your database to the mapping data in its own internal table of locations and boundaries. If your database does not store information consistently, you could run into problems, even if you are using the manual matching process. You can correct a handful of mismatches using the Analyzer tool, but if you have hundreds of items that need to be manually matched, it is time to go back and look at the source data.

Report designers frequently ask whether they can add their own maps to Crystal Reports. Technically, the answer is yes. The map data that drives the Crystal Reports technology is stored in c:\program files\Seagate software\ MapInfo\MapX\Maps, and you can create your own data file using MapInfo Professional (or some other appropriate tool) and add it to this subdirectory. From that point, you could simply add the layer as usual from within Crystal Reports.

However, if you want to be a mapping power user, you will need to look to a different tool. Crystal Reports integrates a very basic set of tools from MapInfo. If you need to create maps, geocode data, and the like, you probably need to step up to MapInfo Professional or some other MapInfo tool created specifically for that task.

Note

Through a reciprocal arrangement, MapInfo Professional uses Crystal Reports as its reporting tool, so you won't be too far out of your league.

Developers also often want to know why a particular region, state, city, or other location is not available. Crystal Reports ships with sample map data and layers that have been provided by MapInfo, and it is not always the most complete or up-to-date data available. You can purchase additional data sets relating to your locale or specific interest directly from MapInfo at www.mapinfo.com.

Project 14-1: Inserting an Advanced Map Based on Geographic Field Values

If you don't have a group or summary inserted into your report, you can still use geographic mapping by selecting a geographic field from your database, along with a break field and value to be displayed. This type of geographic map is called an advanced map, and in this project, we are going to add an advanced map to the Customer by Country report we created in Module 4.

Tip

You can download a copy of this report in the folder for this module, available from the Osborne Web site at www.osborne.com.

Step-by-Step

1. Open the Customer by Country drill-down report you created in Project 4-2.

2. Select Insert | Map.

3. Click the Advanced layout option.

4. From the list of available fields, select {Customer.Country} as the geographic field to use for this map. Highlight the field and click the first right arrow (>) to move the field to the Geographic Field box.

5. Select the field that will serve as the On Change Of field. If {Customer.Country} isn't in the On Change Of box already, highlight the field and click the second right arrow to move the field to the box.

6. Locate the {Customer.Last Year's Sales} field, which contains the values we want to show on the map; then highlight it and click the last right arrow in the dialog box to move the field to the Map Values box. The dialog box should now look like the one shown in Figure 14-14.

7. Choose the section you want your map placed in from the drop-down menu at the top of the dialog box. In this case, place the map in the header.

8. Click the Type tab to continue.

9. Select the Ranges map type and set any related options.

10. Click the Text tab to continue.

11. Enter **International Sales** as the map title and set the Compact Legend option for the legend.

14

12. Click OK to accept your changes and return to your report design or preview. Your map should be inserted into the section you specified. When you preview your report, a map similar to the one shown in Figure 14-15 should appear, allowing you to navigate to a particular area of interest.

13. Save your report as **Customer by Country Map Ch14-1.rpt**.

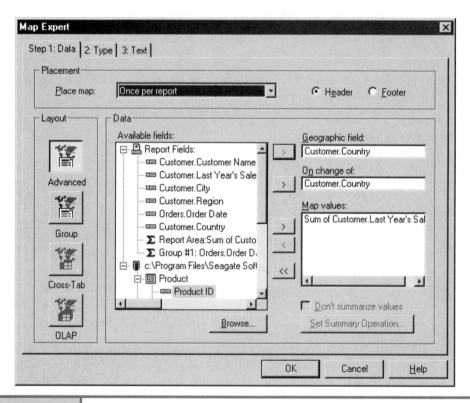

Figure 14-14   Advanced mapping options

☐-■Sum of Customer.Last Yea

Figure 14-15 The finished product

Project Summary

Geographic maps can add values to reports, providing an easy way to summarize geographic data. Whether a map is based on a group, fields from your database, or a cross-tab, maps can provide at-a-glance analysis for report users.

☑ Mastery Check

1. What are the four types of map layout?

_____

_____

2. Which of the following is not a map type:

A. Ranges

B. Dot density

C. Nonlinear

D. Graduated

3. What does the term *pan* mean?

_____

_____

4. How can mismatched data be resolved?

_____

_____

5. What are map layers?

_____

_____

databases or tables, the only join (or link) available between two or more tables in the Linking Expert is a left-outer join (meaning that all of the information from the table on the left will be read first, and any matching items from the table on the right will also be shown).

This can be limiting if you have created a truly relational database design using one of the database file types. The options for looking up two or more tables, shown in Figure 15-3, are as follows:

- Look Up Both at the Same Time

- Look Up All Of One, Then All of the Others

- Look Up All of the Combinations of the Two Files

If the relationships between tables in your database require a different type of join or lookup, you may want to consider using an intermediary table or query.

Figure 15-3   Options for linking two PC-type databases or tables

15

Relational Databases

By far the most popular data access method uses a native or ODBC connection to a relational database. Crystal Reports ships native drivers for the most popular RDBMSs, including these:

- IBM DB2, DB2/2, DB2/400, and DB2/600

- Informix

- Lotus Notes and Domino 4.5 and above, R5

- Microsoft SQL Server

- Oracle 7.x and 8.x

- Sybase SQL Server releases 10 and 11

Most of these native drivers require that the standard database client be installed and configured before they can be used. Your database or system administrator should be able to help you with the client installation. Chances are good that you probably already have the correct software installed on your machine. An easy way to tell is to check the Data Explorer to see whether your data source appears under the heading More Data Sources.

Tip

For more information about working with direct database connections within Crystal Reports, check out *Crystal Reports 8.5: The Complete Reference* by George Peck (McGraw-Hill/Osborne, 2001).

In addition to using native driver access, you can also access these data sources through an ODBC driver. To access a database through ODBC, you will need to configure the appropriate ODBC driver through the ODBC Administrator (accessed through the Windows control panel). Again, your database or system administrator should be able to help you with this or at least point you in the right direction.

Once you have set up an ODBC driver, your database should appear in the Data Explorer in the ODBC section and allow you to report from the tables within your database.

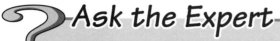

Ask the Expert

Question: What ODBC drivers are included with Crystal Reports?

Answer: Crystal Reports 8.5 includes a number of ODBC drivers for popular data formats and DBMSs, including ASCII, Dbase, IBM DB/2, Informix releases 5 and 7, Microsoft Access, Microsoft Excel, Microsoft FoxPro, Microsoft Visual FoxPro 3.0, Microsoft SQL Server, Oracle, Paradox, and Sybase SQL Server releases 10 and 11.

OLAP Data Sources

OLAP data (sometimes called multidimensional data) can be accessed through OLE DB for OLAP, a standard interface for accessing OLAP data, or through a number of native OLAP drivers that are included with Crystal Reports, including these:

- Hyperion Essbase

- IBM DB/2

- HOLOS HDC

OLAP data provides a summary of information that is held within a relational database and can provide insight that millions of rows of data normally do not.

Tip

For more information about working with OLAP data sources within Crystal Reports, check out *Crystal Reports 8.5: The Complete Reference*, also from McGraw-Hill/Osborne.

Enterprise Data Sources

Enterprise resource planning (ERP) systems generally run on top of a relational database but have their own business rules and data structures. Crystal Reports has a number of data drivers available for ERP systems, including these:

- SAP

- Baan

15

- PeopleSoft
- JD Edwards

Note

Some of these drivers may be sold separately from Crystal Reports 8.5.

To configure these drivers and access information, you will definitely need the help of your database or application administrator, as the setup is not for the faint of heart. A number of technical white papers are available at the Crystal Decision Web site (http://community.crystaldecisions.com) that provide the technical background necessary to get started.

MetaData

Crystal Dictionaries and Seagate Infoviews provide summarized views of your database and generally make report design easier for end users who may not be familiar with your data structures. Crystal Reports can report from two file types:

- Crystal Dictionaries (.dc5)
- Seagate Infoviews (.civ)

Tip

See Appendix B for more information on the Crystal Dictionaries tool and working with dictionary files.

To use either a Crystal Reports dictionary or a Seagate infoview, use the Data Explorer to navigate to the Metadata section and browse for the file you want to use. After you have selected a file, Crystal Reports will add all of the available tables to your report, and you can create your report as you normally would.

Other Data Sources

Crystal Reports also includes a number of drivers for nontraditional data sources, including SalesLogix Act!, Microsoft Exchange, and Microsoft Logs. Most of these data sources have their own unique setup and configuration requirements and do not fit into the standard data source categories that can be accessed through a native or ODBC driver. The following are some of the formats available:

- Act! 2.0, 3.0, and 4.0

- Microsoft Exchange

- Microsoft IIIS

- Microsoft SMS

- Microsoft Windows NT Event Logs

- Web Server Activity Logs (NCSA format)

All of these data formats are available in the Data Explorer in the Other Data Sources section, and most require some additional parameters (file name, location, server name, and so on).

Tip

For a complete list of the information required by these data sources, check out the Crystal Reports help file.

Setting Database Options

Crystal Reports has a number of options that are specific to the databases you will be reporting from. To view these options, select File | Options and click the Database tab to view the options shown in Figure 15-4.

Select the database objects you want to show when creating a Crystal Report. These are your options:

- Tables

- Views

- System Tables

- Synonyms

- Stored Procedures

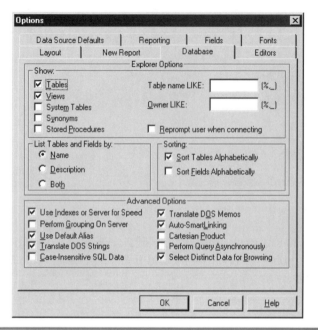

Figure 15-4 You can set the defaults for the database objects available for reporting

Set the filter for database objects with the Table Name LIKE and Owner LIKE text boxes; use the % symbol to indicate multiple characters and the underscore (_) to indicate a single character. If you are looking for all objects owned by user DMCAMIS, for example, the Owner LIKE text box would look like this: DMCAMIS%. You can also use the check box located under the Owner LIKE box to indicate whether a user should be reprompted when connecting.

With the options in the middle of the dialog box, you can select whether to list the tables and fields by their name, description, or both, and you can use the check boxes beside these options to sort table and field names alphabetically.

At the bottom of the dialog box, in the Advanced Options area, you can select from the following options and settings:

● **Use Indexes or Server for Speed** Use existing database indexes or the database server itself for processing where a performance improvement could be gained.

- **Perform Grouping on Server**   If you have created a summary report with none of the details showing and no drill-down capabilities, you can push the grouping of that report back to the server. A GROUP BY clause will be inserted into the SQL that Crystal Reports generates.

- **User Default Alias**   Use the default database alias.

- **Translate DOS Strings**   Translate any DOS strings that may appear in your database.

- **Case-Insensitive SQL Data**   By default, Crystal Report is case sensitive, meaning that {Customer.Country}="ca" and {Customer.Country}="CA" return different data sets. This setting eliminates that case sensitivity for SQL databases.

- **Translate DOS Memos**   DOS used a special memo format that can be translated and viewed from within Crystal Reports using this default setting.

- **Auto-SmartLinking**   When working with multiple databases or tables, Crystal Reports will attempt to create the linkage between these objects based on a common key or field name. This is known as smart linking. For databases that have multiple fields that are the same but not necessarily keys (LastUpdate, for example), turning off this option eliminates the need to continually remove incorrect links.

- **Cartesian Product**   This setting is applicable to OLAP data sources. Requesting a Cartesian Product brings back all possible combinations of a data source.

- **Perform Query Asynchronously**   Some database servers support asynchronous queries, where data is passed back and forth while records are being read. Checking this option allows supported databases to use this communication method, making it easier to stop running queries.

- **Select Distinct Data for Browsing**   When you are browsing for data from pull-down or browse dialog boxes, this option ensures that only a distinct record set (that is, no duplicates) is returned.

Note

Some of these options relate directly to the database you are working with, so you may need to log off and log back on to make them take effect.

15

When working with a PC or file-type database or a Crystal Reports dictionary file, you can also set a default database or data file so that with every new report you create, this default is used. To set the default, click the Data Source Defaults tab and, using the dialog box shown in Figure 15-5, click the Browse button to locate the default data directory for file databases.

You can also add any recognized extensions to the database file filter and select a file filter for any indexes that may be associated with PC-type databases you are using (for example, .ndx, .idx, and so on).

If you use Crystal Reports dictionaries, you can go to the Crystal Dictionaries section and use the Browse button to locate the default dictionary for any future reports. When you are finished, click OK to return to report design or preview.

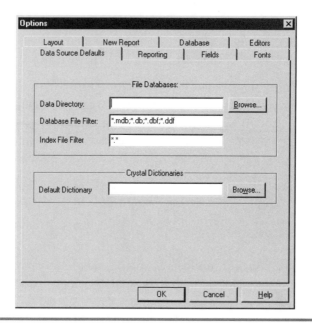

Figure 15-5 You can select a default PC or file-type database to be used when creating new reports

Working with Databases and Tables

When you are working with databases or the tables within them, Crystal Reports provides a number of tools that can make your work much easier. Some of these tools and techniques are described in this section.

Logging On or Off of a Database Server

Crystal Reports logs on to your database to retrieve information and perform queries. Frequently, when you close a report and leave Crystal Reports open, the database connection will remain open as well. To log on or off of a database server, select Database | Log On/Off Server.

Tip

If you do not have a report open, this menu item will appear on the File menu.

From that point, the Data Explorer opens, and you will need to expand the Current Connections node to see all of the databases you are currently logged onto. Select the database you want to log on or off of and click the Log On or Log Off button at the upper right of the dialog box. When you are finished, click Close to close the Data Explorer and return to your report. The connection to the database will be closed until the next time you refresh your report.

Adding a Database or Table to Your Report

When designing a report, you will sometimes need to add databases or tables. To add a database or table to your report, select Database | Add Database to Report. This will open the Data Explorer. Locate the type of database you want to add and expand the appropriate node, as shown in Figure 15-6.

15

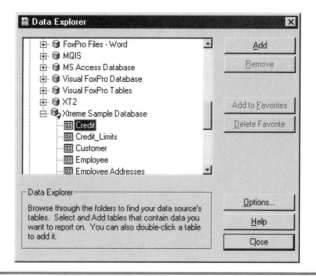

Figure 15-6 The Crystal Reports Data Explorer

A list of data sources and sections is listed here for your convenience:

- **Current Connections**   This section of the Data Explorer shows any databases or sources that you are currently logged on to.

- **Favorites**   If you are familiar with the concept of Favorites in Internet Explorer, you will be familiar with this option; it works the same way. Instead of saving frequently viewed Web pages, however, the Favorites option in the Data Explorer allows you to save frequently used data connections.

- **History**   This section of the Data Explorer automatically saves connections you have recently used.

- **OBDC**   Most databases can be accessed through ODBC. Crystal Reports ships with a number of ODBC drivers for the most popular database formats, including Informix and SQL Server. You need to install and configure the appropriate ODBC driver for your database.

- **Database Files**   You can also access some personal computer databases through a native connection, which eliminates the need for an ODBC driver. These databases include Xbase, Dbase, Paradox, Microsoft Access, and Btrieve.

- **More Data Sources**   In addition to reporting from standard relational databases, Crystal Reports can also report from the local file system, message tracking logs, Internet Information Server (IIS) proxy logs, Windows NT event logs, Microsoft Exchange, Microsoft Outlook, and more. You will find all of these data types under More Data Sources, as well as OLE DB, which is used to access relational databases, OLAP data sources, and nonstandard data sources. A number of native drivers for relational databases also appear under this heading if you have the appropriate database client installed.

- **Metadata/Query**   This is another option for creating reports using Crystal Reports dictionaries or Crystal Reports SQL queries.

Once you have located the type of data source you want to add to your report, expand the node and locate the database or table you want to add. Double-click the database or table name and a green check mark should appear, indicating that the database or table has been added to your report.

When you are finished selecting additional databases or tables, click Close. This will open the Visual Linking Expert. Using the Visual Linking Expert dialog box, draw the link(s) to indicate the relationship between the new tables you have added to the tables currently in your report.

Note

Some types of data cannot be joined together. For instance, you cannot join a file system table to an ODBC data source. One of the solutions to this problem is the subreport. For more information, see Module 11.

When you are finished indicating the relationships between your databases and tables, click OK to exit the Visual Linking Expert. This will return you to your report design or preview. As a final step, preview your report to verify that the links you have drawn are working and that the data set you were expecting is returned. If it is not, you may need to correct the linking in the Visual Linking Expert or consult your database administrator for more information on how the tables should be joined together.

Removing a Database or Table from Your Report

At times, you will need to remove a database or table from your report. To do so, select Database | Remove from Report. In the dialog box shown in Figure 15-7, highlight the database or table you want to remove from your report and click the Remove button.

If fields from the database you are trying to remove have been used in your report, you will receive the warning message "There are fields in the report from this file. Continue?" Click OK to continue and remove the file or Cancel to leave the database or table in your report. When you are finished, you will be returned to your report design or preview. Be careful with this feature; once a database or table is gone, it is really gone!

Note

If the database or table you have removed has been used as an intermediary link between two other tables, you may need to visit the Visual Linking Expert to fix your report.

Figure 15-7   You can remove unused database tables or files from your report

Setting a Database Alias

Aliases are used when you need to reference a table in a report more than once. For example, suppose you have an employee table containing supervisor IDs that are also the employee IDs. To get Crystal Reports to reference the same table twice, you need to add it a second time to the report and give it an alias (such as EmployeeSupervisor). To set a database alias, select Database | Set Alias. You can then select the database or table to which you want to apply the alias and click Set Alias. A dialog box will open, prompting you for the new alias name.

Tip

If you attempt to specify an alias that already exists in your report, Crystal Reports will return the error message "Alias already exists" and will prompt you again for a unique alias name.

You can then enter a new alias and click OK. When you are finished, click the Done button to return to your report. Your database or table will then be globally referenced by the new alias you have created, even in existing formulas.

Changing a Database Location

Another handy feature is the ability to change the database location of your reports. You can design a report on your test database, for example, and then later point it to a production database where your data resides. To change the database location of your report, select Database | Set Location and from the dialog box shown in Figure 15-8, select the database or table you want to point to a new location.

Click the Set Location button to open the Data Explorer and, using the Data Explorer, locate the data source and database or table you want to change, highlight it, and click the Set button.

Note

If you are using PC or file-type databases in your report, you can choose Same as Report, meaning that the database is in the same location as the report file, or use Convert to UNC to convert a location from a drive-letter reference (such as H:\ Database\Sales.dbf) to a UNC path (such as \\Server\database\sales.dbf).

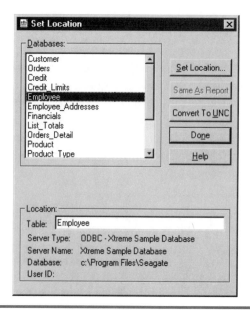

Figure 15-8 You can change the location of your database using the Set Location functionality shown here

If you are using multiple databases or tables in your report, a prompt will appear with the question "Propagate database and server changes across tables with the same original information?" Clicking Yes sets the location for all of the other databases or tables in your report; clicking No changes the location of only the one particular database or table you have chosen.

When you are finished setting the location, click the Close button to return to your report design or preview. The data for your report should now come from the new data source you have selected.

Note

If the data structures differ between the old database or table and the new location you have selected, the Map Fields dialog box will appear, and you must map any unfound fields in your report to fields in the new database structure.

Verifying Database Structures

As your database structures evolve and change, reports you have created from these structures may no longer work because of different field names, types, and so on. To ensure that the changes made in the database are reflected and accounted for in your existing reports, you will need to verify the database that they were created from by selecting Database | Verify Database. If you have databases or tables in your report that are not used, you may receive the message "Verify files in report that are not used?" Click Yes to proceed.

Tip

If you are working with a database that is subject to frequent changes and additions, select Database | Verify on Every Print to verify your report each time it is previewed or printed.

At this point, Crystal Reports will run through the data structures in your report and verify that nothing has changed. If all of the data structures are unchanged, you will receive the message "The database is up to date."

If anything has changed in the data structures, you will receive the message "The database file *xxx* has changed. Proceeding to fix up the report."

If Crystal Reports finds simple changes such as a database field that has been extended or a decimal place that has changed, it will simply update its version of the data structures and display the message "The database is up to date."

If Crystal Reports finds a major change (such as a field name missing or a changed field type), it will open the Map Fields dialog box shown in Figure 15-9.

A list of unmapped fields will appear in the upper-left corner of this dialog box. These are fields that are currently in your report that Crystal Reports could not find when it attempted to verify the underlying data structure. To resolve any mismatched fields, select a field from the Report Fields list, locate its counterpart in the list on the right, and click Map.

Tip

If the type of the field has changed as well as the name, turn off the Match Type option to show all fields.

15

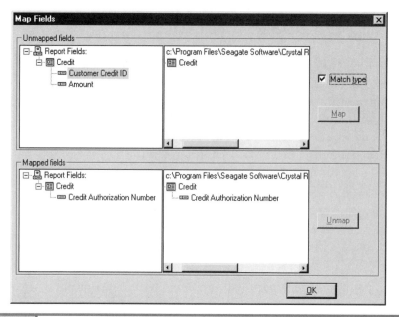

Figure 15-9 Mapping fields ensures that any changes in your database structure are accounted for

When you are finished mapping all of the fields not found in the verification of the data structures, click OK to return to your report design or preview.

Working with the Visual Linking Expert

Relational databases are usually split into a number of different tables. These tables can be joined back together to create complex queries. In Crystal Reports, these joins are created by using the Visual Linking Expert to visually draw a line between two key fields. To change the database linkage in your report, select Database | Visual Linking Expert.

Using the dialog box shown in Figure 15-10, you can draw links between the databases and tables in your report to indicate the relationship between each. To draw a line between two fields, drag the first field and drop it on top of the second. You will know that you have the field positioned correctly when the mouse pointer turns into a Z.

⊥*Tip*

If you make a mistake, you can remove a link by clicking the line to highlight it and then pressing the DELETE key, or to clear all links, click the Delete button on the right side of the expert. This option is especially handy when Crystal Reports automatically attempts to smart-link the tables you have selected.

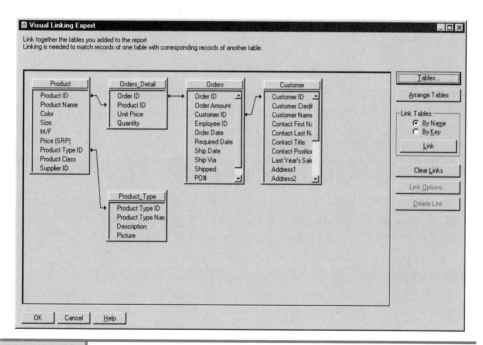

| **Figure 15-10** | Use the Visual Linking Expert to indicate the relationship between your database tables or database files |

By default, Crystal Reports will join two SQL tables with an Equal join. To change the default join type, right-click directly on top of the line drawn between the two tables and select Options from the right-click menu. Using the Link Options dialog box, select a join type for this link from the list:

- Equal

- Left Outer

- Right Outer

- Greater

- Less

- Greater or Equal

- Less or Equal

- Not Equal

Tip

Crystal Reports provides a number of good examples of the different join types in the help file. You can find the examples by opening the help file and searching for the keyword *joins*. Your database or system administrator should also be able to tell you the correct joins for the tables you have selected.

When you are finished editing the links and join types, click OK to accept your changes and return to your report design or preview.

Tip

At any point, you can click the Arrange Tables button to arrange the Visual Linking Expert layout for readability.

Ask the Expert

Question: Is there any way to edit the SQL statement that Crystal Reports generates?

Answer: There will be times when you need to directly edit the SQL statement generated by Crystal Reports. For example, you will want to edit it if you want to use the Union operator to join two identical sets of data. In the Crystal Reports user interface, there is no way to perform this SQL operation. You would need to insert the Union operator and remaining text yourself. To edit the SQL statement generated by Crystal Reports, follow this procedure. First, select Database | Show SQL Query. Next, edit the SQL query within the window shown, making sure to edit only the FROM, WHERE, and ORDER BY clauses of the statement. If you make a mistake or want to return to the SQL statement generated by Crystal Reports, click the Reset button to return to the original statement. All of the standard Windows shortcuts for cut, copy, and paste operations are available, or you can click the icons at the bottom right of the Show SQL Query dialog box.

Finally; when you are finished editing your SQL statement, click OK to accept your changes and return to your report design or preview. Note that Crystal Reports will return an error message if any part of the SQL statement is incorrect. If you need to edit the SQL statement generated by Crystal Reports, it is recommended that you first edit and troubleshoot the statement in a full-blown SQL editor and then copy and paste that text into Crystal Reports.

Project 15-1: Setting Up an ODBC Data Source

Most databases are accessed through ODBC, and you will need to set up an ODBC driver before you can report from your database. In this project, we are going to set up an ODBC driver for our sample Access database and then use it to create a report.

─┤*Note* ──────────────

These instructions are for Windows 95/98. If you are using Windows ME/2000/XP, consult your system administrator for ODBC setup instructions.

Step-by-Step

1. Open the Windows control panel and then open the ODBC Data Source Administrator, shown in Figure 15-11.

2. Select the System DSN tab and then click the Add button

3. In the next dialog box, select Microsoft Access (.mdb) as the data source type.

4. Using the dialog box shown in Figure 15-12, enter a name for your data source. In this example, enter **My Data** and use the Select button to locate and select the sample Xtreme database that ships with Crystal Reports (usually located under C:\Program Files\Seagate Software\Crystal Reports\Samples\En\ Databases\xtreme.mdb).

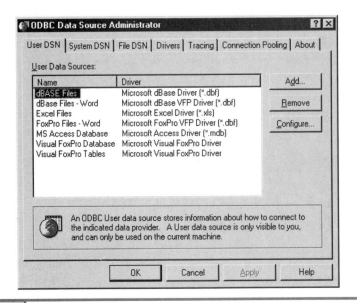

| **Figure 15-11** | The ODBC Data Source Administrator |

5. Click OK to accept your changes. Your new data source should now appear within the ODBC Administrator, under System DSN.

6. Exit the ODBC Administrator and open Crystal Reports from the Start menu.

7. Select File | New and select the Standard Report Expert.

8. On the Data tab of the Standard Report Expert, click the ODBC option, and you should see the ODBC data source you have just created.

9. Select the tables, fields, and so on that you want to see in your report, complete the report expert, and preview your report.

Project Summary

Crystal Reports provides a number of data access methods, the most popular being ODBC. Before you can create a report through an ODBC connection, you first need to set up an ODBC driver that points to your database. With that done, all of the data held within the database is available for reporting.

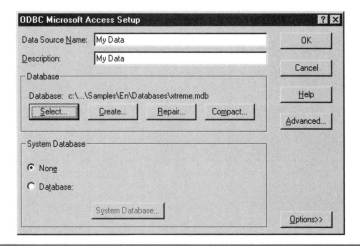

| **Figure 15-12** | A typical ODBC setup dialog box |

✓ Mastery Check

1. What is the difference between a native database connection and an ODBC database connection?

   _____

   _____

2. Which database formats are considered PC-type formats?

   _____

   _____

3. What does the Verify Database command do?

   _____

   _____

4. The complete SQL statement generated by Crystal Reports can be edited.

   A. True

   B. False

5. When will the Map Fields dialog box appear?

   _____

   _____

Appendix A

Mastery Check
Answers

Module 1: Getting Started

1. What are the five phases of report design?

- Defining the concept.
- Sourcing the data.
- Creating the design.
- Developing and testing the design.
- Deploying and operating the report.

2. Why is it important to create a report prototype before actually creating the report itself?

To have a blueprint for the report you are going to create in the development stage.

3. Where are the sample report files that ship with Crystal Reports located?

C:\Program Files\Seagate Software\Crystal Reports\Samples\En\Reports

4. Subreports can be used to:

C. Both A and B (That is, subreports can be used to display related information from two or more different sources in one single report and display unrelated information from two or more different sources in one single report.)

5. What is a drill-down report?

A report that provides a summary view of the data and the ability to drill down into the details that make up that summary.

Module 2: Creating a Simple Report

1. How many report experts are available?

A. 8

2. What does ODBC stand for?

Open **d**atabase **c**onnectivity.

3. What types of summary operators are available within Crystal Reports?

Sum, Average, Minimum, Maximum, Count, Distinct Count, Standard Deviation, Median, Mode, and others.

4. Why do you need to use record selection in your report?

To cut down the number of records returned and focus the report on a specific piece of information.

Module 3: Working with the Report Design Environment

1. What are the four methods you can use to navigate through a report preview?

You can navigate by using the group tree on the left side of the screen (if groups are present), by using the Page Up and Page Down icons, by selecting Report | Go to Page (or pressing CTRL-G), or by searching for a particular value by selecting Edit | Find (or pressing CTRL-F).

2. How many toolbars are available within Crystal Reports?

Four

3. The autosave feature is enabled by default:

B.   False

4. What is meant by "format by example"?

Selecting a format for a field based on a list of examples showing the various formatting options being used.

5. Which of the following can be combined with text objects?

D.   All of the above

Module 4: Organizing Your Report

1. Which type of field cannot be used when inserting a group?

D.   Running total fields

2. How many groups can you have inserted in your report?

As many as you like.

3. When grouping on a date or date-time field, what is the default period that will be used?

A.   Group by day

4. Where can you find the setting to repeat the group header on every page?

Select Report | Change Group Expert; you can then change the group options.

5. What is the difference between *hiding* the details and *suppressing* them?

Hiding a section still allows drill down; suppressing does not.

6. How do you create a page break between groups?

Use the options of New Page After or New Page Before under Format | Section.

Module 5: Analyzing Report Data

1. Which record selection operator allows you to select a list of values to be included?

Is One Of

2. When you use the Select Expert to create record selection on more than one field, what is the default relationship between these criteria?

B.   AND

3. Why can you *not* enter a value when using the operator In the Period?

The periods are predefined within Crystal Reports and cannot be changed.

4. What is the difference between a summary field and a formula?

A summary field does not require any formula to be created and is limited to the simple summary types (Sum, Average, Count, and so on). A formula can be created to perform the same operations, but is much more complex and provides more options through the formula language, functions, and so on.

5. Why might you want to use the Highlighting Expert?

To highlight exceptions or interesting information for the user.

Module 6: Using Parameter Fields

1. What are some of the uses for parameter fields?

To display a report user's name, to facilitate record selection, and so on.

2. Which of the following is *not* a valid value type for a parameter field?

   C. Binary

3. How do you get Crystal Reports to prompt for a new parameter value?

   Click the Refresh button and select the option Prompt for New Parameter Value.

4. Do you have to enter the descriptions for default values every time (even when you are using the same descriptions in other reports)?

   No; you can export a pick list that contains these values and reimport the list into other reports.

5. How can you tell whether a field in your report is a parameter field?

   Parameter fields are marked with a question mark (for example, {?ParameterField}).

Module 7: Distributing the Results

1. Which of the Crystal Reports export formats provides a WYSIWYG view of your report?

   Portable Document Format (PDF) (You also could save the report with data and distribute the report file.)

2. Do you need to pay any additional licensing costs when manually distributing your report using Adobe Acrobat format?

   No.

3. What is the best format available for exporting to Microsoft Word when you want to retain the majority of the formatting features within your report?

   B. Rich Text Format (RTF)

4. What are the two options for exporting your report to Microsoft Excel?

   Excel standard or Excel extended.

5. Before you can export and e-mail a report from within Crystal Reports, what do you need to check first?

   You need to check that the computer where you have installed Crystal Reports has a default mail client and that it works properly.

Module 8: Formulas and Functions

1. What are the two ways to check the syntax of your formula?

When you exit the formula editor, Crystal Reports will check the syntax, but you can also check it at any point using the X+2 button on the toolbar.

2. What is the difference between the two Save options on the formula editor toolbar?

One is for saving the formula; the other is for both saving the formula and closing the formula editor.

3. Where can you find a list of all Crystal Reports functions?

In the Crystal Reports help file, by searching for the keyword Functions.

4. Which of the functions listed here can be used to convert numeric type fields to text?

C. ToText( )

5. What operator can be used to concatenate string and numeric fields?

The ampersand (&).

6. Where can you find the correct syntax for an If…Then statement?

By looking in the Operators pane of the Crystal Reports Formula Editor.

Module 9: Advanced Record Selection

1. What is the relationship between record selection criteria you create using the Select Expert?

And

2. Which operator is used to denote not equal to?

<>

3. Where can you find the settings to control the formula editor's appearance and behavior?

Under File | Options | Editors.

4. Which of these record selection formulas is correct?

A.   {Customer.Country} in ["USA", "Canada", "Mexico"]

5. Where would you find the setting to select only distinct records?

Under Database | Select Distinct Records

Module 10: Working with Sections

1. If you insert a section below the Page Header a section, what will that section be called?

Page Header b.

2. What happens to the objects within a section when it is deleted? Merged?

When a section is deleted, the objects are deleted as well; when a section is merged, the objects are moved into the newly merged section.

3. When you change the order of a section, do you need to change the location of all of the objects within the section as well?

No; they are moved along with the section.

4. How do you invoke the Section Expert?

Choose Format | Section.

5. Which of these is not a formatting option within the Section Expert:

C.   Print at Top of Page

6. Which section supports multicolumn layout?

The Details section only.

Module 11: Using Subreports

1. What is the difference between linked and unlinked subreports?

A linked subreport passes a parameter between the main report and subreport and shows related data; an unlinked subreport does not pass a parameter, and the two reports can show unrelated data sets.

2. Can you insert an existing report as a subreport?

Yes, by selecting Insert | Subreport and choosing Insert an Existing Report.

3. Which of the following is a benefit of on-demand subreports?

C. Delays processing of the subreport until it is needed.

4. What type of field is used for to link subreports with a main report?

A parameter field.

Module 12: Cross-Tab Analysis

1. What are the four grouping options for cross-tabs?

Ascending, Descending, and Specified

2. How do you change the size of a column within a cross-tab?

By resizing the field within that column.

3. How do you display the option for pivoting a cross-tab?

Right-click directly on top of the cross-tab object.

4. Which of the following options cannot be performed within a cross-tab:

A. Suppress the summarized field

5. Can you drag and drop columns within a cross-tab?

No; you would need to change the underlying cross-tab definition to change the column order.

Module 13: Charting and Graphing

1. What are the four types of chart layouts available?

Group, Advanced, Cross-Tab, and OLAP Grid.

2. What must be inserted in your report before you can create a group graph?

A group and a summary field.

3. What values are required to create an advanced graph?

An X value and a Y value (in Crystal Reports, labeled On Change Of and Show Value).

4. How can you change a chart from full color to black and white?

By selecting Black and White from the options in the Chart Expert.

5. Where would you find the option to change the size of a chart element:

C.   Chart Analyzer

6. What types of graph allow drill down?

Group pie graphs and bar graphs.

Module 14: Geographic Mapping

1. What are the four types of map layout?

Group, advanced, cross-tab, OLAP grid.

2. Which of the following is not a map type:

C.   Nonlinear

3. What does the term *pan* mean?

To move the viewpoint reference—in this case, on a map.

4. How can mismatched data be resolved?

By using the Map Analyzer and matching the data in your database to the correct location stored within the mapping-data tables.

5. What are map layers?

Representations of map data that can be placed on top of each other to display country and ocean boundaries, major highways, and so on.

Module 15: Working with Data Sources

1. What is the difference between a native database connection and an ODBC database connection?

A native connection goes directly to the source of the data, whereas an ODBC connection goes through a translation layer.

2. Which database formats are considered PC-type formats?

Dbase, Paradox, Access, and so on.

3. What does the Verify Database command do?

It verifies the databases and tables that are used within your report and will initiate a process to fix up the report if it encounters any changes since the last verification.

4. The complete SQL statement generated by Crystal Reports can be edited.

B. False (Only the WHERE and ORDER BY clauses can be edited.)

5. When will the Map Fields dialog box appear?

When you have attempted to verify that a database or table and the underlying data structures have changed.

Appendix B

Crystal Reports Dictionaries

After you have been creating reports for a while, you will start to understand how your database is arranged. You'll understand its little nuances, how tables are joined together, which fields contain what information, and so on. An easy way to pass that knowledge on to other users (and make things a bit simpler for them in the meantime) is to create a Crystal Reports dictionary for others to use for reporting.

Just as a regular dictionary defines words and phrases, a Crystal Reports dictionary defines the tables, links, fields, and so on within your database. Using the Crystal Dictionaries tool, you can select tables from your database and pick fields, alias fields, rearrange fields, and even assign pop-up help text to describe the values that can be found in each field. You can also select commonly used graphics (such as your company logo) and give users a sample data set to browse, to help them understand what values are contained within the fields you have defined.

When you are finished, users can report directly from the dictionary file you have created and don't need to worry about understanding the underlying tables and relationships—you have done the hard work for them!

Installing the Crystal Dictionaries Tool

Before you can begin working with dictionaries, you need to check to make sure you have installed the Crystal Dictionaries tool. If it is installed, it should appear on the Start menu under Crystal Reports Tools, as shown in Figure B-1, and you can skip to the next section.

Chances are good that the tool has not been installed yet. It is not included on the default setup options for Crystal Reports. To install this tool, you will need to locate your Crystal Reports CD-ROM and rerun the program setup. As soon as you insert the CD-ROM in the drive, the splash screen shown in Figure B-2 should appear. Click Install Crystal Reports.

If you have installed Crystal Reports before, the setup program will give you these options: Add/Remove, Remove All, or Reinstall. Select Add/Remove, as you want to add the Crystal Dictionaries tool to your computer.

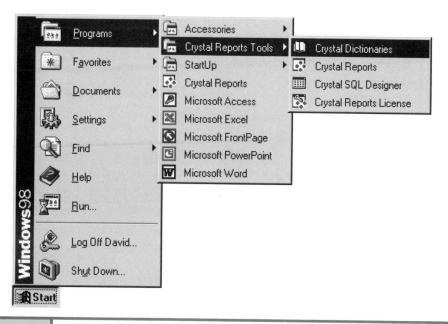

Figure B-1 The Crystal Dictionaries tool will appear under the Crystal Reports Tools program group

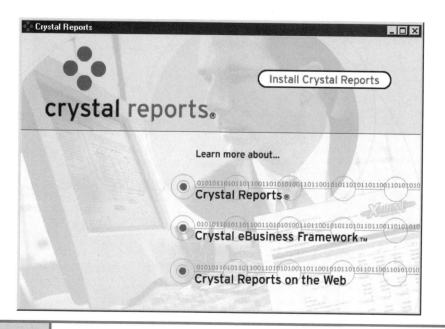

Figure B-2 The initial splash screen for installing Crystal Reports

In the Select Features dialog box shown in Figure B-3, right-click the component for Crystal Dictionaries and select Will Be Installed on Local Hard Drive from the drop-down menu that appears.

---**Tip**---

If you want to use the Crystal SQL Designer, you could also select the option to install it now and save some time later!

When you click Next, the setup program will begin installing the Crystal Dictionaries tool. When the file installation is complete, you should see the option for Crystal Dictionaries under Crystal Reports Tools on the Start menu.

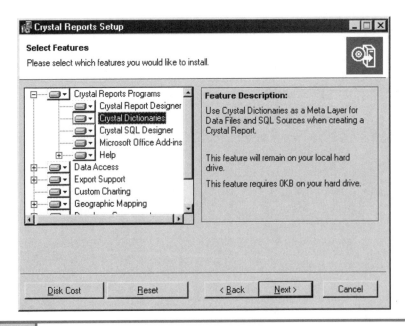

Figure B-3   Select Crystal Dictionaries from the list of components

Creating Crystal Reports Dictionaries

When you first start the Crystal Dictionaries tool, you can create a new dictionary file by selecting File | New, which will open the expert shown in Figure B-4.

The first step in creating a Crystal Reports dictionary is selecting the databases and tables where the data resides. You can create dictionaries from data files (PC-type databases) and through a SQL/ODBC connection.

If you select the Data Files option, a dialog box opens allowing you to select a database file. For a database accessed through SQL/ODBC, you select the ODBC data source name for your particular data source or database.

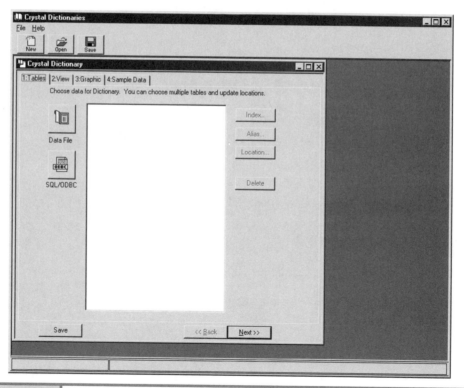

| **Figure B-4** | The Crystal Dictionary Expert |

Tip

If you are creating a dictionary from data files, you can also select the index for your database by clicking the Index button on the right side of the dialog box.

Once you have selected a data source name (and logged onto your database, if required), a list of tables will appear, as shown in Figure B-5.

Highlight the tables you want to use in your dictionary and click Add to add them to the dialog box. When you are finished, click Done.

If you select more than one table for your dictionary, a separate Links tab will open and allow you to use visual linking to specify the joins between your databases or tables.

Tip

If you are unable to locate a table you have added, click the Locate button to find a particular table within your linking diagram.

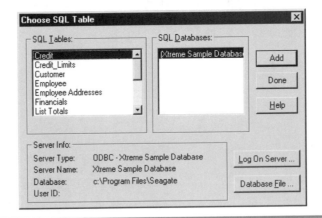

Figure B-5 You can select multiple tables from your database

Using the dialog box shown in Figure B-6 you are going to draw links between the databases and tables in your report to indicate the relationship between each. To draw a line between two fields, drag the first field and drop it on top of the second. You will know you have the field positioned correctly when your cursor turns into the Z icon.

┤*Tip*

If you make a mistake, you can remove a link by clicking the line to highlight it and then pressing the DELETE key.

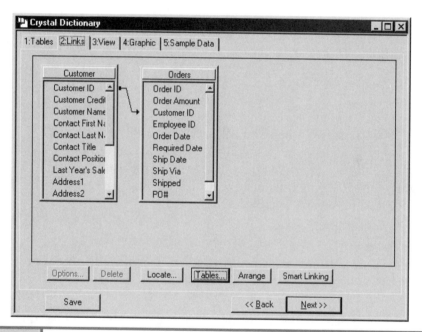

Figure B-6   Use the Links tab to indicate the relationship between your database tables or database files

By default, the Crystal Reports dictionary will join two SQL tables with an Equal join. To change the default join type, right-click directly on top of the line drawn between the two tables and select Options from the right-click menu. Using the Link Options dialog box, select a join type for this link from the list:

- Equal

- Left Outer

- Right Outer

- Greater

- Less

- Greater or Equal

- Less or Equal

- Not Equal

When you have finished editing the links and join types, click the View tab to move on the next step, where you will specify the fields that you want to appear in your query. To select a field, highlight it in the list on the left, as shown in Figure B-7, and click the right arrow to move it to the list on the right. To alias or rename a field, highlight the field and click the Alias button at the bottom of the list, enter a new name, and click OK.

Tip

If you are unsure about the contents of a particular field, use the Browse button to view the field contents, type, length, and so on.

You'll notice that the first time you add a field, a heading will be added titled New Field Heading. Crystal Dictionaries allows you to create field headings to help organize the fields you have selected for your dictionary. When creating a report from a dictionary, Crystal Reports will display the fields you have selected using the notation Field Heading.Field Name. One example of where you would use field headings is shown in Figure B-7, where the information from a single table has been separated into field headings for Customer Information and Contact Information.

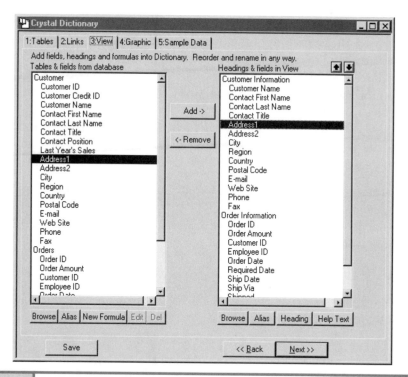

Figure B-7   The fields you select are the fields that the user will have access to when reporting from the dictionary

You can add new field headings by clicking the Heading button located at the bottom of the list on the right. To move fields around within the headings, use the arrows located at the upper right or drag and drop the fields into position.

Another key feature of Crystal Dictionaries is help text. You can associate up to 255 characters of text with a field, so when you move your mouse over the field, the help text appears, as shown in Figure B-8.

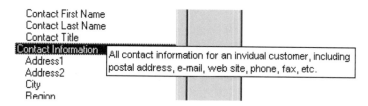

Figure B-8   Help text in action within the Crystal Dictionaries tool

You can also add formula fields to your dictionary by clicking the New Formula button located on the bottom of the list on the left. You will need to give your formula a name, and then a scaled-down version of the Crystal Reports Formula Editor will open, as shown in Figure B-9.

The editor itself can be divided into four main areas:

- **Fields**   The field list appears on the left side of the formula editor and contains a list of all fields present in your report, followed by a node for your data source and all of the tables and fields contained within.

- **Operators**   On the right side of the formula editor, the Operators list contains a hierarchical view of all of the operators available within Crystal Reports, including all of the arithmetic operators, variable declaration, comparison operators, and so on.

Note

Some of the operators—such as +, –, / , and *—you may find easier to just type, but you can double-click any operator in this list to add it to your report.

- **Functions**   In the middle is a list of all of the functions that are available for use. These range from functions for simple summaries (such as sum and average) to type conversion and field manipulation functions to complex statistical and financial analysis functions.

- **Formula Editor**   The largest section in the Formula Editor belongs to the formula text itself. The large text box at the bottom of the formula editor is reserved for formula text that you enter. This area behaves in a manner similar to other text editors (like Notepad) or word processing applications you may have used in the past. The buttons at the bottom of the window provide the tools you need to work with your formula text.

Once you have finished entering your formula text, you can use the Check button to check your formula syntax and click the Accept button to accept your formula text and exit the editor.

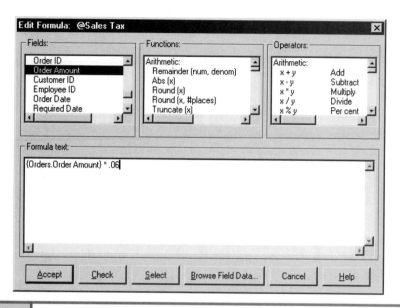

Figure B-9   The Crystal Dictionary Formula Editor

Tip

Remember that these checks will not guarantee that your formula will work. Syntax checking ensures that all of the functions and fields have been spelled correctly and that you have used the correct operators, parentheses, and so on. A good practice is to try your formula in a Crystal Report first and then copy and paste the formula text into your dictionary formula field.

The next step, adding graphics, is optional. You can click the Add button to search for a graphic file to be included with your Crystal Reports dictionary. Crystal Dictionaries supports the following file types:

- Windows Bitmap (.bmp)
- JPEG (.jpeg, .jpg)

● TIFF (.tif, .tiff)

● TARGA (.tga)

● PC Paintbrush (.pcx)

After you have added a graphic to your dictionary, you can use the Alias button to give the graphic a meaningful name (such as Corporate Logo-Black and White). If you ever decide to move the graphic from the location you have specified, you can use the Location button to choose a new directory and/or file name for the graphic.

The final step in creating a dictionary is also optional. The Sample Data tab can be used to collect sample data for the fields within your dictionary file. When a user clicks the Browse Data button within Crystal Reports, the user will actually be browsing the data you have provided and not the underlying data contained within your database.

Note

For fields for which you don't collect sample data, Crystal Reports will query the database for a sample data set.

To collect sample data for your dictionary, highlight a field in the list of fields on the left side of the dialog box shown in Figure B-10 and click the Collect button. A query will be submitted to the database, and the results will be displayed in the column on the right side of the dialog box.

You can edit the values shown by highlighting a value in the list and clicking the Edit button. Likewise, if the values shown are not representative of what should be entered into the database (for example, if values are misspelled, use incorrect capitalization, and so on), you can click the Edit button to edit the values that are shown to the user.

Tip

If you need to delete multiple values, you can use the standard Windows shortcut of using the SHIFT key to select contiguous items in a list and the CTRL key to select distinct items.

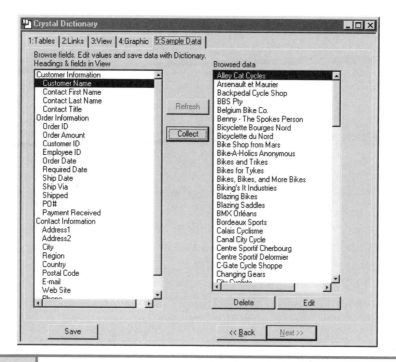

Figure B-10   You can collect or refresh sample values that are displayed when
the user clicks the Browse button within Crystal Reports

Finally, with your dictionary design finished, you will need to save the
dictionary file by selecting File | Save or clicking the Save icon on the toolbar.
Crystal Reports dictionaries are saved with a .dc5 extension and can be used
by Crystal Reports 8.0 or 8.5.

Working with Dictionaries

From time to time when working with Crystal Dictionaries, you will need to
perform administration tasks. The suggestions described here should help reduce
the amount of administration needed and keep your users happy.

Creating a Master Dictionary

A common practice when working with Crystal Dictionaries is to create one dictionary that serves as the master dictionary, containing all of the tables, links, and so on within your database. From that point, you can create many different slices or views of the data by opening the master model, deleting some of the tables and links, and then using Save As to save the dictionary with a different name. For example, this capability might come in handy when you are working with accounting data. Chances are good that you will want to create a view for the controller that shows all of the tables and fields available, but for the accounts payable staff you may want to create a dictionary that shows only the tables and fields related to their work.

This strategy means that when new fields are introduced and you need to update the accounts payable dictionary, you can simply update the master dictionary, delete a few unneeded elements, and save a copy. Likewise, you could save a different copy for accounts receivable, sales, marketing, and so on. Otherwise, you would have to go through each individual dictionary and make the same changes.

Verifying Your Dictionary

As applications and databases are upgraded and changed, you need to verify your dictionaries from time to time. Verifying a dictionary file is similar to verifying a database used within Crystal Reports. When you select File | Verify Dictionary, the Crystal Dictionaries tool will check all of the database tables and fields that are referenced in the dictionary and make sure that they are all still the same. Where a database table or field has changed, the dictionary will be updated with the new details.

Tip

If your application or database is in development, you may want to periodically verify the dictionary files used for reporting, just in case any changes may have been made that you missed.

Using Crystal Dictionaries with Seagate Info Views

For scheduling and distributing reports, Crystal Decisions has created another product, called Seagate Info, which is built on the same architecture as Crystal Reports and can take advantage of any Crystal Reports dictionaries that you have created.

Tip

Seagate Info provides a scheduling and distribution method for reports and has been superseded by Crystal Enterprise. Check out the Crystal Decisions Web site at www.crystaldecisions.com for more information on working with Crystal Enterprise.

Seagate Info offers a feature similar to Crystal Dictionaries, called Infoviews. An infoview is similar to a Crystal dictionary, and the two share a common file format, but infoviews go a step farther and add row and column security to the data represented within the view.

You can use Crystal Reports dictionaries with Seagate Info by opening the Seagate Info View Designer, opening a Crystal Reports dictionary, and using the Save As functionality to save your Crystal Reports dictionary (.dc5) file as a Seagate infoview (.civ) file.

Creating Reports from Dictionaries

To see how to create a report from a Crystal Reports dictionary file, we are going to create a new report and let the Standard Report Expert guide us. To get started, click the New icon on the standard toolbar or choose File | New to open the Crystal Report Gallery. Then select the Standard Expert and click OK.

The first step in creating a report using the Standard Report Expert is choosing the dictionary on which the report will be based. To select your data source, you use the Data Explorer, shown in Figure B-11. The Data Explorer itself is really just a number of different views of the data sources that you have available to use in your report. You will find the option to work with Crystal Dictionaries

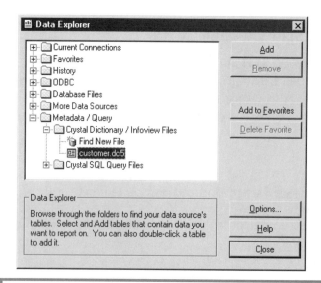

The Crystal Reports Data Explorer

(Crystal Dictionary/Infoview Files) under the Metadata/Query node. Immediately underneath this node is the Find New File option, which will open a browse dialog box and allow you to select a Crystal Reports dictionary (.dc5) file.

Tip

Regardless of how many tables your dictionary is based on, Crystal Reports does not open a Linking tab for you, as the links have already been created within the Crystal Dictionaries tool itself.

Choosing Fields

The Fields tab of the Standard Report Expert, shown in Figure B-12, is split into two sections. The left pane lists all of the fields that are available from your dictionary to be inserted into your report, grouped under their Field Heading names. To add a field to your report, you need to move the field from the left pane to the right pane. You can accomplish this by double-clicking the field name or by highlighting the field and clicking the Add button. Additional buttons are also available to add or remove one or all fields.

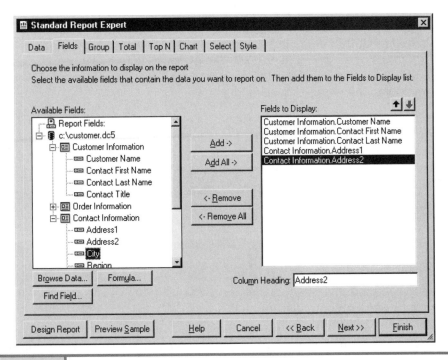

Figure B-12   Using the Fields tab to select the fields for your report

---

Tip

To select multiple fields, hold down the CTRL key while clicking.

If you are unsure of a field's definition or contents, you can use the Browse Data button to display a sample of the field's contents. If you have collected sample data within your dictionary on a particular field, that is what will be shown. If you select a field that has no sample data associated with it, keep in mind that the underlying database table will be queried and those results shown.

Another key feature of the Fields tab is the Find Field button, at the bottom left. This button allows you to search the selected tables for a field that matches your criteria. To see the help text in action, click to select a field and then leave the cursor over the field for a few seconds. A small box should appear, displaying the help text you entered in your dictionary file.

Tip

Keep in mind that the fields within a dictionary file can be used as if they were fields from the underlying database. You can use them in formulas, with functions, and so on. They will always have the notation {Field Heading.Field Name} when used within your report or formula text.

To change the order of the fields you are inserting in your report, you can use the up and down arrows that appear in the upper-right corner of the dialog box to move fields up and down. You can also change the column heading associated with a field (although hopefully you will have done a good job of creating aliases for the fields themselves within the dictionary).

Grouping and Sorting

The next step in creating a report using the Standard Report Expert is selecting the sorting and grouping to use in your report, using the Group tab, shown in Figure B-13. This tab is similar to the Fields tab. To select a field, you move it from the list on the left to the list on the right.

By specifying a field on the Group tab, you can add control breaks or groups to your report. For example, if you were to group on the State field, your report would be printed with all the records for each state together, with a break between each state.

After you select a field, notice that you have a choice of sort orders:

- **In Ascending Order** This option groups the records by the field you have specified and orders those groups from A through Z, 0 through 9, and so on.

- **In Descending Order** This option groups the records by the field you have specified and orders those groups from Z through A, 9 through 0, and so on.

- **In Specified Order** Using this option, you can name and define your own grouping criteria.

- **In Original Order** If your database has already performed some sorting on the data, this option leaves the records in their original order.

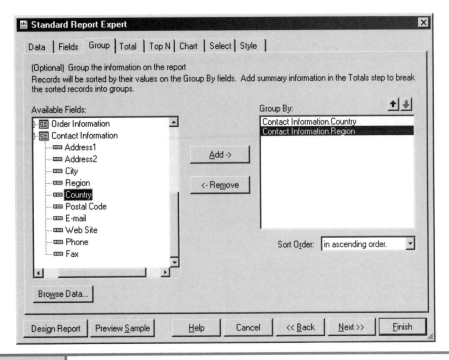

Figure B-13 Choosing the grouping and sorting for your report

Inserting Summaries

The Total tab, shown in Figure B-14, is used to insert Crystal Reports summary fields into your report. Crystal Reports provides these summary fields so that you do not have to create a formula every time you want to insert a sum, average, and so forth.

Note

If you have used any formula fields in your dictionary, keep in mind that Crystal Reports will treat these fields differently based on their outcome. For example, if your formula field returns a string value, different summary operations are available than if it returned a numeric value. You may need to revisit the dictionary design to make sure that any formulas you created return the correct values.

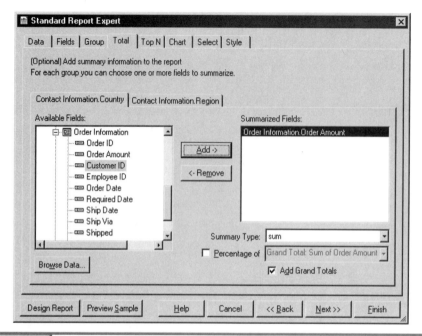

You can insert a number of summary fields into your report; the types of summaries vary based on the type of field, as shown in Table B-1.

For some of the statistical functions, you are asked to provide additional information, such as the value for N. For other functions, you specify that a summary is a certain percentage of a particular field.

When you add a summary to your report using the Standard Report Expert, the summary appears immediately following each group, showing the summary for only that particular group. The option at the lower right of the dialog box, Add Grand Totals, adds the same type of summary field at the end of the report and shows the value for the entire report.

Previewing Your Report

With the Data, Fields, Group, and Total tabs complete, your report design is almost finished. The next three steps of the Standard Report Expert, for Top-N analysis, charts, and record selection, are optional, so we will skip these for now.

Summary Type	With Numeric Fields	With Other Field Types
Sum	X	
Average	X	
Maximum	X	X
Minimum	X	X
Count	X	X
Distinct Count	X	X
Sample Variance	X	
Sample Standard Deviation	X	
Population Variance	X	
Population Standard Deviation	X	
Correlation	X	
Covariance	X	
Weighted Average	X	
Median	X	
Pth Percentile	X	
Nth Largest	X	X
Nth Smallest	X	X
Mode	X	X
Nth Most Frequent	X	X

Table B-1   Crystal Reports Summary Types and Usage

The final tab in the Standard Report Expert, shown in Figure B-15, is Style. You can give your report a title and can apply a predefined style, including coordinating colors, fonts, and so forth. If you select any of the predefined styles shown, you see a preview of what that particular style looks like on the right.

With the report expert settings complete, it is time to take a look at the report you have created by clicking one of the buttons at the bottom of the tab, shown in Figure B-15. You can go straight to the design of your report by clicking the Design Report button, or you can preview your report by clicking the Preview Sample or Finish button. The only difference between Preview Sample and Finish is that Preview Sample allows you to select the number of records that are returned, whereas Finish retrieves the whole data set for your preview.

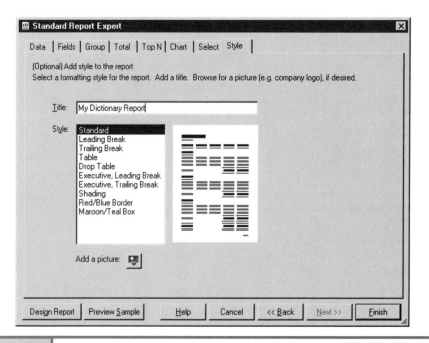

Figure B-15   You can apply a preformatted report style to your report

Distributing Crystal Reports and Dictionaries

When distributing a report created from a Crystal Reports dictionary, you will need to provide the recipient with both the Crystal Reports (.rpt) file and the dictionary (.dc5) file. You also need to be careful about where the recipient places these two files. When the report was created, Crystal Reports stored the location of the dictionary file and will look in that location first. If it cannot locate the dictionary file, it will look in the same directory where the report itself is saved. A good practice is to either establish a central location for reports and their associated dictionaries or always place the report file and dictionary in the same directory.

Appendix C

Crystal SQL Designer

When you are working with different applications and databases, there are going to be instances when a particular report cannot be created using Crystal Reports alone. Although Crystal Reports has a number of powerful features for working with databases, sometimes you will need to create complex SQL statements to get the results you need.

To help you with this problem, Crystal Reports ships with its own SQL Designer tool, which allows you to create complex SQL joins and write SQL statements that are not possible using just Crystal Reports. Once you create a query using the SQL Designer tool, you can use it as the basis for reports using Crystal Reports.

Tip

If you are just starting out creating reports using databases and SQL, you may need some help from your application or database administrator to create and troubleshoot your SQL queries.

Installing the Crystal SQL Designer Tool

Before you can get started working with queries, you need to make sure you have the Crystal SQL Designer tool installed. If it is installed, it should appear on the Start menu under Crystal Reports Tools, as shown in Figure C-1, and you can skip to the next section.

Chances are good that the tool has not been installed yet. It is not included in the default setup options for Crystal Reports. To install this tool, you will need to locate your Crystal Reports CD-ROM and rerun the setup program. As soon as you insert the CD-ROM in the drive, the splash screen shown in Figure C-2 should appear. Select Install Crystal Reports.

If you have installed Crystal Reports before, the setup program will give you these options: Add/Remove, Remove All, and Reinstall. In this instance, select Add/Remove; you want to add the Crystal SQL Designer tool to your computer.

C

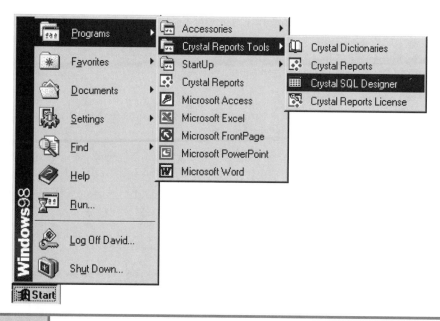

Figure C-1   The Crystal SQL Designer tool appears in the Crystal Reports Tools program group

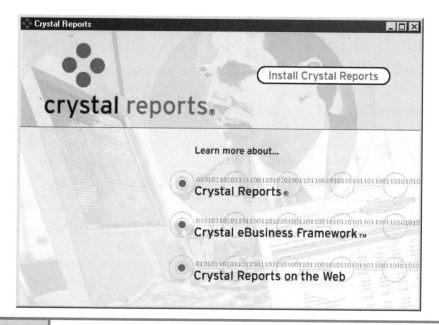

Figure C-2   The initial splash screen for installing Crystal Reports

In the Select Features dialog box, shown in Figure C-3, right-click the component for Crystal SQL Designer and select the option Will Be Installed on Local Hard Drive from the drop-down menu that appears.

Tip

If you want to use the Crystal Dictionaries tool, you can also select the option to install it now and save some time later.

When you click Next, the setup program will begin installing Crystal SQL Designer. When the file installation is finished, you should see Crystal SQL Designer listed under Crystal Reports Tools on the Start menu.

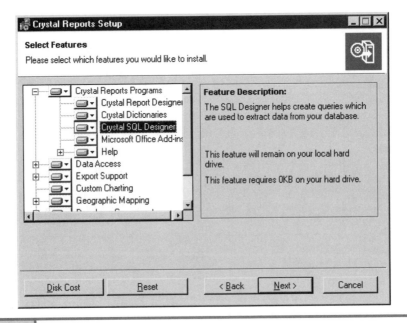

Figure C-3   Select Crystal SQL Designer from the list of components

Creating SQL Queries

When you first start Crystal SQL Designer, you can create a new query by selecting File | New. You will be presented with three options, as shown in Figure C-4.

- **Use SQL Expert**   Like the experts provided with Crystal Reports, the Create SQL Expert guides you through creating your SQL query.

- **Enter SQL Statement Directly**   Enter a SQL statement without using an expert (for example, you can directly enter SELECT * FROM CUSTOMER WHERE CUSTOMERID = 1).

- **Start from Existing Seagate Query**   Use another query file as the starting point for a new query.

   Most queries are created using the Create SQL Expert and then edited as needed. In this case, select the Use SQL Expert option, which opens the dialog box shown in Figure C-5. As you go through the steps of the Create SQL Expert, a

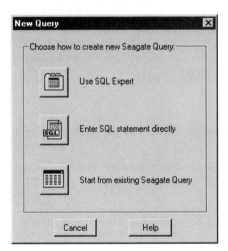

Figure C-4   You have three options when working with Crystal SQL Designer

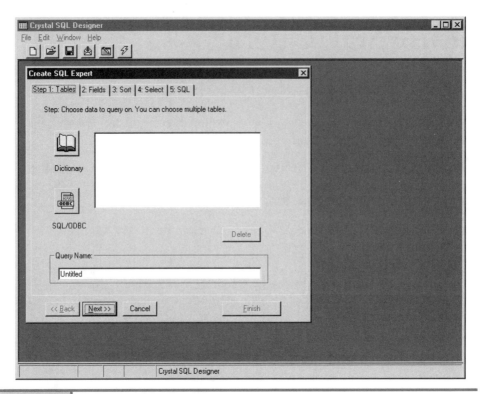

Figure C-5 The Create SQL Expert

SQL query will be written in the background; you can submit this to the database, and a result set will be returned.

The first step in creating your query is selecting the dictionary or data source where the data resides.

Tip

For more information on working with Crystal Reports dictionary files, see Appendix B.

If you have created a dictionary based on your database tables, you can click the Dictionary button to locate and select a dictionary file (.dc5) to use; otherwise, select the option for SQL/ODBC. This opens another dialog box that allows you to select the tables for your query and add them to the Create SQL Expert. When you are finished, click Done to continue.

If you select more than one table for your dictionary, a Links tab will open that allows you to use visual linking to specify the joins between your databases or tables.

Using the dialog box shown in Figure C-6, draw links between the databases and tables in your report to indicate the relationship between each. To draw a line between two fields, drag the first field and drop it on top of the second. You will know that you have the field positioned correctly when the cursor turns into a Z.

Tip

If you make a mistake, you can remove a link by clicking the line to highlight it and then pressing the DELETE key.

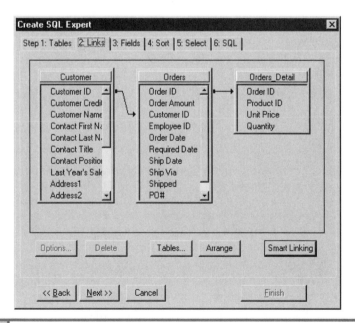

Figure C-6   Use the Links tab to indicate the relationships between your database tables and database files

By default, Crystal SQL Designer joins two SQL tables with an Equal join. To change the default join type, right-click directly on top of the line drawn between the two tables and select Options from the right-click menu. Using the Link Options dialog box, select one of the following join types:

- Equal

- Left Outer

- Right Outer

- Greater

- Less

- Greater or Equal

- Less or Equal

- Not Equal

Once you have created the links between the tables in your query, click the Fields tab to specify the fields that you want to appear in your query.

On the Fields tab, highlight the fields that you want in your query and use the Add button to add them to the list of query fields. You can add all of the fields by clicking the Add All button (you can also use the Remove and Remove All buttons to remove fields if you make a mistake).

Tip

If you are unsure of the contents of a field, you can use the Browse button to view a data sample, which also shows the field type, length, and so on.

At this point, you can also add SQL expressions to your query. SQL expressions are similar to Crystal Reports functions, except they are written using SQL (instead of the Crystal Reports formula language), and they are always evaluated on the database server itself. To add a new SQL expression, click the Expression button, enter a name for the expression, and click OK. The SQL Expression editor, shown in Figure C-7, will appear and allow you to enter your SQL expression.

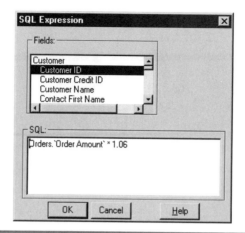

C

| **Figure C-7** | The SQL Expression editor |

┼*Tip*

You can double-click a field name within the SQL Expression editor to insert a field reference in your expression.

When you are finished entering your SQL expression, click OK to return to the Fields tab of the Create SQL Expert. If you need to calculate any summaries within your SQL query, you can use the built-in aggregate functions by selecting a query field and then choosing a summary function from the drop-down list marked Total. The following aggregate functions are available within the Create SQL Expert:

- SUM
- AVG
- MAX
- MIN
- COUNT

You can also select distinct records by clicking the check box immediately below the drop-down function list. Checking this option will add the word DISTINCT immediately after your SQL query's SELECT statement.

The Sort tab of the Create SQL Expert lets you select the sort order for your query. To select a field for sorting, highlight the field and use the Add button to add it to the list of group fields. Once you have added a field, a drop-down box will appear, as shown in Figure C-8, with the following sort order options:

- Ascending

- Descending

- Original

The Select tab of the Create SQL Expert is used to specify the record selection criteria for your query. Again, you select the field you want to use for record selection and use the Add button to move it from the list of available fields on the left to the list of selection fields on the right.

Once you have selected a field, a second set of options will appear, as shown in Figure C-9, allowing you to select a record selection operator and enter a value (or values). Table C-1 lists these operators and their uses.

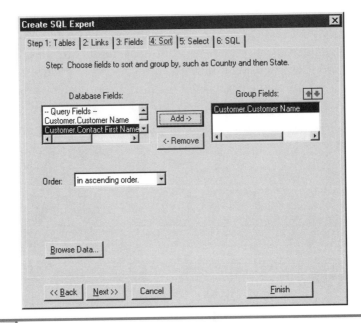

Figure C-8   Choose sorting options from the Order drop-down menu

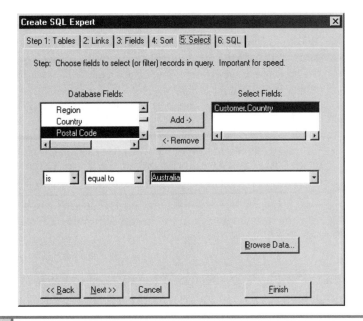

| **Figure C-9** | The Select tab specifies record selection for your query |

The final tab in the Create SQL Expert lets you view the SQL that has been generated for you, as shown in Figure C-10.

Operator	Description
Is any value	Default option for record selection, allowing all records to be returned, regardless of the value.
Is equal to	Looks for an exact match to the criteria entered.
Is not equal to	Looks for all records *except* those matching the criteria specified.
Is one of	Used to build a list of criteria, allowing you to select multiple values from one field (for example, is one of USA, Canada, and Mexico).
Is not one of	Used to build a list of criteria you *don't* want. (for example, is not one of Australia, New Zealand, and Japan).
Is less than	Brings back any records less than the criteria entered.
Is less than or equal to	Brings back any records less than or equal to the criteria entered.
Is greater than	Brings back any records greater than the criteria entered.
Is greater than or equal to	Brings back any records greater than or equal to the criteria entered.

| **Table C-1** | Record Selection Operators in the Create SQL Expert |

Operator	Description
Is between	Used to specify inclusive values as criteria. Any records between the two inclusive criteria are returned.
Is not between	The opposite of Is between. Any records outside the two inclusive criteria are returned.
Is Starting With	Looks at the start of a string, and if the value entered matches, returns that record.
Is Like	Used to specify values with wildcards that can represent any character; _ is used to represent single characters (for example, Is Like _ave will return Dave, Save, Rave, and so on), and % is used to represent multiple characters (for example, Is Like Dave* will return Davey, Daveys, Daves, and so on).

Table C-1   Record Selection Operators in the Create SQL Expert (*continued*)

You can edit the SQL that has been created and then finish with the Create SQL Expert by clicking the Finish button at the lower right of the dialog box. When you click Finish, you will be asked whether you want to process the query

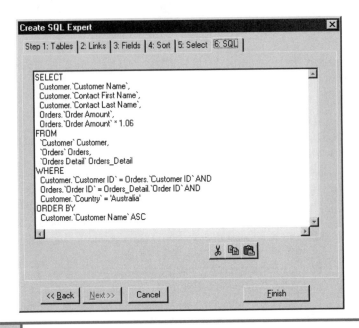

Figure C-10   SQL generated by the Create SQL Expert

now. If you select Yes, the SQL statement you have created using the Create SQL Expert will be submitted to the database, and a result set will be returned. If you select No, your database query will not be processed, and you will be shown a blank result set. If you click Cancel, you will be returned to the Create SQL Expert.

When you do process your query, a result set should be returned, as shown in Figure C-11.

You can refresh your query at any point by clicking the Refresh icon or pressing F5. You can also return to the Create SQL Expert by selecting Edit | Query.

C

Note

If you have made any changes to the SQL statement that the Create SQL Expert cannot represent using its own tabbed interface, the expert may display only the SQL statement that you have created and not allow you to use the other tabs to edit your SQL query.

You can save your query by selecting File | Save. Crystal SQL Designer saves query files with the .qry extension.

Customer Name	Contact First Name	Contact Last Name	Order Amount	SalesTax
Bruce's Bikes	Bruce	Hyde	17.50	18.55
Canberra Bikes	Craig	Stobbs	479.85	508.64
Down Under Bikes	Dave	Flynn	45.00	47.70
Kangeroo Trikes	Sandra	Anderson	107.80	114.27
Koala Road Bikes	Nathan	Wu	64.42	68.29
Peddles of Perth	Vanessa	Jacobsen	5,879.70	6,232.48
Tasmanian Devil Bikes	Todd	Llyod	3,305.72	3,504.06

Figure C-11   Your query results are displayed in a grid

Working with SQL Queries

With your first query finished, it is time to look at some of the most common administrative tasks performed when working with SQL queries.

Verifying SQL Queries

From time to time, as applications and database structures change, you may need to verify your queries. Select File | Verify Query, and the Crystal SQL Designer will look at your query structure and then compare it to the underlying database structures. If any of the tables, fields, and so on have changed, the verification process will find the changes and update your query accordingly.

Note

If tables or fields have been deleted or renamed, you may need to edit your query to ensure that these changes are picked up.

Exporting Query Results

One of the most common questions when working with Crystal SQL Designer is "How do I print the results?" To print the results of your query, you can save the query and create a Crystal Report from the query file. A much easier method for printing the results is to export the results and print them from another application.

To export your query results, select File | Export to open the Export dialog box, shown in Figure C-12.

Select an export format and destination and click OK to export your results to the format and destination you have specified.

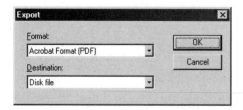

Figure C-12 To export query results, select a format and destination

Tip

For more information on exporting, see Module 7, which discusses export formats and destinations.

Creating Reports from SQL Queries

To see how to create a report from a Crystal query file, create a new report and let the Standard Report Expert guide you. To get started, open Crystal Reports and click the New icon on the standard toolbar or choose File | New to open the Crystal Report Gallery. Then select the Standard Report Expert and click OK.

The first step in creating a report using the Standard Report Expert is choosing the query on which the report will be based. To select your data source, you use the Data Explorer, shown in Figure C-13. The Data Explorer itself is really just a number of different views of the data sources that you have available to use in your report. You will find the option to work with Crystal query files under the Metadata/Query node. Immediately underneath this node is the Find New File option; click this option to open a browse dialog box and select the Crystal query (.qry) file you want to use.

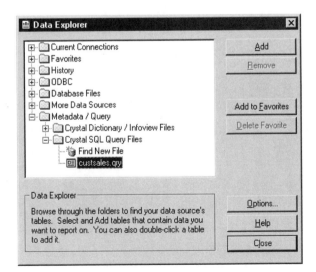

| **Figure C-13** | The Crystal Reports Data Explorer |

Choosing Fields

The Fields tab of the Standard Report Expert, shown in Figure C-14, is split into two sections. The left pane of the dialog box lists all of the fields that are available from your query to be inserted into your report, grouped by their field heading name. To add a field to your report, move the field from the left pane to the right pane. You can accomplish this by double-clicking the field name or by highlighting the field and clicking the Add button. Additional buttons are also available to add or remove one or all fields.

Tip

To select multiple fields, hold down the CONTROL key while clicking.

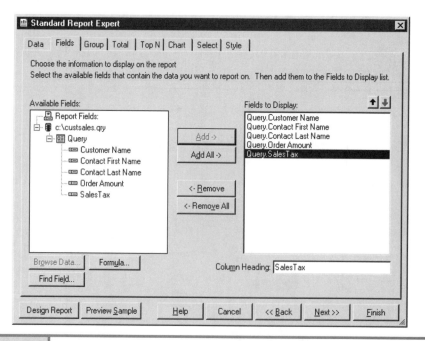

Figure C-14   Use the Fields tab to select the fields for your report

If you are unsure of a field's definition or contents, you can use the Browse Data button to display a sample of the field's contents.

Another key feature of the Fields tab is the Find Field button, at the bottom left. This button allows you to search the selected tables for a field that matches your criteria. To see the help text in action, click to select a field and then leave the mouse over the field for a few seconds. A small pop-up box should appear displaying the help text you have entered in your query file.

Tip

Keep in mind that the fields in a query file can be used as if they were fields from the underlying database. You can use them in formulas, with functions, and so on. They will always have the notation of {Field Heading.Field Name} when used within your report or formula text.

To change the order of the fields you are inserting in your report, you can use the up and down arrows that appear in the upper-right corner of the dialog box to move fields up and down. You can also change the column heading associated with a field.

Grouping and Sorting

The next step in creating a report using the Standard Report Expert is selecting the sorting and grouping to use in your report, using the Group tab. This tab is similar to the Fields tab. To select a field, you move it from the list on the left to the list on the right.

By specifying a field on the Group tab, you can add control breaks or groups to your report. For example, if you were to group on the State field, your report would be printed with all records for each state together, with a break between each state.

After you select a field, notice that you have a choice of sort order, as shown in Figure C-15:

- **In Ascending Order**   This option groups the records by the field you have specified and orders those groups from A through Z, zero through nine, and so forth.

- **In Descending Order**   This option groups the records by the field you have specified and orders those groups from Z through A, nine through zero, and so forth.

- **In Specified Order**   Using this option, you can name and define your own grouping criteria.

- **In Original Order**   If your database has already performed some sorting on the data, this option leaves the records in their original order.

Inserting Summaries

The Total tab, shown in Figure C-16, is used to insert Crystal Reports summary fields into your report. Crystal Reports provides these summary fields so that you do not have to create a formula every time you want to insert a sum, average, and so forth.

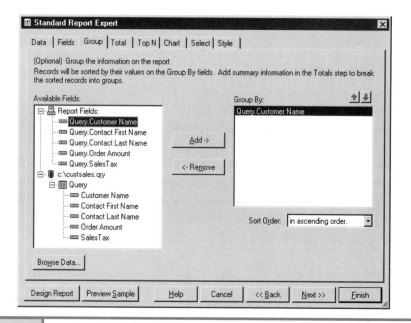

Figure C-15   Choosing the grouping and sorting for your report

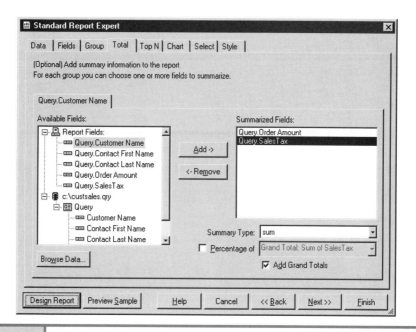

Figure C-16 | Inserting summary fields into your report

You can insert a number of summary fields into your report; the types of summaries vary based on the type of field, as shown in Table C-2.

For some of the statistical functions, you are asked to provide additional information, such as the value for N. For other functions, you specify that a summary is a certain percentage of a particular field.

When you add a summary to your report using the Standard Report Expert, the summary appears immediately following each group, showing the summary for only that particular group. The option in the lower-right corner of the dialog box, Add Grand Totals, adds the same type of summary field at the end of the report and shows the value for the entire report.

Previewing Your Report

With the Data, Fields, Group, and Total tabs complete, your report design is almost finished. The next three steps of the Standard Report Expert, for Top-N analysis, charting, and record selection, are optional, so we will skip these for now.

Summary Type	With Numeric Fields	With Other Field Types
Sum	X	
Average	X	
Maximum	X	X
Minimum	X	X
Count	X	X
Distinct Count	X	X
Sample Variance	X	
Sample Standard Deviation	X	
Population Variance	X	
Population Standard Deviation	X	
Correlation	X	
Covariance	X	
Weighted Average	X	
Median	X	
Pth Percentile	X	
Nth Largest	X	X
Nth Smallest	X	X
Mode	X	X
Nth Most Frequent	X	X

Table C-2   Crystal Reports Summary Field Types and Usage

The Style tab in the Standard Report Expert, shown in Figure C-17, is for setting the report style. You can give your report a title and can apply a predefined style, including coordinating colors, fonts, and so forth. If you select any of the predefined styles shown, you see a preview of what that particular style looks like on the right.

With the report expert settings are complete, it is time to take a look at the report you have created. As shown at the bottom of Figure C-17, you have three options: you can go straight to the design of your report using the Design Report button, or you can check out a preview of your report by clicking the Preview Sample or Finish button. The only difference between the last two is that the Preview Sample button allows you to select the number of records that are returned, whereas the Finish button retrieves the whole data set for your preview.

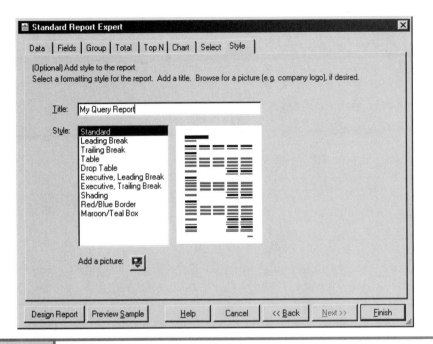

C

Figure C-17 You can apply a preformatted report style to your report

Distributing Crystal Reports and Queries

When distributing a report created from a Crystal query, you will need to provide the recipient with both the Crystal Reports (.rpt) file and the query (.qry) file. You also need to be careful about where the recipient places these two files. When the report was created, Crystal Reports stored the location of the Crystal query file, and it will look in that location first. If it cannot locate the query file, it will look in the same directory where the report itself is saved. A good practice is to either establish a central location for reports and their associated queries or always place the report file and query in the same directory.

Appendix D

Troubleshooting (FAQ)

This appendix lists some of the most common problems encountered when creating or editing reports. If the questions and answers listed here don't cover your particular problem, you can go to Crystal Decision's Web site at http://community.crystaldecisions.com and search the Crystal Knowledge Base. Alternatively, you can post a question in one of the forums available on the Crystal Decisions Web site or using the forums or message boards of user group Web sites such as the following:

- Crystal Decisions User Group North America (www.cdugna.org)
- Mid-West Crystal Decisions User Group (www.mwcug.org)
- Crystal Decisions Australasia User Group (www.cdaug.org)
- Crystal User.com (www.crystaluser.com)
- Crystal Reports Special Interest Group (www.crystalsig.org)

Crystal Decisions also has a number of technical support plans and options available for free or for purchase. The Web site (www.crystaldecisions.com) should have the full details of which plan or option best suits you.

My report runs slowly. What can I do?

This is a tricky issue, as any number of problems could be causing your report to run slowly. First look at your record selection formula. Try to avoid using formulas within record selection because Crystal Reports will need to read all of the database values first, then calculate the formula, and then apply record selection. Another culprit may be the linkage between the tables in your report. Review the links you have created with your database or application administrator to make sure that you have only the tables you require and that you have created the correct links between them. Another likely culprit is subreports. Be careful where you place subreports in your report. A subreport placed on the detail line will run once for every record in your report! Likewise, a subreport placed in the group header or footer will run once for each group, and so on. A last word of advice: use subreports as sparingly as possible.

When I refresh my report, it doesn't show any records. What gives?

First, try to refresh your report using F5 or the refresh icon. If that doesn't work, a good place to start looking is your record selection formula (Select Report | Select Expert). Has your record selection criterion narrowed the selection so far down that no records are returned? Try changing the record selection so that some records are returned and work from there. After ruling out a problem with record selection, try selecting Database | Verify Database to make sure that the database structures haven't changed.

When my report runs, the first (or last) page is blank. What can I do?

This problem is easy to solve, and fairly common. Remember: On the front and rear of every report is a report header and report footer. Check to see if you are throwing a page break after the report header (select Format | Section and look under the New Page Before/After properties for the report header or footer). Another possible culprit is the Keep Together setting on a section; this feature will sometimes force a blank page to appear.

My Preview tab has disappeared. How can I get it back?

If your preview tab has disappeared, chances are good that you have accidentally closed it. If you look on the toolbar near the Page Forward and Page Back buttons, you will see a red X icon that closes additional tabs you may have open. To get your Preview tab back, click the Preview or Refresh icon or select File | Print Preview.

When I go to the Select Expert, it won't let me edit the fields and criteria I have picked and gives a message about a composite expression. What have I done wrong?

When you receive a message about a composite expression in the Select Expert, Crystal Reports has noticed that you have modified some part of the record selection formula itself, and this is its way of telling you that you need to go back and edit the formula instead of using the Select Expert interface. From the Select Expert (Report | Select Expert) , you should be able to click the Show Formula button to display the formula you have created and then click the Formula Editor button to invoke the Crystal Reports Formula Editor to help edit your record selection formula.

When linking two tables, I get the message "File Link Warning: The specified fields may not link successfully due to different type" (or "different length"). What does this mean?

When you are working with multiple tables in a report, Crystal Reports prefers that the fields you create links with have the same type and length. This is really not a Crystal Reports requirement, but is just good database design and practice. Crystal Reports will display the File Link Warning error message, but will still allow you to link two fields that may have different types or lengths.

I was moving fields around, and now one of my database fields is stuck inside a text object. How do I get it out?

Believe it or not, this is a feature. Whenever you move a database or other field close to a text field, Crystal Reports assumes that you want to place that field within the text field. Everything probably happened too quickly, but you may have noticed that your cursor turned into the page icon, indicating that Crystal Reports was ready to insert a field into a text object. For an immediate fix, you can use CTRL-Z to undo the operation and get the field out of the text field, or you can double-click the text field to place it in Edit mode and then drag the field out.

The print date on my report is wrong—what gives?

The print date is a system-generated field and relies on the settings found under Report | Set Print Date and Time. If this setting is set to Today's Date/Time, the print date field on your report will correspond to the system date on your computer. If this setting is set to another date and time, Crystal Reports will always display that specific date and time for the print date field, regardless of the system date on your computer.

When I am in the Visual Linking Expert, I get the error "A link cycle will be created." What did I do wrong?

Crystal Reports does not allow you to link a table back to itself. To reference information that is held within the same table, select Database | Add Database to Report and add the same table to your report. Crystal Reports should display a warning message, alerting you to the fact that this table has already been added. Edit the alias name for your table and click Yes to add this table to your report a second time. You can then reference the table by the alias name and use it as you would any other table in your report.

I have a memo type field in my database, but it doesn't appear in the formula editor. Why?

Memo fields are unavailable when working with the Crystal Reports Formula Editor. In addition, you can't browse memo fields as you would other fields. If you do need to work with values contained within a memo field, ask your database administrator or developer to change the type of field to text or to truncate the information within the memo field and put it into a string field for you.

Index

INTERNATIONAL CONTACT INFORMATION

AUSTRALIA
McGraw-Hill Book Company Australia Pty. Ltd.
TEL +61-2-9417-9899
FAX +61-2-9417-5687
http://www.mcgraw-hill.com.au
books-it_sydney@mcgraw-hill.com

CANADA
McGraw-Hill Ryerson Ltd.
TEL +905-430-5000
FAX +905-430-5020
http://www.mcgrawhill.ca

**GREECE, MIDDLE EAST,
NORTHERN AFRICA**
McGraw-Hill Hellas
TEL +30-1-656-0990-3-4
FAX +30-1-654-5525

MEXICO (Also serving Latin America)
McGraw-Hill Interamericana Editores S.A. de C.V.
TEL +525-117-1583
FAX +525-117-1589
http://www.mcgraw-hill.com.mx
fernando_castellanos@mcgraw-hill.com

SINGAPORE (Serving Asia)
McGraw-Hill Book Company
TEL +65-863-1580
FAX +65-862-3354
http://www.mcgraw-hill.com.sg
mghasia@mcgraw-hill.com

SOUTH AFRICA
McGraw-Hill South Africa
TEL +27-11-622-7512
FAX +27-11-622-9045
robyn_swanepoel@mcgraw-hill.com

**UNITED KINGDOM & EUROPE
(Excluding Southern Europe)**
McGraw-Hill Education Europe
TEL +44-1-628-502500
FAX +44-1-628-770224
http://www.mcgraw-hill.co.uk
computing_neurope@mcgraw-hill.com

ALL OTHER INQUIRIES Contact:
Osborne/McGraw-Hill
TEL +1-510-549-6600
FAX +1-510-883-7600
http://www.osborne.com
omg_international@mcgraw-hill.com

O S B O R N E

Now you can learn all the major development languages with Osborne's Beginner's Guides

Break
The Language Barrier

SQL:
A Beginner's Guide
FORREST HOULETTE, PH.D.
0-07-213096-2

JAVA 2:
A Beginner's Guide
HERB SCHILDT
0-07-212742-2

HTML:
A Beginner's Guide
WENDY WILLARD
0-07-213026-1

JAVASCRIPT:
A Beginner's Guide
JOHN POLLOCK
0-07-213140-3

PERL:
A Beginner's Guide
R. ALLEN WYKE &
DONALD B. THOMAS
0-07-212957-3

XML:
A Beginner's Guide
DAVE MERCER
0-07-212740-6

ASP 3.0:
A Beginner's Guide
D. MERCER
0-07-212741-4

LINUX PROGRAMMING:
A Beginner's Guide
R. PETERSEN
0-07-212743-0

WEB DESIGN:
A Beginner's Guide
W. WILLARD
0-07-213390-2

FRONTPAGE 2002:
A Beginner's Guide
K. CHINNATHAMB
0-07-213491-7

JSP:
A Beginner's Guide
G. BOLLINGER & B. NATARAJAN
0-07-213319-8

PHP4:
A Beginner's Guide
W. McCARTY
0-07-213371-6

$29.99 each

Purchase your Osborne/McGraw-Hill books at book stores and online retailers everywhere.

For more information on these and other Osborne/McGraw-Hill titles, visit our Web site at www.osborne.com